Yale Historical Publications

Miscellany, 98

For Toni

The New England Mind
in Transition

Samuel Johnson
of Connecticut, 1696–1772

Joseph J. Ellis

New Haven & London, Yale University Press, 1973

Library of Congress catalog card number: 73–77149
International standard book number: 0–300–01615–8

Designed by Sally Sullivan
and set in Baskerville type.
Printed in the United States of America by
The Colonial Press Inc., Clinton, Massachusetts.

Published in Great Britain, Europe, and Africa by
Yale University Press, Ltd., London.
Distributed in Latin America by Kaiman & Polon,
Inc., New York City; in Australasia and Southeast
Asia by John Wiley & Sons Australasia Pty. Ltd.,
Sydney; in India by UBS Publishers' Distributors Pvt.,
Ltd., Delhi; in Japan by John Weatherhill, Inc., Tokyo.

Contents

List of Illustrations
following page 180

Preface

This is not a story of the English Samuel Johnson, the eighteenth-century lexicographer and wit immortalized in the famous biography by James Boswell. It is, instead, the story of an American colonist of the same name who lived at roughly the same time. The American Johnson was a fat, red-faced scholar who first achieved a kind or prominence when he denounced the Puritan churches in 1722. He then toiled in relative obscurity as an Anglican missionary in Connecticut for over thirty years before he gained a measure of fame as the first president of King's College, now Columbia University. Among a small number of Anglicans in New England and New York he was regarded as a great leader, but Ezra Stiles probably summed up the majority opinion when he said that some thinkers "with half the Observation and Reading of Dr. Johnson would make ten times greater Men." Another contemporary, when asked to comment on Johnson's scholarly achievements, remarked that "Dr. Johnson was always of the opinion of the last book he read." He does not seem to have been a particularly brilliant or original character.

He was, however, a peculiarly sensitive intellectual. As I have found him, he was concerned with the central religious and philosophical questions of his day. What had Puritanism come to mean in New England during the first half of the eighteenth century? How and to what extent had earlier Puritan conceptions of the church and the ministry undergone revision? What was the intellectual heritage of the eighteenth-century Puritan? What were the tensions between that heritage and the Enlightenment or, as Johnson called it, the New Learning?

These are difficult questions. Twentieth-century historians have yet to answer them with any precision. Nor was Johnson, who spent most of his life wrestling with his own formulations of these intellectual problems, wholly satisfied with his answers. By the end of his life he was a frustrated and defeated old man who had abandoned the intellectual enterprise in favor of the comforting certitude of the Old Testament. For most of his life, however, he read widely, thought about what he had read, and wrote down what he thought. This is what first attracted me to the man: his earnest exploration of an intellectual milieu that many scholars have assured us was a kind of ice age. A number of distinguished historians have recently begun to chip away at this glacial stereotype, so that it is no longer possible to explain the intellectual development of the maturing colonies by means of a casual reference to the pragmatic wisdom of Benjamin Franklin or the convoluted piety of Jonathan Edwards. In part because of the work of Bernard Bailyn, Richard Bushman, David Hall, and Edmund Morgan, I came to Samuel Johnson with a strong preconception that the period during which he lived was an important stage in the development of American intellectual history and that Johnson's curious mind was one barometer of the intellectual pressures of the times.

I have tried to write what some might call an "intellectual biography." By this I mean that I have focused on what Johnson thought. I felt that this was an appropriate approach, not only because Johnson always fancied himself an intellectual, but also because there are already two published accounts of his life extant. Although these accounts are riddled with pro-Anglican sentiment and other interpretive flaws, they do a commendable job of detailing the facts of the narrative. I felt that their existence freed me from some of the traditional duties of the biographer and allowed me to write what Perry Miller has called a "life of the mind."

This does not mean that I regard Johnson's intellect as something wholly separate from his personal life. I have tried to be sensitive to the ways in which Johnson's ideas were affected by his experiences as a father, pastor, and teacher. It seemed clear to me, for example, that Johnson's idealized conception of the church underwent drastic revision due to his experiences as an Anglican missionary. Similarly, the death of his wife, his son, and many of his friends from smallpox caused him to disavow his earlier estimate of God's rationality. Unfortunately, many of Johnson's personal papers were destroyed by fire during the American Revolution, so that no record of his childhood experiences and family relations—evidence that a clinical psychologist might have found revealing—was available. The blanks in the historical record, then, make a clinical analysis of Johnson's personality impossible. Although I have concerned myself with what John Higham has called "the inner happenings," by this I mean the relationship between different ideas, not the relationship between ideas and deep-rooted psychic needs. I have also tried to look beyond the ideological lacework and take account of the way ideas were translated into action.

In the course of this study I have been forced to come to terms with the inherent ambiguity of language. Some readers might object to the absence of any systematic definition of the word "puritan," a term that appears at regular intervals in the text. I can only take solace in the fact that a flock of prominent historians have faced the same dilemma. Samuel Eliot Morison, for example, felt compelled to stop his account of John Winthrop in mid-passage in order to "talk of puritanism and the puritans." In part because of the work of historians like Morison, Perry Miller, and Edmund Morgan, I feel absolved from rushing into the breach with my historical dictionary. But, in all honesty, a dictionary would not suffice. Previous histories of colonial New England and Tudor-Stuart England have made it abundantly clear that Puritanism was a vast and flexible network of beliefs and attitudes that provoked bitter disagreement over its meaning then and will fit into no convenient verbal receptacle now. I have attempted to use the word with some precision, explaining its implications for theology, polity, philosophy, and education. One of the principal intentions of the book is to enrich our understanding of what happened to Puritanism in the eighteenth century. In a sense, the chapters that follow are an attempt to build toward a definition of the troublesome term.

The central theme of this book is the way certain habits of thought that had been firmly established in seventeenth-century New England were challenged and, in some cases, changed. I have tried to suggest that the challenge came not only from Locke,

Newton, and the emerging English Enlightenment, but also from within New England, from the practical exigencies created by a maturing society, exigencies that forced the New England ministers to confront the ambiguities of their religious legacy. After his conversion to episcopacy in 1722, Johnson himself became a challenge to orthodoxy, and a considerable part of this volume is devoted to an analysis of the response he provoked. The title of the book, then, is meant to refer not only to Johnson and his mental development, but also to the intellectual alterations that orthodox Puritan ministers made in response to Johnson.

Another theme that runs throughout the following chapters is the slow and surreptitious nature of intellectual change in eighteenth-century New England. So much of Puritan theology and polity was a matter of subtle emphasis that a slight shift in perspective was capable of producing fundamental religious change. Moreover, when new ideas were introduced into New England their impact was often delayed for several decades while men like Johnson mulled them over. For example, in Johnson's philosophical writings, as in the college curricula of the period, antithetical ideas rested side by side in apparent harmony. During all this period the liberal religious ideas of the English latitudinarians, the Lockean model of perception, and the Newtonian prescription for scientific knowledge were waging a kind of guerrilla war against the medieval categories on which established religious and philosophical doctrines rested. For many years it was unclear to Johnson how much of the old learning would have to be sacrificed to the twin gods of reason and science. Only toward the end of his life did he realize the extent to which an emphasis on rational inquiry corroded man's sense of depravity. Most of his productive years were spent in a vain effort to integrate the insights of reformed Christianity with what he called the New Learning. In this sense I believe he serves as a useful device for an analysis of the uneasy transition from Puritanism to the Enlightenment.

There are other themes in this book—the provinciality of colonial culture, the problems of a New England missionary, the secularization of colonial education, the relationship between religion and politics. These are large issues that I have not dealt with ex-

haustively, but rather as they relate to the story of Samuel Johnson. I do not think that Johnson's opinion on these issues was
always profound. The man's character had a certain shallowness
as well as great depth. Nor would I claim that Johnson's thoughts
were "typical of the times." He was, after all, a well-educated and
well-read person who took ideas much more seriously than did
the bulk of his contemporaries. He was also a convert to Anglicanism and, therefore, an intruder in the heartland of New England Puritanism. But these two distinguishing characteristics—
his intellectualism and his alienation from the New England
mainstream—allowed him to have insights denied to others.
Johnson always believed that men at all times and in all places
shared certain archetypal experiences. But the problems that obsessed him and the tentative solutions he worked out occurred at
a specific time and in a specific place. This book is intended less
as a demonstration of the timeless character of Johnson's ideas
than as an attempt to relate those ideas to colonial culture in the
formative years prior to the American Revolution.

My intellectual debts, thank heavens, are easier to recognize
than the subtle transitions in American intellectual history. Since
it has taken a considerable time to get this book out of me and
into print, my list of creditors is quite long. Somewhere near the
top of the list belong William Abbott and Thad Tate, for they
were the first teachers to expose me to the history of colonial
America. I first became acquainted with Samuel Johnson in
David Hall's graduate seminar at Yale. Later on Professor Hall
let me read an early draft of his book on the New England ministry and provided me with several research leads. Sydney Ahlstrom forced me to revise and sharpen my thoughts on Johnson's
theology. Bruce Kuklick read the chapter that deals with Johnson's philosophy and let me corner him into some lengthy discussions of George Berkeley. Murray Murphey also read the material
on Johnson's philosophy and allowed me to see an unpublished
piece of his on the same subject.

A few friends and colleagues deserve special mention. Richard
Warch not only sustained me spiritually throughout the research
and writing, but also enriched my appreciation of the ecclesiasti-

cal and theological debates. Without him I would never have understood what all that talk about Arminianism meant. William McFeely read the entire manuscript and was always there when it counted. During two crucial stages of my budding career, when I was ready to leave Samuel Johnson's story buried in the filing cabinet, C. Vann Woodward took the time to offer counsel that sustained the project.

The respective staffs of the Archives of the Episcopal Church in America, the Columbia University Library, the Connecticut Historical Society, the Records Division of the Guilford Town Hall, and the Yale University Library were always able to locate relevant material and usually able to provide me with a congenial place to work. Alice Bonnell of the Columbiana Room was especially considerate. Among the helpful people at Yale Press, Edward Tripp and Nancy Paxton ushered the manuscript through to publication with demonstrable concern for the author and a careful eye for detail. I would also be remiss if I neglected to thank the editors of two scholarly journals in which earlier versions of portions of this book were first published. Chapter 6 appeared as "The Anglicans in Connecticut, 1725–1750: The Conversion of the Missionaries," *New England Quarterly* 44 (1971): 66–81. Chapter 8 was published as "The Puritan Mind in Transition: The Philosophy of Samuel Johnson," *William and Mary Quarterly*, 3rd ser. 28 (1971): 26–45.

A special debt is owed to Edmund Morgan. He has shown me what it means to be a historian and waited patiently for me to begin to learn. He shepherded me through each stage of this study and demanded more of each draft by forcing me to ask more of myself. To him I owe my professional and personal acquaintance with the Puritan ethic.

Ann Granger not only typed several drafts of the entire manuscript, but also offered helpful suggestions about format. My wife, an ardent advocate of sexual equality, steadfastly refused to type a word unless she was paid. Fortunately for me and the book, she and I agreed that there were other and better ways for a wife to help a prospective author.

South Hadley, Massachusetts   J. J. E.

1

Tradition and Turmoil: School and Churches

In 1653 William Johnson moved from New Haven, Connecticut, to Guilford, a new settlement in the same colony, which a group of English colonists had recently purchased from the Indians for "four coats, two kettles, four fathoms of wampum, four hatchets and three hoes."[1] The Mohegans had called the area Menunkatuck, after one of their legendary chiefs, but as colonists continued to trickle into the area and the population grew to around five hundred, the English name became more appropriate. William Johnson contributed ten children of good English stock to the growing settlement. He also worked hard at farming, bought more land, and gradually developed a reputation as one of the leading citizens of Guilford. In 1673 he was chosen deacon of the First Congregational Church. Three years later, when the town needed a clerk, the selectmen chose Johnson. When the townsmen decided to build a new grammar school, they commissioned Deacon William to survey the land and supervise construction. In 1685 they requested him to defend the town patent before the Connecticut General Court. When the master of the grammar school died in 1687, William agreed to carry on instruction until a replacement could be found. Somehow he found time to serve eighteen terms as deputy in the semiannual meetings of the General Court, drill the militia, and draw up a new series of maps for the colony.[2]

1. *Guilford Records,* B : 138. The records are located in the Guilford Town Hall.
2. Ralph D. Smith, *The History of Guilford* (Albany, 1877), pp. 9, 20, 30; Bernard C. Steiner, *A History of the Plantation of Menunkatuck* (Baltimore, 1897), pp. 112–13, 292, 397, 420, 512.

In 1694 William Johnson's youngest son, Samuel, married Mary Sage; in October 1696 Mary gave birth to a son and named him after his father.[3] Samuel Jr. spent his childhood and all but ten years of his adult life in the same part of colonial Connecticut that his grandfather had helped to build. It was "a mountainous country, full of rocks, swamps, hills and vales. Most that is fit for planting is taken up. What remaynes must be subdued, and gained out of the fire as it were, by hard blowes and for small recompense." [4] Madame Sarah Knight, who traveled through Connecticut in 1704, reported that the people were mostly rural folk, "generally very plain in their dress . . . and follow one another in their modes." [5] According to one contemporary observer, most of Connecticut's farmers enjoyed "very little elegance . . . but more of necessaries." [6] A farmer summed up the experience of his neighbors: "We labour in tilling the ground and by that time a yeare's travel and labour hath gathered some small parcell of provision, it is transported to the market at Boston." [7] It was a rough country, but it could keep a man and his family alive, provided the man was a diligent worker and his family pitched in. The rocky land tended to reward men who possessed the harder virtues, witness Deacon William. As a product of this "land of steady habits," young Samuel Johnson probably broke some stones, planted some seeds, and learned the basic skills required of a New England farmer.

But from the beginning the Johnson boy seemed destined for a career other than farming. He had "an impatient curiosity to know everything that could be known," [8] and his grandfather

3. Johnson's genealogy is found in the family Bible formerly in the possession of Dr. William Carmalt of New Haven, Connecticut; see also Herbert Schneider and Carol Schneider, eds., *Samuel Johnson: His Career and Writings,* 4 vols. (New York, 1929), 1 : 56–59. Hereafter cited as *Career.*

4. J. H. Trumbull and Charles J. Hoadley, eds., *Public Records of the Colony of Connecticut,* 15 vols. (Hartford, 1850–90), 3 : 296. Hereafter cited as *Conn. Recs.*

5. Sarah K. Knight, *The Journal of Madame Knight* (New York, 1935), pp. 43–44.

6. John J. Carman, ed., *American Husbandry* (New York, 1939), p. 50.

7. *Conn. Recs.,* 3 : 301.

8. *Career,* 1 : 3.

fed this curiosity with passages from Scripture and the Lord's Prayer. When Samuel learned these by heart, Deacon William took him around town for recitations. By the time he was four, the boy could read and write. This was enough to convince a proud grandfather, who convinced all of Guilford, that the Johnson boy was a prodigy. If there was any doubt, Samuel dispelled it when he began to study Hebrew at the age of five.[9]

Neither William Johnson nor Samuel's father believed this scholarly interest to be a waste of time. No one tried to convince Samuel that the family farm or their newly founded tailoring business was more important than Hebrew. As Deacon William observed, since the boy read more proficiently than he sewed, perhaps God had ordained that the Johnson family should produce a scholar. The grandfather had tried to inculcate in Samuel the basic virtues of diligence and industriousness; the fact that the boy exercised these virtues most visibly in academic pursuits was a sign that no God-fearing Puritan could afford to ignore. The year he died, William Johnson obtained a promise that his favorite grandchild would be given the opportunity to pursue his education.[10]

Fortunately, the colony had a school system that met young Johnson's needs. The founders of Connecticut had been English Puritans who were undaunted by the problem of preserving a culture while carving farms out of the wilderness. They insisted that their children learn to read the Bible and understand the minister, as well as combat the primitive conditions of the frontier and "that old deluder Satan." Charles Chauncy, president of Harvard, warned New Englanders that parents who "account it their happiness to live in the vast howling wilderness, without . . . schooles, and means of education for their posterity," ran the risk of having their children "go native." Civilization was essential if succeeding generations were to overcome the barbarism of the frontier environment. And schooling was essential if English civilization was to survive in the new

9. Ibid., p. 4.
10. Steiner, *Menunkatuck*, pp. 113–14.

world. Parents who forced their children to "drudge . . . at plough, or hough, or such like servil imployments" and ignored the need for education, said Chauncy, were guilty of having "sacrificed their sonnes and daughters unto Devils." Five years before Chauncy delivered his warning, Connecticut had taken steps to avoid the devilish temptations of the wilderness. In 1650 the Connecticut General Court had ordered that all towns with fifty families or more establish a school at which children could learn to read and write. Towns with one hundred or more families were required to set up a grammar school with a master capable of teaching Latin and Greek.[11]

Since the leaders of Connecticut believed that the skills learned in the grammar school were essential for everyone who wished to understand God's biblical pronouncements, they did not leave the support of the schools in the hands of private citizens. If sanctity was a matter of public concern, so was the school system that made sanctity possible. Each town was required by law to tax its inhabitants at the rate of 40 shillings per £1000, thereby assuring the maintenance of the school system and educational standards. In fact, by 1672 all the settled territory of New England, with the exception of Rhode Island, was under a compulsory system of education financed by public taxes.[12]

As a result, Johnson's early inclination toward learning fitted nicely into a strong Puritan bias for education, a bias which had been institutionalized in Connecticut and which was still alive at the beginning of the eighteenth century. More than any other group, the religious leaders of the colony regarded themselves as the protectors of this scholarly tradition. In the election sermons delivered at Hartford in May of each year, the colony's most prominent ministers demonstrated their persistent belief in the value of education. In 1712 John Woodward predicted that neglect of "the religion and good Education of our Youth"

11. *Conn. Recs.*, 1 : 554–55; Robert Middlekauf, *Ancients and Axioms* (New Haven, 1963), pp. 7–8. See Samuel Eliot Morison, *The Intellectual Life of Colonial New England* (New York, 1956); Thomas G. Wright, *Literary Cultures of Early New England* (New York, 1920). James Truslow Adams, *A Provincial Society* (New York, 1927), has another opinion.

12. *Conn. Recs.*, 1 : 554–55; Morison, *Intellectual Life*, p. 69.

would result in "a succeeding Ignorant and Barbarous Generation." [13] The next year John Bulkley made the same point,
warning that an uneducated populace would lead to the aban-
donment of the cherished traditions of the Puritan founders of
Connecticut.[14] In 1724 Samuel Woodbridge announced that
"the Education of our Youth is of the last importance to our
future flourishing in Vertue, in Piety, in Arts, in Wisdom &
Reputation." [15] During this period the clergy regarded religion
and learning as allies. There was as yet no sense of tension
between science and Scripture. Not until the Great Awakening
did a sizable segment of the Puritan ministry question the direct
correlation between education and moral behavior.

But at the precise time that Johnson was ready to begin his
formal schooling, the Connecticut schools needed more than
sentimental support. They needed money. Money was in short
supply primarily because Connecticut was engaged in a war
against the Indians. The colonists called it King William's War
and, when William III died, Queen Anne's War. Coastal towns
such as Guilford were in little danger of attack, but they were
obliged to send men and supplies to the inland towns of Dan-
bury, Waterford, Simsbury, and Deerfield. The resulting shortage
of manpower put a strain on many of the local institutions in the
coastal towns.[16] Since the school system was supported by public
taxes, it was affected by the economic pressures generated by
the Indian wars. The General Court was forced to increase the
annual assessments for defense. In Guilford these taxes continued to mount until they reached a high of £480 in 1704.[17]

13. John Woodward, *Civil Rulers Are God's Ministers for the People's Good*
(Boston, 1712), p. 44.
14. John Bulkley, *The Necessity of Religion in Societies* . . . (New London,
1713), p. 48.
15. Samuel Woodbridge, *Obedience to the Divine Law* . . . (New London,
1724), p. 22.
16. *Conn. Recs.*, 4 : 331; *Guilford Records*, C : 76, 77, 85, 95; A Bill of
Mortality for the Town of Guilford, no pagination, located in the Guilford
Town Hall. Cotton Mather, *Duodecennium Luctuosum* (Boston, 1714), pp.
7–13, discusses the war's effect on local life. See also Francis Parkman, *A
Half-Century of Conflict* (Boston, 1893), pp. 52–90.
17. *Conn. Recs.*, 4 : 521, 534. The tax increase is clearly seen in ibid., pp.
302, 317, 329, 398, 440, 466, 488, 519.

By 1706 the increased taxation had not only emptied the pockets of most colonists, but had also carried all but £2000 of Connecticut's circulating currency out of the colony and forced most business transactions to be concluded in farm goods and "country pay." When the local collectors failed to obtain the annual assessment for schooling, the colony treasurer appointed an investigation committee. It reported that there was no money to be collected. Education, like everything else, would have to wait for better times.[18]

Johnson also had to wait, since the Guilford grammar school was open only periodically between 1702 and 1707.[19] As a result, he did not start school until he was eleven years old, three or four years later than was the custom in New England. His first master, Jared Eliot, a future member of the Royal Society, gave up the job after only six months in order to accept the ministry at Killingworth. Since Johnson's parents agreed that it was imperative for the boy to get on with his Latin, they decided to send him to Upper Middletown to attend classes under Joseph Smith. Upper Middletown was further inland, very susceptible to Indian attack, and Smith's classes were often postponed. Johnson returned to Guilford in 1708, thoroughly convinced that "in a manner, he had lost a year." [20] During the next two years he made up for lost time. Under Daniel Chapman and his successor, John James, Johnson attended classes regularly at the Guilford grammar school.

The curriculum was traditional. It consisted almost entirely of training in Latin and Greek. Chapman and James taught Johnson to memorize the rules of Latin grammar, to parse and construe, and to translate Latin into English and back again.

18. The colony-wide effect of the depression on the schools is best seen in *Conn. Recs.* 4 : 30–31, 50, 97, 331, 408, and 5 : 213, 353, 463; Clifford K. Shipton, "Secondary Education in the Puritan Colonies," *New England Quarterly* 8 (1934): 652; Benjamin Trumbull, *History of Connecticut,* 2 vols. (1818), vol. 1, chap. 17. The currency problem is discussed in Henry Bronson, "A Historical Account of Connecticut Currency," *Papers of the New Haven County Historical Society* (New Haven, 1865), 1 : 171.

19. *Guilford Records,* C : 77, 101.

20. *Career,* 1 : 4–5; E. E. Beardsley, *The Life and Correspondence of Samuel Johnson* (Hartford, 1873), pp. 3–4; Steiner, *Menunkatuck,* p. 398.

Johnson puzzled over the Greek alphabet, translated from Greek to English, and eventually was required to write original essays in Latin and Greek. This was the classical curriculum as taught in England and Massachusetts, as well as in Connecticut. It was not designed to inform, but rather to instill a set of disciplined mental habits which would enable a student to investigate substantive topics later in his educational career. It was assumed that the best students, once they were "duly prepared and Expert in Latin and Greek," would continue their education at the Collegiate School at Saybrook, twelve miles up the road from Guilford.[21]

So when Johnson was graduated from grammar school and announced his intention to attend college, he was following a well-marked path that other Connecticut boys had traveled earlier. And the course that lay before him was equally prescribed. A college education was supposed to prepare a man for leadership in the colony, perhaps as a civil magistrate, but more probably as a Puritan minister. Tradition provided direction at most of the crucial junctures of a young man's life, and Puritan tradition encouraged the best of its youth to aspire to a ministerial career. That seemed to be where Johnson was heading, but he was doing so at a time when the religious traditions that had shaped Connecticut Puritanism were facing serious challenges and changes.

What was being challenged and changed was the basic conception of the church and the ministry as defined by the Puritan founders of New England. While these founders had bequeathed to Johnson's generation a consistent commitment to education, they had also passed on a legacy of ecclesiastical inconsistency and confusion. The first Puritan settlers had tailored their religious institutions to fit their understanding of the human search for sanctity. They were especially concerned that the specific form of church polity which they devised be able to

21. Middlekauf, *Ancients and Axioms*, pp. 77–83; Kenneth B. Murdock, "The Teaching of Latin and Greek at the Boston Latin School in 1712," Colonial Society of Massachusetts, *Transactions* 27 (1932): 21–29. The quotation is from Yale's entrance requirements.

harness the religious fervor of the church members without at the same time creating a cumbersome network of institutional offices and agencies that would impede rather than facilitate the individual's pursuit of godliness. Although most Puritans acknowledged their kinship with the Church of England, they decried the excessive ritual and ceremony, the proliferation of bishops, archbishops, and minor church officers, the incompetent but entrenched clergy, and the corrupt membership of the Anglican church. In Puritan eyes the Church of England was still overloaded with institutional remnants of Catholicism; it was clear to the founders of the Massachusetts Bay Colony that the visible church in England stood too far from the invisible; it included obvious sinners as well as saints; it needed to be purified. The first generation of New England Puritans, then, were bound together by their common disgust with Anglican church procedures and by their desire that ecclesiastical considerations be subordinated to the more pressing quest for personal salvation.[22]

Upon arriving in New England the Puritans had to transform this commitment to a personal polity from an instrument of opposition to one of control. Equipped with an arsenal of ideas about the church that they had built up in their opposition to episcopacy in England, they had limited experience in the application of these ideas. Since religion was the dominant force in the lives of the Puritans—at least contemporary diaries, letters, published treaties, and the bulk of the historical record lead to this conclusion—many of their basic ideas about social organization and the relationship between social order and individual freedom found expression in their writings on church polity and in the structure of their churches. Moreover, since the way they translated their ideas into religious institutions was so influential for Johnson and his generation, it is nec-

---

22. The literature on early Puritan views of the church is immense. Among a host of distinguished works, I have been guided most directly by Edmund S. Morgan, *Visible Saints* (Ithaca, 1963), pp. 1–32, and *Roger Williams: The Church and the State* (New York, 1967), pp. 3–27; also Perry Miller, *Orthodoxy in Massachusetts* (Cambridge, Mass., 1933), passim.

essary to take some care in tracing the broad outlines of New England polity as it developed in the seventeenth century.

In 1648, five years before Johnson's grandfather moved from New Haven to Guilford, the religious leaders of New England formalized their position on church polity in a document entitled the Cambridge Platform. It represented the distillation of their experience in the New World, an attempt to build a church on purely biblical precedents, and their effort to enclose Puritan piety within a social institution. The guiding principle of the Platform was the recognition that power rested with the congregation. It provided for no supervision by bishops or civil magistrates. Members were obliged to imbibe the word of God and to discipline one another. Although the Platform acknowledged that "churches have the right to preserve church-communion one with another," it insisted that one church did not have dominion over another. Neither the decision of a synod (a gathering of ministers to discuss church problems) nor the advice of civil authorities was binding on a congregation unless the majority of members approved. Moreover, the church members selected the minister. If he proved unworthy or delinquent, they could depose him. The ordination ceremony consisted of an "Imposition of Hands" upon the elected minister by representatives of the congregation. Since this informal ceremony invested him with no permanent spiritual power, when a minister left one church he was not regarded as a minister until elected and ordained by his new congregation. Finally, an individual member was required to demonstrate that he possessed saving grace before he was admitted as a full member. This was the most innovative element of early New England polity; both English Anglicans and English Puritans rejected such a pure criterion for membership. According to the New Englanders a church was not a place where men could come in search of salvation; it was a place where those who were already saved gathered for "the mutual edification of one another." [23]

23. All information and quotations are from Williston Walker, *The Creeds and Platforms of Congregationalism* (Boston, 1960), pp. 205-30.

None of the Puritan founders were behavioral scientists. They justified their institutional creations to one another in biblical rather than sociological terms. They claimed that their churches were modeled on the "pure and unspotted" churches established by the apostles in the early Christian Era. From a modern perspective it seems clear, however, that the early Puritans found most meaningful those passages from the New Testament that affirmed their disgust with the hierarchical and centralized organization of the Church of England.

But by limiting membership to the saints, they had unwittingly deprived the church of its evangelical function. Unlike the New England schools, which were intended to nourish the rational faculties, discipline the passions, and alter behavior, the main mission of the church was not to make people behave differently. Nor did the minister claim to convert sinners. Granted, the non-elect were required to attend services on the assumption that their chances of salvation might be improved by exposure to the Word, but the early Puritans did not believe that the church was primarily an instrument for conversion. Its main function was to bring those who possessed saving grace together. And the infusion of grace, unlike education, was not within the province of public institutions. It was a private matter between the individual and God.

The ways in which these ideas about the church were found wanting and seriously modified during the remainder of the seventeenth century established the ecclesiastical context for Johnson's later religious crisis. Since the Puritans insisted that all the activities of their community be subservient to the common quest for godliness, social and political controversies tended to spread to the church, producing schisms and disputes that the congregational polity could not resolve.[24] But the paramount crisis of the second generation concerned the problem of church membership. In 1662 a synod decided to admit to the church all grandchildren of saints who led moral and scandal-free lives,

---

24. Richard L. Bushman, *From Puritan to Yankee: Character and the Social Order in Connecticut, 1690–1765* (Cambridge, Mass., 1967), pp. 162–82, contains an excellent analysis of the impact of political, economic, and social dissension on the churches.

despite the fact that their parents had been unable to demonstrate their own election. Neither these new members nor their parents were allowed to receive communion or vote in church affairs—they were only "halfway members"—but their inclusion guaranteed that church membership would not shrink to nothing if future generations of Puritans did not produce their share of saints. Implicit in the synod's decision was the recognition that the subjective mystery of salvation was less detectable than the architects of the Cambridge Platform had realized, that a pure membership was a flimsy foundation on which to construct an ecclesiastical system, and that the restraining influence of the church on the entire community was more important than the preservation of a congregation of saints.[25]

By the beginning of the eighteenth century the implications of the Half-Way Covenant had been made explicit and institutionalized in many of Connecticut's churches.[26] Solomon Stoddard, the powerful minister of Northampton, Massachusetts, had even abandoned all distinctions between full and halfway members and admitted all upstanding citizens of the area to communion. And Stoddard had not stopped there. He had also claimed that participation in church services and reception of the Lord's Supper was a means of grace by which an unconverted man might become regenerate. A church was not a gathering of persons who had discovered sainthood on their own, but an institution which facilitated sainthood. Salvation, like education, was dependent on public institutions.[27]

Finally, Stoddard insisted that the minister, not the membership, was the center of authority in the church "and it is not

25. Walker, *Creeds and Platforms*, pp. 238–339; Morgan, *Visible Saints*, pp. 113–38; Perry Miller, "The Half-Way Covenant," *New England Quarterly* 6 (1933): 676–715. Robert G. Pope's "The Half-Way Covenant: Church Membership in the Holy Commonwealth, 1648–1690" (Ph.D. diss., Yale University, 1967), analyzes the implementation of the synod's policy. The Connecticut legislature's acceptance of the synod's findings is in *Conn. Recs.*, 2 : 109.

26. Walker, *Creeds and Platforms*, p. 282; Bushman, *Puritan to Yankee*, pp. 148–49.

27. Solomon Stoddard, *The Doctrine of Instituted Churches . . .* (Boston, 1700), pp. 8, 21; also Stoddard, *An Appeal to the Learned . . .* (Boston, 1708), p. 25; Perry Miller, "Solomon Stoddard, 1643–1729," *Harvard Theological Review* 34 (1941): 277–330

the work either of the Brethren or Ruling Elders anyways to intermeddle . . . or limit him." Decades of squabbles within and between churches had convinced Stoddard that "the community are not fit to judge & rule in the Church," that church order required clerical rather than congregational autonomy.[28]

In 1708, the year Johnson returned from Upper Middletown to attend school at Guilford, the leading ministers of Connecticut gathered at Saybrook and announced the creation of the ecclesiastical machinery to control the larger and more diverse church membership brought about by the Half-Way Covenant and the adoption of Stoddardean policies. The Saybrook Platform established four county organizations, known as consociations, to oversee the activities of Connecticut churches. These consociations, controlled by the clergy, were empowered to decide all disputes between churches and to review the ordination of new pastors. If a congregation did not follow the consociation's decision, it lost the legal right to raise taxes to support its minister. The second section of the Platform created a "General Association," another layer of ministers empowered to supervise colony-wide church practice and settle "Questions & Cases of Importance" that the consociations had been unable to resolve.[29]

Like the Cambridge Platform, the Saybrook Platform was part of the Puritan effort to institutionalize piety; but unlike the Cambridge Platform it focused attention on the institution rather than the piety. Over seventy-five years of experience in the new world had convinced the Puritans that sainthood was neither so detectable nor so easily institutionalized as the founders had believed. Although concern for personal piety remained strong, the churches had subordinated their initial mission of nourishing the elect to the more practical task of monitoring the behavior of all members. A church was no longer a covenanted community of visible saints gathered together for mutual edification. It was an interlocking network of congregations and con-

---

28. Stoddard, *The Doctrine of Instituted Churches*, p. 12.
29. Walker, *Creeds and Platforms*, pp. 504–05. See Sydney E. Ahlstrom, "The Saybrook Platform: A 250th Anniversary Retrospect," *Bulletin of the Congregational Library* 11, no. 1 (1959): 5–10; no. 2 (1960): 3–15.

sociations, all under the authority of a clerically controlled Association designed to maintain order and uniformity. Since the Connecticut Puritans still believed that the biblical mode of church organization was eternal and absolute, it was difficult for them to admit that the Saybrook Platform was a departure from the Congregationalism of their fathers. It was even more difficult for them to admit that, by the beginning of the eighteenth century, they had constructed an ecclesiastical establishment similar to the one from which their fathers had fled.[30]

There is no reason to believe that, as a twelve-year-old boy, Samuel Johnson knew what the Saybrook Platform meant. He was too busy with his Latin and Greek, preparing for college. But whether or not he was conscious of the currents of ecclesiastical opinion that were blowing through Connecticut, he was soon to be buffeted by those same winds. For Saybrook had not put an end to the half-century of debate over the church and the ministry; it had merely provided an institutional framework within which ecclesiastical bickering could continue.[31]

In good time Johnson would find himself disturbed by the same issues that had troubled New Englanders for so long. For

30. I am not suggesting that the Puritan jeremiads, the laments over the loss of piety tirelessly repeated at the turn of the seventeenth century, were wholly accurate descriptions of what was happening. There is evidence that many church members retained their religious zeal; that they had such an elevated conception of what was required for sainthood that they never felt capable of testifying. My contention is that by 1708 the leaders of the Connecticut churches were convinced that piety required church order, and church order demanded a clerical bureaucracy with coercive power. Religion was still, in my opinion, the dominant influence in a New Englander's life. For that reason I regard the gradual shift in thinking about the ways to organize a church as an excellent early indication of Puritan ideas about the state. For an analysis of the emergence of a more conservative or court conception of politics, see T. H. Breen, *The Character of the Good Ruler: Puritan Political Ideas in New England, 1630–1730* (New Haven, 1970), pp. 203–39; also Perry Miller, *The New England Mind: From Colony to Province* (Cambridge, Mass., 1953), pp. 367–84.

31. The New Haven County churches refused to surrender their congregational prerogatives to the consociations, and many churches throughout the colony resented the unprecedented clerical authority. Walker, *Creeds and Platforms*, pp. 508–13; *Conn. Recs.*, 5 : 55–56; *Contributions to the Ecclesiastical History of Connecticut* (New Haven, 1861), pp. 41–42; Bushman, *Puritan to Yankee*, pp. 151–56. See below, chap. 4.

the present, he was having enough trouble mastering the intricacies of the subjunctive mood. Deacon William was dead and gone, but the hopes he had expressed for his grandson needed to be fulfilled. Land still had to be cleared and younger sisters needed help from big brother with their school work. The neighbors and family had come to expect a lot of the Johnson boy. He was not going to disappoint them.

2

Curricular and Universal Order

The Collegiate School at Saybrook was only twelve miles up the Post Road from Guilford. In 1710 it had not yet been renamed Yale College; nor had it grown into a great center of learning. The college consisted of ten acres of land and a small, wooden-frame building where two tutors, Joseph Noyes and Phineas Fisk, lived and held classes for fifteen young men. Enrolment had been held down by the Indian wars, despite the fact that the Assembly had excused college students from service in the militia. The rector or president, the Reverend Samuel Andrew, remained at his Milford parsonage thirty miles away. He made an annual appearance at commencement, but left effective control of the college in the hands of the tutors. There was no dormitory; students were obliged to find rooms with families in Saybrook. The library consisted of about forty dated volumes donated by the first rector, Abraham Pierson. Little wonder that when Caleb Heathcote visited the school he concluded that it was not a college at all, but "a thing which they call a college." [1]

1. *Conn. Recs.*, 4 : 440. See Franklin B. Dexter, ed., *Documentary History of Yale University under the Original Charter of the Collegiate School of Connecticut, 1701–1745* (New Haven, 1916), p. 59 (hereafter cited as *Doc. Hist.*) for a letter from Noyes to Andrew indicating that the rector's duties were only ceremonial. See Franklin B. Dexter, *Biographical Sketches of the Graduates of Yale College with Annals of the College History*, 6 vols. (New York, 1885–1912), 1 : 97–117 (hereafter cited as *Yale Biographies*) for the size of the classes. See also Heathcote to Secretary, 9 November 1705, in Francis L. Hawks and William S. Perry, eds., *Documentary History of the Protestant Episcopal Church in the United States of America, Containing Numerous Hitherto Unpublished Documents Concerning the Church in Connecticut*, 2 vols. (New York, 1863–64), 1 : 10 (hereafter cited as *Conn. Episcopacy*).

In September 1710 Johnson and eight other first-year students
arrived at the Collegiate School and began to settle into the
daily routine of college life. They rose at around five-thirty in
the morning and walked to the college building for assembly
at six o'clock where they recited morning prayers in Latin. The
assembly then broke up into classes, with Johnson and the other
freshmen following tutor Fisk into his study for recitations. They
emerged an hour later for breakfast, a short half-hour meal,
then returned to the classroom where they spent the remainder
of the morning. The big meal of the day was dinner at noon,
after which students had an hour and a half off for recreation.
By two o'clock the students were back at work, either reciting
for Fisk or preparing for recitations. There was a light meal at
sundown, followed by evening prayers and a reading from Scripture, all in Latin. Johnson and his fellow students then returned
to their lodgings in town to study until eleven, when they were
obliged by the college rules to put out their lights and rest for
the next day.[2]

There were breaks in the routine. Two or three times a week
the upperclassmen were required to conduct a public debate.
In these disputations one student was pitted against another and
obliged to argue the validity of a logical principle, a theological
proposition, or the meaning of some biblical passage. The debates were often held after meals, so that a freshman could observe the older students in action and get an introduction to the
subjects he would soon be studying. Every Saturday the entire
student body gathered to hear a lecture on theology by Fisk
or Noyes. The students had Sunday off, except that everyone was
expected to attend services at the Saybrook Congregational

2. There is no complete account of student life at Saybrook. This description is based on Edwin Oviatt, *The Beginnings of Yale, 1701–1726* (New Haven,
1926), pp. 237–40, and Franklin B. Dexter, "Yale College at Saybrook,"
Miscellaneous Historical Papers (New Haven, 1918), pp. 253–54. There is
an unpublished manuscript by E. P. Morris in the vault of the Yale Library
that deals with early colonial education. Chapter 2 is especially useful. For a
comparison with Harvard, see Samuel Eliot Morison, *Harvard in the Seventeenth Century*, 2 vols. (Cambridge, Mass., 1936), 1 : 74–110.

Church.[3] It was a full schedule, but Johnson managed to find the spare time to ice-skate with classmate Benjamin Lord during the winter. And in the warmer months he liked to swim in Long Island Sound.[4]

The trustees who devised the college rules were all ministers. They were, by and large, the same ministers who had drafted the Saybrook Platform, the same men who controlled the consociations and the Saybrook Association. In their minds there was no tension between the official goal of the Collegiate School—"the Liberal & Religious Education of Suitable Youth"—and the more practical function: namely, to reinforce rather than challenge intellectual assumptions and thereby provide a steady flow of orthodox ministerial candidates who would help bring order out of the current ecclesiastical chaos.

The four-year college program was a model of academic order. The freshmen were to spend their time with languages, polishing up their Latin and Greek and mastering the grammatical rules of Hebrew. Either at the end of the first or the beginning of the second year, the students began logic, which they continued to study throughout their sophomore year. As juniors they were to read natural philosophy or physics. By the time they were seniors they were ready to tackle the intricacies of mathematics and metaphysics. Training in theology was to continue on each Saturday throughout the four years.[5]

3. For an account of disputations, see David Potter, *Debating in the Colonial Chartered Colleges* (New York, 1944). Johnson wrote out two of his disputations: "An Analysis of the Nineteenth Chapter of Mark" and "An Analysis of the Second Chapter of Matthew." Both are in the Johnson MSS. See also James J. Walsh, "Scholasticism in the Colonial Colleges," *New England Quarterly* 5 (1932): 483–90. For Harvard, see Morison, *Harvard in the Seventeenth Century*, 1 : 179–84.

4. *Career*, 1 : 5.

5. There is no adequate account of the Saybrook curriculum. For general information, see Colyer Meriwether, *Our Colonial Curriculum 1607–1766* (Washington, 1807). The official report of the trustees on the curriculum is in *Yale Biographies*, 1 : 348–49. The most detailed account of the early Saybrook curriculum is in a letter from Benjamin Lord to Ezra Stiles on 28 May 1779, in ibid., pp. 115–16. Helpful are Oviatt, *The Beginnings of Yale*; Ebenezer Baldwin, *Yale College: A Sketch of Its History* (New York, 1879), 2 : 496–97; Alexander Cowie, *Educational Problems at Yale College in the*

There was no room in this program, as there was in the Harvard curriculum, for either rhetoric or astronomy. The trustees of the Collegiate School apparently felt that their charges would get enough rhetorical training in their class recitations and disputations. Since they regarded astronomy as a physical science, the trustees preferred to have it taught in the third year as a part of the physics course. Otherwise, the subjects offered at the Collegiate School and the order in which they were offered were quite similar to the courses in the Harvard curriculum, which was modeled on Cambridge and Oxford.[6]

But the college curriculum inculcated a vision of order that transcended the discipline of the daily schedule and the systematic arrangement of subjects. Languages, logic, physics, mathematics, and metaphysics were the intellectual components of a medieval conception of universal order. The disconcerting discoveries of Copernicus and Galileo had as yet no place in the curriculum. A young graduate of the Collegiate School accepted the scholastic vision of a cosmos ruled by God with the earth at its center. Every planet, person, animal, and element occupied a divinely ordained place. Although the quest to decipher God's will could produce anxiety, especially in a devout Puritan, a young man knew that the quest was not in vain, that there was a cosmic scheme in which he had a place, just as there was a divinely sanctioned blueprint for church order. All was not right in the world, but there was a right and it was in heaven with God. During his college years Johnson would learn to expect things to fit together, to regard disorder as a symptom of human ignorance, and to explain natural events in supernatural terms.

Before any member of the class of 1714 was introduced to the more challenging disciplines, he had to endure a year of gram-

---

Eighteenth Century (New Haven, 1936). For the best insight into the content of the subjects, see *Career*, 2 : 55–187, and Johnson's college notebooks in the Johnson MSS. Full of new information on college life and the curriculum is Richard Warch's "Yale College, 1701–1740" (Ph.D. diss., Yale University, 1968).

6. The Harvard curriculum for 1723, as reported by tutor Henry Flint, is in Morison, *Harvard in the Seventeenth Century*, 1 : 146–47. See James B. Mullinger, *A History of the University of Cambridge* (London, 1888), pp. 159–70. For Oxford, see G. C. Broderick, *A History of the University of Oxford* (London, 1891), pp. 181–201.

Of course, this is a historical judgment made from a modern perspective, after the broad intellectual movements of the eighteenth century have crystalized. From Johnson's point of view, Ramist logic was not an amalgam of medieval and modern ideas, but rather a required subject. To judge from the notes he took during his college years, it seems clear that Johnson accepted the pseudoprinciples of Ramus at face value, conscientiously copying the definitions into his notebook without considering their import for philosophy or science. He was a dutiful, not an imaginative student. He did not question the arbitrary series of dichotomous categories of *Dialecticae*. For him, as for most Puritan scholars, these categories *were* knowledge. In later years, the recollection of his total acceptance of meaningless Ramist terms and other "Scholastic cobwebs" caused him to condemn the entire New England intellectual tradition.[21] He was never conscious of any connection between Ramist logic and, for example, Newtonian physics.

The entire third year at Saybrook was devoted to the study of physics according to the Ramist method. Physics, according to student Johnson, was "the art of becoming thoroughly acquainted with, understanding and inquiring into nature, and the structure and actions of all things in nature." [22] With the definition established, Johnson went on to put other lessons of Ramist logic to work. He began to look for "catholic rules, by whose light the nature of things is understood." [23] Ramus had assured him that physics, like Latin and logic, was essentially the study of principles or "whatever has a nature generated from principles." [24] In order to understand everything there was to know about physics, all Johnson had to do was discover the principles

---

21. Ramus defined an "argument" as "quod aliquid arguendum affectum est." According to this definition anything could be an "argument." Although there were obvious differences between kinds of "arguments," Ramus provided no way to distinguish one from the other. Because he based his entire system on this nondiscriminatory definition, Ramus introduced chaos into his logic at the very outset. For the definition, see Ramée, *Dialecticae*, p. 1.

22. From a physics manuscript by Johnson, "Synopsis Philosophiae Naturalis," *Career*, 2 : 27.

23. Ibid., p. 25.

24. Ibid., p. 29.

that governed natural objects "where they exist in a fundamental way, and not merely in the human mind or books" and then arrange them "in a methodical and orderly way." [25]

The notion that there are patterns imbedded in the natural world which can be deciphered by rational men, and that these patterns underlie all celestial and terrestrial phenomena, had already led Isaac Newton to develop empirical and mathematical postulates that would alter dramatically the medieval conception of natural philosophy. Unfortunately, the Collegiate School offered a version of natural philosophy which was neither empirical nor mathematical. The principles and patterns that Johnson was taught to search for were speculative, based on topical charts drawn up by logicians and metaphysicians like Ramus and Keckermann. Johnson and the other students never heard of Newton or his work. This left them twenty-five years behind their counterparts at Harvard, where Charles Morton's *Compendium Physicae,* adopted for use in 1687, blended the modern scientific discoveries of Newton with the old Scholastic hypotheses. Neither Harvard nor the European universities was quick to embrace the pioneers of modern thought wholeheartedly. At the Collegiate School, Galileo, Boyle, Kepler, Newton, and Huygens were completely ignored.[26]

Johnson and the other budding physicists at the Collegiate School had to search for physical principles in an archaic intellectual environment. The textbook in physics at Saybrook in 1712 was a manuscript of Abraham Pierson based on his old Harvard notes.[27] These notes had been taken in 1667, when Pierson was a senior sophister and Johannes Magirus (?–1596) was the reigning authority in physics at Harvard. As a result, the physics taught to Johnson was a secondhand version of

25. Ibid., p. 25.

26. *Publications of the Colonial Society of Massachusetts,* vol. 33 (1940) contains the *Compendium.* See also Morison, *Harvard in the Seventeenth Century,* pp. 223–52; A. Wolf, *A History of Science, Technology, and Philosophy in the 16th and 17th Centuries* (New York, 1935), p. 54.

27. The manuscript itself is lost, but the notes on which it was based are in the memorabilia room of the Yale University Library.

Magirus' *Physiologicae Peripateticae,* itself a hundred-year-old summary of Aristotle's *De Anima.*[28]

Tutor Fisk lectured on the definition of matter and form, the arrangement of the four elements—earth, air, fire, and water—and the distinction between genus and species. Motion was summarily explained as "a successive change by which there is a progress from a terminus *a quo* to a terminus *ad quem.*"[29] This was pure Aristotle, as were the lectures on astronomy, in which Johnson learned that the earth was at the center of the universe, surrounded by the other planets and the orbit of stars.[30] At only one point did the Saybrook curriculum veer from the scholastic notion of physics, and that was to correct the "heathen Aristotle" for not including a discussion of heavenly spirits in his account. Here Johnson's notes referred to Scripture as the final authority in order to verify the nine distinguishing characteristics of an angel.[31]

At the end of his third year, when Johnson reviewed his notes on physics, he was able to discern the principles of physical nature, but they were scholastic, not Newtonian, principles. The world was an "ordered structure of all nature being dependent on one principle and tending to one end."[32] The message of Aristotelian physics, like that of Ramist logic, was natural order,

28. I have used the edition of Magirus published at Cambridge, England, in 1642. Magirus was discarded by Harvard in 1671 and replaced by the Cartesian text of Heereboord. Morison, *Harvard in the Seventeenth Century,* p. 233. For colonial physics, see Louis McKeehan, *Yale Science, the First Hundred Years 1701–1801* (New York, 1947), and Theodore Hornberger, *Scientific Thought in the American Colleges 1638–1800* (Austin, 1945).

29. *Career,* 2 : 39.

30. *Career,* 2 : 51. Harvard had long since abandoned Ptolemy for Copernicus. The first recorded exposition of Copernicus in the colonies is by Zechariah Brigden, "A Brief Exposition and Proof of the Philolaick System," *New England Quarterly* 7 (1934): 9–12, first published in 1659. Morison, *Harvard in the Seventeenth Century,* pp. 214–15.

31. *Career,* 2 : 45. The Ramist belief that all knowledge arranged itself into a dichotomy conflicted with the hierarchical order of Aristotelian physics, but Ramus did not carry his attack on Aristotelian logic into an attack on scholastic physics or astronomy. The tensions between Ramist logic and Aristotelian physics went unnoticed at Saybrook.

32. *Career,* 2 : 157.

but the order took the form of a hierarchy rather than a dichotomy. Johnson believed that he lived in a universe in which insects and meteors ranked below metals and minerals, in which plants ranked below animals and men, in which all material and spiritual objects were judged according to their resemblance to God. Physics, as taught at Saybrook, accepted the medieval habit of directing attention not towards experimentation and empirical analysis of nature, but toward speculation on the supernatural. Science was dependent on theology.[33]

Johnson had been studying theology since freshman year. Either he or one of his classmates had read selections from the Bible aloud at every meal, and the bulk of his Hebrew assignments had come from the Old Testament. More importantly, he had been listening to a theology lecture by Noyes or Fisk on every Saturday of the school year. The Saybrook trustees believed that a good deal of harm had been done by those people who had tampered with the doctrines of New England Puritanism. A heavy dose of William Ames was the trustees' cure for doctrinal instability among the students of the Collegiate School. Every week, Johnson listened to the tenets of religious orthodoxy, as they were found in Ames' *Medulla Theologicae* and *Cases of Conscience* or Johann Wollebius' *Abridgment of Christian Divinity*. These were old texts. The founders of New England Puritanism had used them, and succeeding generations of Puritans had done the same. Eighty years after the founding of New England, Ames and Wollebius still represented those theological doctrines that a devout Puritan accepted as orthodox. The contentiousness that divided New England society over the question of proper ecclesiastical order had no parallel in theology.[34]

Johnson learned that God was an all-powerful being who had created Adam and endowed him "with the most illustrious wisdom." [35] Although God had provided man with a rational

---

33. Ibid., p. 27.

34. Johnson mentioned that Saybrook students were not allowed "to vary an ace in their thoughts from Dr. Ames *Medulla Theologiae* and some writings of Wollebius." *Career*, 1 : 6.

35. *Career*, 2 : 59.

faculty and made a "covenant of works" with Adam that
promised salvation in return for obedience to divine law, Adam
had allowed the imperfect, irrational aspects of his nature to
take precedence over the rational. The result was original sin,
which doomed all his descendants to "the habitual transgression
and deviation . . . from the law of God." [36] The all-merciful
Creator could not allow man to writhe helplessly in a state of
depravity, so he formed a new covenant, the "covenant of grace,"
which promised salvation in return for faith, while also obliging
man to make every effort at perfect obedience, no matter how
impossible it seemed. Obedience to God's law was not completely
impossible for a depraved man, because Adam had once possessed
the ability to perform holy actions, "and after the Fall some
little sparks of it remained." [37] Those who successfully prepared
their souls evidenced signs of election. The others were condemned to hell.[38]

Over and above the specific theological points, the lectures on
Saturday served as the chief interdisciplinary course in the Collegiate School's curriculum. Theology, like logic, was a series of
numbered paragraphs, headings and subheadings, definitions and
demonstrations designed to reveal a pre-existent divine pattern
which New England Puritanism most nearly embodied on earth.
Like Ramus, Ames admitted a concern for "Method and logicall
form." [39] Wollebius sounded like Ramus when he asked his
readers "to imprint in their memories the Anatomie of the Body
of Theologie, that in the Common places, in the definitions and
divisions of heavenly doctrine, they may be exact and perfect." [40]

---

36. Ibid., p. 165.
37. Ibid., p. 59.
38. Ibid., p. 175. Johnson's theological section of *Technologia* asserts the
doctrinal and ecclesiastical beliefs of orthodox New England Puritanism. Its
point of view is virtually identical to that of Thomas Hooker's *A Survey of
the Summe of Church Discipline* (London, 1648), which represented the views
of the founders, and to Samuel Willard's *A Compleat Body of Divinity*
(Boston, 1726), which opened up the new century. Perry Miller, "The
Marrow of Puritan Divinity," *Errand into the Wilderness* (Cambridge, Mass.,
1956), pp. 48–98; Norman Pettit, *The Heart Prepared* (New Haven, 1966).
39. William Ames, *The Marrow of Sacred Divinity* (London, 1643), A–3.
40. Johann Wollebius, *The Abridgment of Christian Divinity* (London,
1660), A–2.

None of this seemed unduly abstract or abitrary to Johnson.
It fitted in perfectly with the scholasticism of his other subjects.
Ramus had shown that there was a dichotomous division running through all things. Surely one of the most fundamental
of all divisions was that between the natural and the spiritual.
Aristotelian physics had explored the former. Ames and Wollebius were the academic guides through the latter. A college education was a four-year journey over an interlocking network of
academic roads, all constructed out of medieval materials and
all leading, not to Rome, but to God. And the fourth-year
course in metaphysics, based largely on Ames' *Medulla,* promised
to provide a peek at the blueprint for the entire scholastic grid
system.[41]

Johnson was anxious to learn metaphysics, but he had to learn
mathematics first. He had a lot to learn, since his previous
mathematical training had not gone beyond the simplest forms
of arithmetic. Fisk exposed Johnson to fractions and certain
"numerical principles," such as how to find the lowest common
denominator. The highest level of mathematics which Fisk could
teach was plane geometry. Johnson delighted in the axioms,
rules, and precision of geometric problems, for they quite clearly
seemed to substantiate the notion that there was some essential
order to the entire universe. The lectures on mathematics
stopped at this point, without the mention of algebra, primarily
because Fisk did not know that it existed.[42] Next came metaphysics.

The study of mathematics, even the rudimentary form of it
that Johnson learned, was part of the search for universal rules.
But in mathematics the rules were expressed in numbers,
whereas in grammar, logic, and physics they were verbal. Moreover, there were other obvious discrepancies among the disciplines that had not been explained. The formula that allowed a

41. Morison, *Harvard in the Seventeenth Century,* pp. 253–64, for Harvard
scholasticism.

42. *Career,* 2 : 115–37. The back of Johnson's college notebook and other
papers of this time are covered with simple geometric problems and fraction
reductions. At Harvard "as late as 1725, the senior sophisters had to spend a
month studying Arithmetic in order to qualify for Euclid." Morison, *Harvard
in the Seventeenth Century,* p. 208.

student to discover the area of a triangle bore no apparent relation to the grammar rule one followed to discover the stem of a Latin verb. And grammar rules seemed unconnected with the rule a good Ramist followed to distinguish one side of a logical dichotomy from another. An eighteenth-century philosophe would have explained these discrepancies as the result of a reliance on fictitious medieval categories and authorities. A twentieth-century relativist would have condemned the entire enterprise for its assumption that there were objective standards against which to measure reality. A third-year scholar at Saybrook, lacking the wisdom of a philosophe or the cynicism of a modern man, believed that all discrepancies were to be resolved during the senior course in metaphysics.

Johnson had a fair idea of what metaphysics was all about. Before his senior year he had perused the *Encyclopaedia* of John Alsted (1588–1638) and the systems of Alexander Richardson and Keckermann.[43] Each of these writers was part of that western intellectual tradition that culminated in Diderot's attempt to compile a tableau of all knowledge. Alsted, for example, listed ideas and authors from Aristotle to James I, and defined the parameters of each discipline along the way. By reading these encyclopedic compilations, Johnson could see that specific facts were clustered around general principles. Alsted and Keckermann did not make their underlying principles of synthesis clear, but metaphysics promised to lay bare the structural framework of all thought.[44]

But Johnson studied metaphysics at the college for only a short time. At the beginning of his senior year he left Saybrook in order to take a job as master at the Guilford grammar school. He did not record his reasons for leaving, perhaps because it was not unusual for students at the Collegiate School to leave college at the end of three years and still graduate with their class. Guilford offered him an excellent salary of 40 shillings per

43. *Encyclopaedia Scientiarum Omnium* (Herborn, 1628). Johnson mentions Alsted in *Career*, 1 : 6. See Perceval R. Cole, *A Neglected Mind: Johann H. Alsted* (Sydney, 1910).

44. Keckermann's *Systema S.S. Theologiae* (Hanover, 1615) was in the Yale Library in 1742.

month, which was considerably higher than average, perhaps
too high to resist. Whatever the reasons, he left Saybrook in
November of 1713.[45]

During the next year, while he instructed the grammar school
students of Guilford, he also worked on a philosophical treatise
entitled *Technologia Ceu Technometica*. Written in Latin, it
was intended to be a synthesis of all that he had learned at college. As with most of Johnson's intellectual creations, it sacrificed
originality in favor of a faithful rendering of all that he had
learned. It reflected rather than refracted the scholastic lessons
taught at Saybrook. In addition, it was Johnson's miniature version of Alsted's *Encyclopaedia* or Keckermann's *Systema*, a
student's conception of what the Collegiate School regarded as
metaphysics. Johnson dedicated the treatise to "the most worthy,
most brilliant" Saybrook tutor, Phineas Fisk.[46]

Johnson began his analysis by distinguishing, in good Ramist
fashion, between two kinds of ideas called types and archetypes.[47]
The former were ideas of this world; the latter were ideas located outside this world. Using the techniques learned in his
second-year logic class, Johnson distinguished between two kinds
of types. The first, entypes, were ideas as they existed in physical
objects.[48] The entype of a chair, for example, was the essence
that a man perceived when he looked at the chair. It was the
essential quality or nature of any physical object. The second
kind of type, the ectype, was an idea as it existed in the human
mind, the innate idea or set of ideas with which a man was
born.[49] The existence of ectypes made logic possible, because
they provided all men with an inherent comprehension of universal principles which the study of Ramus would deepen and

45. *Career*, 1 : 6; Smith, *History of Guilford*, p. 398.
46. *Career*, 2 : 57. Years later Johnson added, "Oh! dismal, intolerable, an
hundredth part of this would be enough for him." The word "technologia"
was another conventional term in the Puritan academic vocabulary. Frequently
cited in the commencement theses of eighteenth-century Harvard and Yale, it
was a one-word expression of the idea that all knowledge could be laid out
systematically, usually with the aid of Ramist categories.
47. *Career*, 2 : 65.
48. Ibid., p. 67.
49. Ibid., p. 69.

develop. Logic, then, was "the ectypal art of reasoning well." [50]
All logic was built on an ectypal foundation.

The keystone of Johnson's amateur philosophy was the archetype. All the entypes and ectypes were pale copies of absolute
and eternal standards that Johnson called archetypes. Like the
conception of entypes or innate ideas, Johnson's reference to
archetypes revealed a heavy indebtedness to Plato, a debt which
Johnson failed to acknowledge. While the physics that Puritan
boys learned at Saybrook relied on the Aristotelian division
between matter and form, the metaphysics accepted the Platonic
view that the physical world is but an imperfect image of some
transcendent spiritual reality. Johnson was unfamiliar with the
Timaeus or any of Plato's other writings, however, and had
adopted a fundamentally Platonic philosophy indirectly, by reading the *Medulla* of William Ames. All the metaphysical terminology of the *Technologia* was lifted straight from the *Medulla,*
the sourcebook for Puritan theology. Moreover, Johnson followed Ames in defining an archetype not as a cosmic ideal, as a
classical Platonist would have insisted upon, but as "an idea of
the thing decreed in the divine mind." [51] Archetypes were ideas
as they existed in the mind of God. Every worldly object or type
was not just a reflection of some pristine, impersonal order, but
a mirror of God's will. As Johnson put it, "Things are God's
words in print." Or as Jonathan Edwards was to express this
lesson of Ames, natural events were "shadows of divine things." [52]

The net result of Johnson's metaphysical scheme was to enlist
Platonic philosophy in the service of religion. It encouraged a
young man to use his ectypal powers (logic) to analyze the
entypes (natural philosophy), because such an academic pursuit exposed a student to the messages of God in a diluted form.
These same divine messages would be covered in their pure form
during the theology lectures on Saturday. *Technologia* sanctioned
science as the study of types at the same time that it reinforced
the medieval view that science was the handmaiden of theology,

50. Ibid., pp. 69, 95.
51. Ibid., p. 65.
52. Ibid., p. 67; Ola Winslow, ed., *Jonathan Edwards: Basic Writings* (New
York, 1966), p. 250.

which dealt with the archetypes in their purest form. It clarified
the rationale for the assumed connection between subjects
taught in college: there was an order running through all the
arts because the universe was a reflection of the orderly mind
of God. It had practical utility, for it justified the Puritan
tendency to "read sermons in stones," to regard worldly events
like storms and Indian attacks as a manifestation of some spiritual force. It reaffirmed the belief of New Englanders that there
was an archetypal model for church order that all godly men
must strive to discover and re-create on earth. Finally, it made
William Ames the master metaphysician as well as theologian for
New England, for it insisted that ultimate truth and God were
one. Johnson concluded his *Technologia* by referring his readers to William Ames for answers to all unresolved philosophical
questions.[53]

Because the *Technologia* provided such a fitting capstone to
the program at the Collegiate School, Johnson wanted to have
it finished by commencement. This took place on 8 September
1714, but the *Technologia* still needed two months of work.[54]
Johnson decided to leave it at Guilford and bring only his valedictory oration.

Johnson and his classmates gathered outside the college building in the morning and conducted the final disputations for the
benefit of Rector Andrew, the tutors, and all who cared to observe. When the time came to grant degrees, Andrew presented
a book to each senior sophister, who accepted it as a sign of
his degree, then returned it to the rector so that it might be
used again. The ceremonies ended with Johnson's valedictory,
delivered in Latin, and Andrew's concluding prayer.[55]

It was the end of a successful collegiate performance that

53. *Career*, 2 : 183.
54. He finished it on Thanksgiving, 1714.
55. From Lord's account in *Yale Biographies*, 1 : 116. Another account is
somewhat more critical: "I hear that the Athenian Oracle is held at Seabrook
College that all Notty Questions (altho twisted as hard as the Gordion one)
may be Resolved and untied: and that They'll Do it, altho with Alexander's
Sword." Ebenezer Williams to Thomas Foxcroft, 25, December 1714, in
Connecticut Historical Society MSS.

promised to be only the first step in an illustrious academic career. Connecticut's schools were just beginning to recover from the effects of Queen Anne's War; its churches were still confused over questions of polity. The colony needed scholars who could refurnish the war-torn schools with the traditional intellectual doctrines. The churches needed ministers who could address themselves to troublesome ecclesiastical issues and bring order out of the current chaos. Even more promising was the news announced at commencement that, due to the arrival of a large shipment of books from London, the young scholars of the area would have access to the latest European discoveries in science and theology.[56]

56. Anne S. Pratt, *Papers in Honor of Andrew Keogh* (New Haven, 1938), pp. 13–14. Johnson remembered hearing about the books, which were on the way from Boston. See *Career,* 1 : 6.

3

The New Learning

The Post Road headed southwest out of Saybrook, then wound its way along the coastline past Killingworth and Madison into Guilford. The trip home after commencement took only a few hours, but it was sufficient to remove Johnson from the intellectual stimulus of his college friends and from the newly arrived library. He had a college education and a long list of academic honors, but he also had a job that tied him to the Guilford grammar school and to daily Latin vocabulary drills. It was not the place for an ambitious scholar. For four years he had listened to the praise of his tutors and the pleas of those fellow students who needed his academic assistance. Now, after he had mastered the linguistic skills, developed a taste for philosophy, and begun to take ideas seriously, he found himself too big for his home town. Just when the Collegiate School had made available its new 800-volume library, containing the works of Locke, Descartes, Newton, Boyle, and Shakespeare, Johnson was saddled with the task of teaching ten-year-olds how to read.

The availability of the books at Saybrook provided an opportunity to avoid the intellectual sterility of post-college life and to overcome the provincialism of colonial Guilford. During the ensuing months Johnson traveled back and forth from Guilford to Saybrook, his saddle bags filled with copies of Bacon's *Advancement of Learning,* Locke's *Essay on Human Understanding,* and Newton's *Principia,* and his mind filled with the profound speculations of Europe's most renowned thinkers.[1] No

1. *Career,* 1 : 6–7.

one in Guilford could appreciate what Johnson was doing and learning, but there was Daniel Brown down the road in New Haven. Brown, who was also teaching grammar school, felt the need for intellectual exercise, and Johnson soon had him wholly committed to a zealous program of study. In letters Johnson advised Brown not to study too hard and not "to live wholly without diverting of your mind without [sic] feminine society," but also to "write smaller so as to write more." [2] The correspondents exchanged information, shared impressions, and assured themselves of their scholarly superiority. They dropped names, wrote in Latin, quoted long philosophical passages, made fanciful distinctions, and encouraged each other's intellectual pretensions. When Johnson finished a philosophical essay, he and Brown both agreed that it was of cosmic significance and merited the description "These Are/The System of/Travails of The/Humane/Intellect/In The/Microcosm/& In the/Macrocosm/Sophio-Technology." [3]

In 1715 Johnson and Brown began to meet regularly to discuss specific books and compare notes. Other young ministers and teachers of the neighboring towns soon joined these discussions. Jared Eliot, Johnson's old grammar school teacher, came over from Killingworth, and Samuel Whittlesey rode in from Wallingford. John Hart left his ministry in East Guilford to participate. Further south, James Wetmore of North Haven and Timothy Cutler of Stratford got wind of the enterprise and joined in. The seven-man group was soon immersed in an investigation of books and ideas that Johnson saw fit to call the "New Learning." [4]

Although historians have preferred to call it the Enlightenment, the name is less important than the fact that Johnson and his scholarly allies were involved in an intellectual adventure. It was as if they had been placed in a time machine that carried them from the Middle Ages into modernity. All of the old

---

2. Ibid., 2 (dated 20 June 1715): 193.
3. Ibid., 2 : 201. The treatise was finished on 15 October 1716.
4. Ibid., 1 : 7. The group meetings were informal. There is no record of the precise time when each participant began to attend. Johnson claimed the meetings began around 1715.

authorities were in disrepute; the scholastic reference points learned at the Collegiate School were useless as guides. The methodological chart of Ramus now appeared to Johnson as "a curious cowbeb of distributions and definitions." [5] The heir to Ramus was Francis Bacon, who relegated all fanciful projections of the human mind to the trash heap. Johnson claimed that Bacon's *Advancement of Learning* exposed the elaborate tableaux of Ramus, Ames, and Alsted as relics of the dark ages. The Ptolemaic universe, it turned out, had been discredited by scientists like Copernicus and Galileo, who used the Baconian empirical technique to revolutionize astronomy. The physical theories of Aristotle and Magirus had been eclipsed by Newtonian mechanics, which not only insisted on observation and experimentation, but also developed higher mathematical systems to verify its findings. Lockean epistemology also emphasized the inductive rather than the deductive, and concentrated on the analysis of perceived ideas rather than speculation on cosmic archetypes.[6] The intellectual foundation of New England Puritanism, once a source of comfort and stability for Johnson, became a source of embarrassment. In his autobiography, written over fifty years later, Johnson recalled that the more he studied the New Learning, the more he "found himself . . . emerging out of the glimmer of twilight into the full sunshine of open day." [7] On 16 November 1715, he announced that he "was wholly changed to the New Learning." [8]

It is so very tempting to believe him. The tension between the essentially medieval world view imbibed at Saybrook and the enlightened philosophy contained in the Dummer books was severe. Johnson and his seven friends were reading explosive material that would eventually alter the intellectual landscape of the western world. Like Locke and the "five or six friends" who gathered in London to thrash out the principles of *An Essay on Human Understanding*, Johnson and his coterie might have become the vanguard for the Enlightenment in America.

5. *Career*, 1 : 4.
6. F. H. Anderson, *The Philosophy of Francis Bacon* (New York, 1948).
7. *Career*, 1 : 6.
8. Ibid., 2 : 186.

And Johnson, rather than Benjamin Franklin, might have gained fame as the first American philosophe.

The available evidence is sparse, but it is sufficient to show that Johnson was too cautious and common a man to lead New England into the eighteenth century. He did recognize that the New Learning outmoded the lessons of the Saybrook curriculum and that the metaphysics of his *Technologia* was hopelessly outdated. But the philosophical treatises he composed during the period from 1715 to 1720 also reveal that Johnson did not comprehend the import of the new science or philosophy. The New Learning was a name he used rather than a coherent system he understood. His writings contain a hodgepodge of old and new ideas, a blend of Puritan technologia and English empiricism that represents his attempt, not to champion new discoveries, but to integrate them with the comfortable certainties learned in college. Johnson may have denounced the old learning of Puritan New England, but he devoted the bulk of his intellectual energies to a synthesis of Ames and Ramus with Locke and Newton. If his experience is an accurate measure of the way enlightened ideas established themselves in America, it is clear that this was a phase of American intellectual history fraught with confusion and inconsistency.

In October of 1716, Johnson finished a small book he called "The Revised Encyclopedia." [9] It was intended as a revision of *Technologia* in the light of his self-proclaimed conversion to the New Learning. He had been reading Locke's *Essay* the previous summer, had mentioned his excitement over Locke in letters to Brown, as well as his desire to incorporate facets of Lockean epistemology into a new world view.[10]

There were parts of Locke's *Essay* that blended nicely with the Platonism of Ames and the Puritan metaphysical tradition. In the opening chapters of Book 4 of the *Essay*, Locke affirmed the possibility of a human knowledge that was infinite and universal. He suggested that men were capable of having insights into a transcendental realm of absolute truth. At one point

9. Ibid., p. 201.
10. Ibid., pp. 189–200.

Locke, like Johnson in *Technologia*, asserted that "so far as
. . . ideas . . . agree to their archetypes, so far only is truth
real." Moreover, the critical distinction that Locke drew between
primary qualities (resident in the physical object) and secondary
qualities (resident in the human mind) was very similar to the
distinction Ames made in *Medulla* between ectypes and entypes.[11]

But the thrust of Locke's philosophy was empirical. He did
not deny that reason was a useful faculty, but he did insist that
it was a limited one. It could manipulate the specific ideas that
entered the mind through the senses; it could not transcend
experience. Locke believed that philosophical attention should
be centered on the here and now, on the ideas that men accumulated by experience rather than the fanciful projections of the
human intellect. His most critical comments were directed at
those philosophers who postulated the existence of an archetypal
reality and spent their time musing over its make-up. He did not
deny the possibility that some heavenly region of truth and
beauty existed, but he insisted that philosophers refrain from
making it their chief concern. Human knowledge consisted of
discovering relationships between simple ideas of this world
rather than a hypothetical correlation between earthly types and
cosmic archetypes.[12]

So Lockean philosophy, like Ramist logic, was a blend of old
and new, except in Locke the medieval elements were subordinated to a concern for empiricism. And this empirical bent
not only militated against scholastic schemes that were based
on unverifiable distinctions, it also discouraged the constant re-
sort to divine explanations of natural events. The long-range
impact of Lockean philosophy was to discredit all metaphysical
systems that sought refuge in the supernatural and to encourage
a naturalistic interpretation of religion.

11. John Locke, *An Essay Concerning Human Understanding*, ed. A. C.
Fraser, 2 vols. (New York, 1959), 2 : 157–250. Hereafter cited as *Essay*.
12. R. I. Aaron, "The Limits of Locke's Rationalism," in J. Dover Wilson,
ed., *Seventeenth-Century Studies Presented to Sir Herbert Grierson* (Oxford,
1938), pp. 292–310. See Locke, *Essay*, 1 : 158–60, 183–93, 497–502; 2 : 14,
101–04, 292–303.

Johnson was slow to recognize the implications of Lockean empiricism. In fact, the thoughts expressed in "The Revised Encyclopedia" indicate that Johnson oscillated between a mere mouthing of Lockean terminology and a fascination with the least innovative parts of Locke's *Essay*. He accepted the empirical definition of an idea as "the image or thought of anything set before the mind . . . the intelligence that the mind has of anything coming within its reach." This was a good beginning, a foundation on which Johnson could construct a new epistemology. Instead, he followed up with a vague reference to Locke's analysis of language and the comment that "words are therefore the signs or images of thoughts and thoughts are of things." [13]

What then followed was lifted from the writings not of Locke, but of Jean Le Clerc, a Dutch philosopher who had taken it upon himself to show how Locke's epistemology buttressed traditional Christianity. Johnson could not surrender himself completely to Lockean empiricism because he remained supremely impressed with Le Clerc's exposition of ontology, "or as some others call it, metaphysic." [14] According to Le Clerc, before men experienced sensations or reflections they must possess some primal idea of a supreme being. Johnson cluttered up his tabula rasa with the metaphysical assumption that "God . . . is the very foundation of our wisdom, without which our learning seems but a very groundless, useless and insipid thing." To deny this was both "highly irreligious" and "grossly irrational." [15] The process of affirming it took up much of "The Revised Encyclopedia," enough to replace any analysis of Locke's philosophy. The absence of any substantial discussion of empiricism did not prevent Johnson from concluding that Lockean phi-

---

13. *Career*, 2 : 209–11.

14. An outline of Le Clerc's life and thought is in Rosalie Colie, *Light and Enlightenment: A Study of the Cambridge Platonists and Dutch Arminians* (Cambridge, 1957). See also Locke, *Essay*, 1 : xxxvi. Johnson wrote to Brown in 1716, "I have read a treatise of Mr. J. Clark, Professor of Philosophy in Amsterdam, written in Latin, printed in 1704, dedicated to Mr. J. Locke." *Career*, 2 : 197. Le Clerc's works were in the Dummer collection. The quotation is from ibid., p. 212.

15. *Career*, 2 : 204, 207.

losophy was valuable, not because it revolutionized the scholastic conceptions of perception, but because it enabled men to
understand how God communicated his ideas. Locke made men
more cognizant of the will and plan of their Creator, let them
know "the thing to be done and how it is done." [16] The main
point of empiricism, according to Johnson, was its tendency to
reinforce the lessons of rational theology.

In 1720 he finished the formal treatise which he called
"Logic." It was an attempt to elucidate the complex operations
of the human mind, the kind of problem that Locke himself
liked to tackle, and clearly was based on the solutions that Locke
had provided in his *Essay*. Johnson began with the assertion
that "all ideas come into the mind either by sensation or reflection." [17] After defining these two terms in good Lockean
fashion, he distinguished between simple and complex ideas,
even daring to use the same examples that Locke had used to
clarify the distinction.[18] Johnson then proceeded to sort complex ideas into three categories: "modes, substances, and relations," distinctions lifted straight out of the *Essay*.[19] His discussion of the varying levels of testimony and the skepticism with
which different kinds of evidence should be accepted were also
taken directly from the pages of the *Essay*.[20]

This was old stuff to the circle of scholars who gathered at
Saybrook and Guilford and to anyone else who had read *An Essay
on Human Understanding*. It did show a greater familiarity
with Locke than he had revealed five years earlier. And much
of the moralism of Le Clerc had been removed. Johnson was
clearly striving to digest the main tenets of Lockean empiricism.
As yet he did not sense the extent to which empiricism led toward deism and even atheism. He appropriated huge sections
of the *Essay*, paraphrased certain passages, totally reworded
others. How much Johnson actually understood and how much

16. Ibid., p. 209.
17. Ibid., p. 221.
18. Johnson used color as an example of a simple idea and a centaur as
an example of a complex idea. See *Career*, 2 : 222, and Locke, *Essay*, 1 : 148–50,
390–405.
19. *Career*, 2 : 224.
20. Ibid., pp. 231–33; Locke, *Essay*, 2 : 190–225.

was mere mimickry is difficult to say. It is clear that Johnson's interest in Locke was becoming more intense, even though Locke was getting keen competition from the vestiges of scholasticism.

In the Lockean sections of both "Logic" and "The Revised Encyclopedia" Johnson had to cope with his own older ideas and more established habits of thinking. Despite his conviction that he could turn his back on Ames, Ramus, and the lessons of the Saybrook curriculum, Johnson's philosophical writings were riddled with notions that had no place in the New Learning but which he found difficult to discard. He was fascinated by newness and by current European philosophy, but this was offset by his conservative impulse to retain much of what he condemned as old-fashioned.

First, he did not totally abandon Ramist logic and method. He persisted in the belief, acquired during the sophomore logic course at Saybrook, that all human knowledge could be broken down into different "arts," categorized, and thereby understood. This categorizing instinct allowed him to distinguish between "semiotical" and "real" knowledge as if it were a universal Ramist dichotomy that need not be further explained. Ramist terms such as "eupraxy" and "euprattome" intervened between a discussion of absolute categories and a Lockean analysis of sensation.[21] Definitions of mathematics, logic, grammar, and physics were piled one on top of the other and confused with explanations. The whole morass of terms, categories, and definitions was often represented visually on a Ramist-like chart, as if philosophy could be studied like a family genealogy.[22] Nor was this use of Ramist method simply an unconscious retention of old intellectual habits; Johnson was often aware of what he was doing. In 1720, when someone asked him to recommend a program of study for college students, he suggested that they "begin with logic, reciting first Ramus" and encouraged the sophomores to memorize the Ramist dichotomies.[23]

Secondly, the direct influence of Ames is evident throughout

21. *Career*, 2 : 210.
22. Ibid., pp. 203, 214–15.
23. Ibid., p. 250.

"The Revised Encyclopedia" and "Logic." Intermingled with
attempts to paraphrase Locke's empirical approach to epistemology are various references to archetypes and a priori values. Instead of visualizing the mind as a blank tablet devoid of innate
ideas, Johnson compared it to a mirror "or a glass [which] receive[s] the ideas or images of the rays of the glorious wisdom
and other of the adorable perfections of God in His Works." [24]
Whereas Locke preferred to play down the significance of absolute standards and to regard knowledge as the efficient operation
of finite faculties, Johnson was obsessed by eternal archetypes
and the notion that knowledge consisted in the agreement or
conformity of anything with an infinite standard. He insisted
that "our real ideas are either right or wrong according as they
agree or disagree with the things themselves which they are
taken to represent, even as pictures are true or false representations of their originals." [25] This tendency to emphasize metaphysical explanations and final, as opposed to secondary, causes
added to Johnson's philosophy a strong Platonistic element
which was completely at odds with the inductive approach and
modest goals of Locke's *Essay*.[26] All of this failed to trouble
Johnson, who felt no sense of contradiction in citing William
Ames while also claiming conversion to the New Learning.

   Although Johnson claimed to be a convert to the New Learning and a disciple of Locke, primary evidence shows quite clearly
that he never fully compehended Lockean empiricism. He
recognized that Locke had shattered the scholastic schemes of
Ramus and Ames, but he was attracted to the least innovative
parts of Locke's philosophy, those speculative doctrines analyzed
by Le Clerc. He was groping for a synthesis of these disparate
intellectual elements, an integration of Ramus, Ames, Le Clerc,
and Locke, but his mind was still a melange of old and new.
This philosophical confusion was undoubtedly disturbing to a
man who had once written out a treatise explaining everything

---

24. Ibid., p. 208.
25. Ibid., p. 227.
26. The influence of Plato is evident throughout both treatises. See also
"Miscellaneous Notes," dated 1 July 1718, in *Career*, 2 : 248. Johnson claimed
that he did not read Plato until 1721.

in the universe, but he had little time to iron out philosophical problems after he immersed himself in the hectic affairs of his alma mater.

Although the Indian War had ended in 1714 and Connecticut's economy had begun to rebound from its long depression, neither of these developments had an immediate effect on the college at Saybrook. Progress and reform would take time. The students had more complaints than patience and by the early months of 1716 they threatened to walk out if more proficient tutors were not hired. In the spring of the same year, a smallpox epidemic in Saybrook broke the school in two. Fourteen students left Saybrook to assemble under Elisha Williams at Wethersfield, where they believed themselves removed from the dangers of smallpox and the ineptitude of their former tutors. Thirteen others decided to band around Joseph Hart, the minister at East Guilford, and pursue their education under his direction.[27]

Exactly what role Johnson played in these developments is unclear. The students at East Guilford were only a few miles from his home town and he might have provided some of them with room, board, and academic assistance. It is clear that he knew what was happening and was aware that the survival of the Collegiate School was in danger. In August he received word from Daniel Brown, who was located at the Hopkins Grammar School, that the trustees were making every effort to gather the splintered student groups at New Haven.[28]

New Haven had offered the trustees £500 and eight acres of land if they would relocate the school there.[29] Although two of the trustees, Timothy Woodbridge and Thomas Buckingham, had balked at the offer, a majority decided that this was an excellent opportunity to give their school a permanent home.

27. Trumbull, *History of Connecticut*, 2 : 123; Oviatt, *The Beginnings of Yale*, chap. 6; *Career*, 1 : 6–8.

28. Brown to Johnson, 3 August 1716, in *Career*, 2 : 195–96. Oviatt, *The Beginnings of Yale*, p. 318, reports that Johnson housed and fed many of the students at East Guilford. I have found no evidence to verify or contradict this assertion.

29. Dexter, *Doc. Hist.*, p. 63.

They voted to move the college to New Haven and invited Johnson to come along as tutor.[30] The students at Wethersfield refused to comply with the decision in the hope that Woodbridge
and Buckingham could persuade the Connecticut Assembly to
transfer the college to Hartford, which was more centrally sit-
uated than New Haven and, incidentally, closer to Wethersfield.
Meanwhile, four other students decided to brave the smallpox
and the wrath of the trustees in order to study under Azariah
Mather at Saybrook. These dissenting groups posed a serious
challenge to the supremacy of the college at New Haven and
engaged the entire colony in a series of debates that split the
upper and lower houses of the legislature and the inland and
coastal populace, as well as the membership of the board of
trustees. Johnson decided that the students should not be deprived of an education while their elders haggled over geography. He informed the trustees that he was coming down to New
Haven to accept the post of tutor.[31]

The new post called for him to instruct the first three classes
in all their subjects. It was a difficult and time-consuming chore,
but it did provide him with the opportunity to deal with more
advanced students and to try out some of his ideas in the classroom. Brown's advice and criticism were available, as were
some of the books of the Dummer collection, which Johnson apparently removed from Saybrook for use in his courses and for
his own reading.[32] This was the time when he was digesting his
thoughts and sifting ideas for "The Revised Encyclopedia." It
was an exciting time for Johnson, a time when ideas seemed
alive and vital, if not completely clear. Little wonder that some
of the vitality and confusion found its way into the subjects he
taught and effected an alteration in the college curriculum.

Although Johnson did not teach the senior course in metaphysics, he managed to introduce some ideas from Locke's *Essay*

30. Ibid., p. 68.
31. Ibid., pp. 79, 81–82, 84–88. For a report of the debate in the legislature,
see *Conn. Recs.*, 5 : 529–50. See also *Career*, 1 : 8, for Johnson's account.
32. The Dummer books were not moved from Saybrook to New Haven until
December of 1718. Nevertheless, Johnson was reading many of them before
that date, as is evidenced by his letters to Brown, his autobiography, and the
content of his own treatises.

into the underclassmen's courses. Two of the commencement
theses in physics for 1718 declared

8. Heat, cold, humidity and dryness are not primary qualities.
9. Secondary qualities arise from magnitude, size, motion,
   shape and number of particulars.[33]

Johnson was working on Lockean philosophy, trying to understand it and to incorporate some of its insights into his own
philosophic writings. He undoubtedly carried his own work
into the classroom at times. But he could not bring a sophisticated understanding of the *Essay* or the implications of its
analysis to his students. He himself was probing. His students
were exposed to the existence of a New Learning but not to its
content. They could share in Johnson's intellectual exploration,
but, like him, they did not know where they were going.

Astronomy was different. There had been very little astronomy
taught during Johnson's undergraduate days and what was
taught was badly in need of overhaul. Johnson had learned to
believe in a Ptolemaic universe, cluttered with equants and
spinning epicycles, all whirling about a centrally located earth.
He had accepted this as self-evident until he read William
Whiston and William Derham in 1717.[34] These were not profound thinkers but popularizers and admirers of Newton who,
like Le Clerc, were struggling to reconcile the New Learning
with the assurances of long-accepted theological dogma. The
fixed stars, planetary orbits, gravity, and everything in the universe became a magnificent testimony to God's majesty, a re-
assurance that the discoveries of Copernicus, Kepler, and Newton served only to buttress the doctrines of eighteenth-century
theology. Although their arguments were superficial and their
conclusions moralistic rather than scientific, in the process of
manipulating facts in order to reach these conclusions they

33. The Yale commencement theses of 1718 are the earliest still extant.
They are preserved in the Yale historical manuscripts room, Yale University
Library. All quotations are from a translation from the Latin by Anne
Accardo.
34. *Career,* 1 : 8. Derham's *Astro-Theology* (London, 1715), and Whiston's
Astronomical Principles of Religion (London, 1717) were in the Dummer
collection.

opened Johnson's eyes to the fact that the sun was the center of the universe. This was one of those intellectual discoveries that Johnson was easily able to visualize, understand, and accept. In 1717 he wrote "Mundus Novus" to proclaim his conversion from Ptolemy to Copernicus because "God and nature do nothing in vain." [35]

Johnson's undergraduates soon got the message. Astronomy was considered part of physics, one of the courses which Johnson taught. It was the first course taught at the Collegiate School in which the students learned that they were not the center of the solar system. By 1718 one of the physics theses declared

26. Just as the sun is the center of this system, thus there are fixed stars for other systems.

Apparently, Johnson did more than mention Copernicus; the commencement theses indicate that the entire approach to astronomy became more sophisticated and more mathematical. In place of the descriptive accounts of Aristotle or Ptolemy, the students began to make a gesture at analysis, such as

29. Centripetal force converts the rectilinear movement of the planets into curved movement.

Even the descriptive theses tended to be more specific, proclaiming that

30. The rings of the primary planets are elliptical in shape.
32. Comets are unarranged masses revolving around the sun in a parabolic ring.
33. All predictions of astrology concerning future happenings are both fallacious and foolish.

Revelations about the structure of the universe soon led Johnson to investigate its operation. Derham and Whiston spoke to this point, and spoke most reverently when they mentioned the name of Newton. Here, obviously, was a recognized genius whom Johnson had to read. When he began to thumb through the pages of the *Principia*, however, he soon discovered them

35. *Career*, 2 : 247.

filled, not with the easy and comforting explanations of Derham, but with complex formulas and confusing theorems. This was another one of those books that confronted Johnson with a system that seemed as obscure as a new language, but this time the key to the grammar was mathematics, "a study he was averse to." Nevertheless, "he was resolved to overcome that aversion, and by laborious application he gained the mastery of Euclid, Algebra, and the Conic Sections, so as to read Sir Isaac with understanding and his aversion turned into great pleasure." [36]

The pleasure took a long time to come and so did the understanding. In fact, it was impossible to grasp the Newtonian explanations without higher algebra and calculus. It was possible, however, to understand the conclusions of the *Principia*, to comprehend that there were specific mechanical laws operative on every terrestrial body and that these laws were equally applicable in the celestial realm, without knowing how Newton derived these laws. Brown joined Johnson on the college faculty in 1718 and together they introduced this diluted version of Newton into the curriculum "as fast as they could," probably using Derham and Whiston as texts. [37] Th students were required to absorb that part of the New Learning represented by Newton, or at least to understand his interpreters. Many of the juniors remained content to mouth the memorized platitudes of pre-Newtonian physics (i.e., space is granted where place is not), [38] but others tried to comprehend the principles of the new science. One graduate of 1718 argued the Newtonian principle that

6. Movement is proportional to a force moving by having been pushed.

In an effort to advance himself and his students beyond this crude appreciation of Newton, Johnson began to read more books on mathematics. He forced himself to study *Mathesis Juveniles*[39] by Christopher Sturnius and *Euclid's Elements*[40] by

36. Ibid., 1 : 9.
37. Ibid., p. 8.
38. Physics thesis no. 4.
39. London, 1709, signed "Libris Samuelis Johnsoni."
40. London, 1705, purchased from Brown in 1718.

the great Isaac Barrow, taking notes in the margins and on the
back pages. This was difficult reading for Johnson. He preferred
philosophical endeavors, in which answers were not so terribly
specific and speculation was more valuable than computation.
But since he was convinced that this painful enterprise was a
necessary means to a valuable goal, he persisted. As a result, the
students of the Collegiate School discovered that they were being
required to learn more mathematics than any other undergraduates in the colonies.

Perhaps Johnson simply wanted company in his misery; more
likely he wanted to give his students a better background in
mathematics than he himself had received. Johnson's own mathematical notes for these years consist of detailed drawings and
elaborate geometrical proofs. After he had mastered geometry
and taught his students what he had learned, he went on to
trigonometry and forced his students to follow.[41] Two of the
theses for 1718 read

> 19. When the base and the perpendicular only have been
> given, the angle at the base is not able to be found by use
> of sines.
> 20. Sines of angles are proportionate to the opposite side.

Algebra came next. There is no evidence that it had ever been
taught before in America. Johnson led his classes through the
multiple arrangements of x's and y's, teaching them to isolate
an unknown variable and break down quadratic equations. They
spent so much time at such endeavors that eight of the thirty
mathematical theses for 1718 were algebraic. One of the theses
tried to explain what all the effort was about.

> 6. Algebra is the doctrine which, through a comparison of
> known quantities with unknown quantities, very easily
> occasions the solution of the most obscure questions of
> arithmetic and geometry.

Whether either Johnson or his students assimilated the rules
of algebra "very easily" is questionable. Johnson was simply will-

41. Mathematical Notes 1717–18, in Johnson MSS.

ing to endure a discipline that he abhorred in order to get himself to the point where he could fathom the reasoning of the *Principia*. In the process he revolutionized the mathematics course at the college and made a substantial contribution to colonial education.[42]

Despite all these changes, however, the students at the Collegiate School still studied Ames, Wollebius, and Ramus; still learned scholastic physics; still believed in technologia. The old learning was still there. It was too well established to be overturned by one man. It had, after all, provided Johnson himself with a world view, with a philosophical framework complete with questions and reassuring answers. Johnson himself did not yet understand how new the New Learning was. He did not grasp the impact that Lockean empiricism and Newtonian science would have on Puritan theology. He accepted the comforting view of interpreters like Le Clerc and Derham, who regarded the New Learning as a flying buttress that stabilized revealed religion. Until the implications of Newton and Locke had been fully digested, they were able to coexist peacefully with scholastic ideas they would eventually replace.

The changes wrought by Johnson's introduction of the New Learning into the curriculum found their way into the commencement theses of 1718, but hardly anyone noticed. Other changes in the college were more visible and, at least as far as the trustees were concerned, more consequential. There was finally a building which the college could call its own, an impressive structure three stories high, complete with classrooms and living accommodations for students and tutors. The trustees regarded it as a sign of permanence, an indication that the college was in New Haven to stay. Johnson appreciated it for another reason: it was a new home for him. He and Brown moved in immediately after commencement. At the same commencement, the building and the college were christened with a new name. Clumsy references to "the Collegiate School at New

42. Lao G. Simons, "Introduction of Algebra into American Schools in the Eighteenth Century," United States Bureau of Education, *Bulletin* 18 (1924): 34–40.

Haven" were dropped and replaced by the title "Yale College," in honor of the English benefactor, Elihu Yale. The new name had a distinctive sound, and the happy combination of four letters, together with the construction of the new building, helped to influence the dissident student group at Wethersfield to join forces with the college at New Haven. The General Assembly was undoubtedly even more influential, for it ordered the Wethersfield students to merge with Yale College. But the reasons for the merger seemed less important than the fact that the college was once again unified under one board of trustees, one faculty, and one name.[43]

Johnson observed these changes as a tutor, not as an administrator. He had not involved himself in the debates over the college's location. Now that one faction, the one he happened to be serving, had won out, he expected no serious changes in his academic schedule. There would be more students to teach and better facilities, but no alteration in the content of his courses and no delay in his planned program of readings. Trustees and administrators could make grand decisions about buildings and enrolment, but the core of Johnson's life, the world of ideas, would remain unaffected—or so he thought.

As soon as the Wethersfield students appeared in New Haven, it became evident that Johnson's scholarly pursuits were not sufficient to insulate him from college politics. If Johnson regarded himself as a kind of archetype that transcended the affairs of the world, he was about to discover why Locke discouraged archetypal fantasies. The students had not come to Yale College to learn; they had come to make trouble. A few weeks after their arrival, the Wethersfield students drew up a "Collection of Faults" with the "public Expositions & Disputations & managements of the Tutors," naming Johnson as the most deficient and disappointing member of the Yale faculty.[44] Although their specific grievances were never clarified, the

43. Johnson recorded these events in "Some Historical Remarks Concerning the Collegiate School of Connecticut in New Haven," printed in Dexter, *Doc. Hist.*, pp. 149–63.

44. Dexter, *Doc. Hist.*, p. 160.

students persisted in their criticism of Johnson's work and even requested that their parents be allowed to sit in on his classes. The trustees attempted to settle the matter by rearranging Johnson's teaching load and shuffling his class assignments. None of these evasive actions worked. The students continued to protest Johnson's teaching until 10 January, 1719, when they left Yale and headed back to Wethersfield.

The Yale trustees immediately began an investigation of Johnson's classes. He had been teaching subjects that were not supposed to be included in the curriculum, such as algebra and trigonometry, and he had altered many of the prescribed courses by introducing his students to new texts, new authors, and an entirely New Learning. Perhaps the Wethersfield students were the genuine conservatives who objected to these changes in the traditional curriculum. Or perhaps the new students found Johnson's personality offensive. Perhaps Johnson's explorations into a New Learning suggested only complex questions to students who wanted definitive answers. All of these are possible explanations of the students' disapproval of Johnson. As far as the trustees were concerned, however, he was a capable and responsible instructor. At the end of their investigation the trustees concluded

> that Mr. Johnson, against whose learning it has been reputed that the said scholars had objected, had been for some years approved as a tutor in said college, and was well known to be a gentleman of sufficient learning; and that they cannot but look upon it as a very unworthy part in them, if any of those that have deserted the college have endeavored to scandalize a gentleman in such a manner, whom much more competent judges esteem as a man of good learning.[45]

Johnson could not judge his own abilities or his courses, but the approval of the trustees assured him that the fault lay with the students and not with his teaching. The Wethersfield group had come down to Yale with "a Design to disgrace our College &

45. Ibid., pp. 187–91.

Tutors, and either to unhorse our Tutors & get Creatures of
their own or to return & set up a School of their own." [46] While
Johnson had been reading and studying, the faction at Wethersfield had been jockeying for position. Now, after the Wethersfield students had come and gone, it was clear that they had
come with a score to settle. Johnson's scholarship had become
a pawn in a broader conflict between New Haven and Wethersfield; instead of making him immune to their criticism, it had
served as a convenient means by which the dissident students
registered their bitter feelings toward Yale.

Nevertheless, the college was once again broken in half and
Johnson's presence precluded its reunification. The Yale trustees
were obviously on his side. They knew that he and his tutoring
were merely a foil for Wethersfield's grievances, but knowing
this did not help matters. In March of 1719 they appointed
Timothy Cutler rector of the college.[47] Cutler was a former
pastor of Stratford who had a reputation for scholarly achievement and leadership, two qualities which the trustees hoped
would attract the straying students back to New Haven.[48] Johnson knew Cutler well. When they had met together to discuss
the New Learning, Cutler had demonstrated that he was a man
of ability; but Johnson also knew that no amount of ability
could heal the rift between Wethersfield and New Haven as long
as he remained on the faculty. Soon after Cutler arrived on the
job, Johnson offered his resignation to the trustees. They accepted it reluctantly, "with our particular thanks for his good
service" and granted him a £3 bonus "for his extraordinary service." [49] Neither words nor money could conceal the fact that
Johnson was being sacrificed for college unity. In June 1719,
soon after Johnson left Yale, the students began to trickle down
from Wethersfield to New Haven.[50]

46. Ibid., p. 160.
47. Ibid., p. 190.
48. Clifford K. Shipton, ed., *Biographical Sketches of Those Who Attended
Harvard College*, 14 vols. (Cambridge, Mass., 1873–1970), 5 : 45–67. Hereafter
cited as *Harvard Biographies*.
49. Dexter, *Doc. Hist.*, p. 198. For Johnson's account, see *Career*, 1 : 10.
50. Jonathan Edwards, who was one of the Wethersfield students, wrote to
his sister Mary on 26 March 1719 that "the council and trustees, having

The dispute between Johnson and the Wethersfield faction is tantalizing in its ambiguity, but there is simply insufficient evidence to conclude that Johnson offended the students with his emphasis on the New Learning. In fact, the trustees' defense of Johnson, even after they had investigated his teaching, illuminates the undramatic nature of intellectual change during this phase of New England history. The trustees, like Johnson, apparently saw nothing dangerous about Locke and Newton. There is not one shred of evidence that the trustees advised Johnson to discontinue his classes on Newtonian mechanics or Lockean epistemology. Nor is there any evidence that Johnson or the trustees perceived any tension between the naturalistic thrust of the New Learning and established Puritan theology. Johnson's career as a Yale tutor is, then, an excellent reminder of how surreptitiously one set of ideas replaces another. There is rarely a direct challenge to a system of beliefs and assumptions that produces a clear and cataclysmic struggle in which antiquated ideas are vanquished. At Yale in 1718 new ideas infiltrated without fanfare and began an underground war against Ames, Ramus, and technologia, a war that went unnoticed for several decades.[51]

It was a time, however, when the most sensitive of New England's intelligentsia became conscious of the Enlightenment. Like Johnson, young Benjamin Franklin was just becoming aware of English discoveries in science.[52] And Cotton Mather, the eminent and orthodox Puritan minister in Boston, was fascinated with what he called "Experimental Learning."[53] He was interested in keeping pace with the latest European intellectual fads and declared that Locke's philosophy had revealed Ramist

---

lately had a meeting at New Haven concerning it, have removed that which was the cause of our coming away, viz. Mr. Johnson, from the place of tutor." Dexter, *Doc. Hist.*, p. 192.

51. Hornberger, *Scientific Thought in the American Colleges*, p. 82; Miller, *The New England Mind: From Colony to Province*, p. 445. For an excellent discussion of the relationship between college curricula and intellectual change, see Lawrence Stone, "The Ninnyversity," *The New York Review of Books*, 28 January 1971, p. 23.

52. I. B. Cohen, *Franklin and Newton* (New York, 1956), p. 207.

53. Cotton Mather, *Manuductio ad Ministerium* (Boston, 1726), p. 37.

logic to be a *"Disciplinium Omnium Excrementum."* [54] He advised the future scholars of New England to throw out the scholastic schemes and read Boyle, Hook, Locke, and "the uncomparable Sir Isaac Newton." [55] Johnson, of course, was already embarked on a reading program of his own. And he agreed with Mather that Locke and Newton provided greater intellectual stability for religion. In Johnson's mind, however, the New Learning did raise serious questions about the specific religious doctrines of New England Puritanism. Once he discovered that the intellectual pillars of Puritanism were in need of renovation, Johnson began to examine the entire structure. [56]

54. Ibid., p. 54.
55. Cotton Mather, *The Christian Philosopher* (London, 1721), p. 41.
56. Herbert Schneider, *The Puritan Mind* (New York, 1930), p. 47, minimizes the impact of the New Learning on Johnson. See Theodore Hornberger, "Puritanism and Science," *The New England Quarterly* 10 (1937): 503–15.

4

Anglicization

Whether or not Johnson learned anything from his brush with
the Wethersfield students, it was clearly time to get on with some
career other than college teaching. At twenty-three years of age,
he was already showing signs of a slight paunch and a double
chin; his round face usually carried a solemn expression and
had a reddish tinge that made him appear pompous and em-
barrassed at the same time. He looked, in other words, older
than his years, like a man who had settled his portly frame into
some comfortable niche of colonial society and was waiting for
life to reward him with respectability or even fame.[1]

Appearances were not completely deceptive. Although the
bitter experience at Yale had resulted in his resignation, the job
of tutor was usually regarded as temporary, often as one of the
intermediate steps toward a career in the ministry. In 1716 he
had been granted a preaching license from the Connecticut Association.[2] A year later he received a master's degree from the
Collegiate School.[3] Since these were further steps along New
England's well-traveled route toward ordination, the parishioners
of West Haven, who needed a new minister, soon took notice.
Johnson's physical appearance seemed to embody the dignity
usually associated with the ministry. He not only looked the
part, he also possessed outstanding academic credentials. But

---

1. This description of the young Johnson is based on Steiner, *Menunkatuck*,
p. 481, and a later portrait by Samuel Smibert.
2. Dated 28 March 1716, and signed Samuel Whittlesey, in Johnson MSS.
3. *Career*, 1 : 8; Dexter, *Doc. Hist.*, p. 102.

the people of West Haven wanted more than looks and degrees; they wanted to know how well he preached and where he stood on basic theological issues. Despite his crowded academic schedule, Johnson had taken time to delineate his theological position even before his departure from Yale.

As early as 1715, when he was still teaching grammar school at Guilford, Johnson had been requested to preach a sermon to the local parishioners. On May 22 of that year the Guilford citizens listened proudly as their nineteen-year-old prodigy seized upon the word "Immanuel," his text, to enumerate the distinctive features of Puritan theology.[4] He began, appropriately, with a description of man after the Fall. After Adam's transgression against God, said Johnson, men who lived "in a state of nature" were living in a "low and wretched condition," deprived of God's grace, wholly deserving of eternal damnation, and "grovelling at the dust of humility before God."[5] Johnson told his Guilford neighbors that they could not save themselves, that dependence on God, reliance on his grace, was their only hope for salvation. With regard to God, there was very little the young preacher felt he could say for sure. Men much older and wiser than he had concluded that the Almighty was unfathomable. Ames, for example, warned budding philosophers and scientists not to expect their investigation of God to produce results of the same precision and finality as their investigation of the natural world. And Ames explained why: "The principles of other arts, since they are inborn in us, can be developed through sense perception, observation, experience, and induction, and so brought to perfection. But the basic principles of theology, though they may be advanced by study and industry, are not in us by nature."

An industrious and studious reading of Scripture, supplemented by the theological directives of Ames and Wollebius, did allow Johnson to conclude that God was a creature of "awful majesty"[6] who extended his assistance to certain sinners and

4. *Career*, 3 : 293–313.
5. Ibid., p. 304.
6. Ibid., p. 319. His fifth sermon, preached at West Haven on 10 June 1716.

allowed the others to wallow in their depravity. Some men were elected for salvation and the rest were damned. All men, however, had an obligation to pay homage to this majestic God and to make every effort at holiness. The sad fact, Johnson told his listeners, was that "True faith is the gift of God and it is not in man's power to believe, but notwithstanding man is bound to endeavor after it as if it was in his power." [7] This was simply another way of saying what all orthodox Puritans believed, that justification, the intercession of divine grace, preceded and made possible devout and efficacious human action. Johnson was telling his congregation that God alone could infuse their lives with a meaningful religious spirit. Without God's assistance their efforts to lead holy lives would prove vain and delusive. They must, nevertheless, attempt to restrain their own sinful instincts in the hope that God would intervene in their behalf.

It was a hard message. It showed that Johnson accepted the main doctrinal tenets of Puritan theology, including the sovereignty of God, the depravity of man, and eternal election. Other features were also present in this first sermon, however—features which pointed up the more optimistic implications of his theology. Although deference had to be shown toward the basic theological principles enunciated by William Ames, adopted by the Westminster Assembly, and learned at Yale, a minister's theological stance was very often a matter of phraseology and emphasis as well as strict doctrinal allegiance. Puritan theology was a flexible network of beliefs that left room for differences of opinion and personality. The religious message could vary from minister to minister.

In a colony where the vast majority of ministers and churches accepted the main doctrinal points of Puritanism, congregations looking for a pastor often evaluated an available candidate according to the emphasis he placed on the various parts of the theological system. From the very beginning of his ministerial candidacy, Johnson espoused some doctrines more strongly than others. He preferred to direct his energy and his sermons toward certain issues while ignoring or giving only brief attention to

7. Ibid., p. 310.

those that did not concern him. As a result, his religious message possessed a distinctive tone or character that expressed itself in the topics he chose to discuss as well as the divine and human characteristics he preferred to emphasize.

First, Johnson was impressed with the faculty of reason, both as it regulated God's dealings with man and as it made man a more effectual believer. Since Johnson was exploring the New Learning at the same time as he was preaching at West Haven and Guilford, his emphasis on a reasonable theology might have been influenced by Locke and Newton. But the commitment to a rational pursuit of divinity was also ingrained in Johnson by traditional Puritan religious authorities. And Johnson's early sermons reflect conventional Puritan terminology rather than insights gleaned from the New Learning. For example, Ames had described God's relationship with man as a covenant, an agreement which implied that the Almighty had seen fit to conduct his affairs according to rational and regular procedures. Johnson seized upon this image of the Creator to argue that "this is not a groundless and irrational contentment and satisfaction, but it is a well-grounded and rational happiness which the soul finds in the light and smiles of God's countenance." [8]

There was no greater compliment that Johnson, a man given to philosophy and the powers of the intellect, could pay his maker than to suggest that he was reasonable. He was, to be sure, all other things in addition to being reasonable, but it was his rationality that seemed most godlike to Johnson. Similarly, the the rational faculty was the distinctive characteristic of "the image of God" in man.[9] Although man had lost most of his capacity to think rationally due to Adam's sin, "some little sparks of it [reason] remained." [10] One of the chief benefits of God's grace was its ability to activate the previously inert faculty of reason and thereby oblige men to cultivate rational development as a means to the comprehension of God's will. Johnson envisioned reasoned actions as the primary consequence of justi-

8. Ibid., p. 320.
9. Ibid., p. 315.
10. Ibid., 2 : 59.

fication; he argued that "all moral actions are rational." [11] He preached that "the life of a Saint is a rational life" [12] and "religion without reason won't please God." [13] He defined man's soul as the "rational spirit, the principle of his rational actions," and insisted that it could not expect election until it had exercised what he called its powers of "reflection and intellection." [14]

Secondly, Johnson tended to emphasize the human as opposed to the divine role in the regenerative process. He admitted that men could make "a free choice of what was best" only after God had provided them with grace;[15] but he spent most of his time encouraging his listeners to make every effort at sanctity. He told one congregation at West Haven that "God has been graciously pleased for Christ's sake to make promises of those future glories to our observance of the commands of religion. So that the observance of them entitles us to them by virtue of the promises of God." [16] Johnson seemed to be saying that a man could strive to lead a life of sanctity and use it as a bargaining point in his transactions with God. If the relationship between God and man was contractual, individuals should fulfill their end of the bargain and trust that God would do the same. It was a theological position that approximated the heretical notion that men were capable of earning grace, a heresy known as Arminianism. But New England Puritans had been rubbing elbows with Arminianism for many years; the very idea of a covenant between God and man elevated human capabilities to a level that verged on Arminianism. While it is important to recognize Johnson's early emphasis on the human role in the regenerative process, it is also important to understand that his

11. Ibid., 3 : 321.
12. Ibid., p. 324.
13. Ibid., p. 332, preached at East Guilford on 5 May 1716, and at Springfield on 12 May 1716.
14. Ibid., 3 : 338–40.
15. Ibid., p. 352, preached at West Haven on 16 March 1718.
16. *Career*, 3 : 356, preached at West Haven 3 April 1718. Miller, "The Marrow of Puritan Divinity," pp. 48–99, has the best short treatment of the covenant theology. See also William Ames, *The Marrow of Sacred Divinity* (London, 1642), esp. pp. 175–80; and Pettit, *The Heart Prepared.*

theological statements remained within the bounds of Puritan orthodoxy.

Finally, Johnson developed a distinctive sermon style as a vehicle for his theological views. As he said later in life, he "never liked enthusiasm," and he despised sermons that attempted to appeal to emotions.[17] He preferred to direct his own religious message to the mind rather than the heart and to deliver the sermon in a style that mirrored the message. When Johnson outlined a sermon, he employed the scholastic logic learned at Yale as a way of organizing the cumbersome mass of religious material. Ames himself had called Ramus the "greatest master of the arts" and had advised the use of Ramist techniques in preaching. "There will be some," he said, "who condemn the precision of method and logical form as curious and troublesome. But we wish them sounder reason, for they separate the art of learning, judging, and memorizing from those things which most deserve to be learned, known and memorized."

Johnson continued to follow Ames' advice even after he had denounced the scholasticism which Ames and Ramus typified. Johnson kept extensive notes which show that each sermon was an intricately reasoned piece with a formal logical structure.[18] He was too convinced that "well composed forms were infinitely best" to worry that his delivery appeared stiff or impersonal or that the rigid order he imposed on his preaching might foster boredom as easily as comprehension. He abhorred confusion in the pulpit. Since he made sure that his own sermons were composed and presented with a precision that discouraged emotional outbursts, the only possible grounds on which his congregation could disagree was the content of his theology. And no parish he addressed during his ministerial candidacy found his theology offensive.[19]

17. *Career,* 1 : 11.
18. Notes on Sermons, Johnson MSS.
19. For the emphasis on reason and morality in other Puritan ministers, see Cotton Mather, *Reasonable Religion* (Boston, 1700), esp. pp. 10, 27, 39–41; *A Man of Reason* (Boston, 1718), and *Bonifacius* . . . (Boston, 1710), pp. 20, 31; also Benjamin Colman, *The Divine Compassions Declar'd and Magnified* (Boston, 1715). The best secondary account is Miller, *The New England Mind: From Colony to Province,* pp. 395–437.

The people of West Haven examined Johnson's record as a ministerial candidate, found it acceptable, and approved him as their pastor in March of 1720. Although West Haven was a small congregation that did not provide its ministers with instant fame or widespread recognition, there were compensations. It did give Johnson a permanent pulpit from which to voice his religious convictions. Moreover, he was able to stay close to those precious books in the library at Yale.

This last consideration was critical. Johnson did not want to get stuck in some backwoods settlement where his intellectual interests would have to vie for his attention with Indian attacks and the rudimentary concerns of frontier existence. Erudition had a way of withering in the wilderness, and Johnson felt that he had made too much of an inroad into philosophy to throw it away for the rustic life. West Haven and New Haven looked like provincial outposts when compared with cosmopolitan London, but New Haven did have Yale College, which, in turn, had a large collection of books. The books continued to attract men like Cutler, Brown, Wetmore, and the other members of Johnson's intellectual coterie, who fed his appetite for scholarship. If the West Haven call kept him close to all this, Johnson was willing to swallow his pride and accept a ministry which carried little prestige. On Sundays he preached to his new flock. The rest of the week he read and studied.

He had not lost his interest in the New Learning, "yet he chiefly applied himself to divinity and ethics, and history both sacred and profane." [20] This was in part a reflection of his new interests as a ministerial candidate and in part a reflection of the contents of the Dummer collection. Whatever the reasons, Johnson was off on another intellectual adventure, a pursuit of religious truth that paralleled and borrowed from his quest for the New Learning. This time his chief authorities were not modern scientists and philosophers, but seventeenth-century English theologians and churchmen. And this time he was more concerned with the implications of early Christian history than contemporary scientific discoveries. In the end, the impact of

20. *Career*, 1 : 12.

his extensive reading in English sources (he read 162 books from
1719 to 1722) when combined with his analysis of the discrepancies in New England Puritanism, resulted in a dramatic conversion to Anglicanism.[21] In order to understand the reasons for
Johnson's conversion—certainly the most consequential act of
his life—it is necessary to examine the religious doctrines of the
English latitudinarians and the ecclesiastical problems that troubled Johnson's clerical contemporaries in New England.

The term "latitudinarian" was as vague as the philosophy it
came to connote. Originally, it had been used as an epithet, "a
convenient name to uproach a man that you owe a spite to;
'tis what you will, and you may affix it upon whom you will; 'tis
something that will serve to talk of, when all other discourse
fails." [22] The first Englishmen to be called latitudinarians were
academicians at Cambridge University who also labored under
the label "Cambridge Platonists." Richard Cudworth and Henry
More were the most prominent representatives of this group of
moderate Puritans who criticized the nonconformist tradition
from within. They were eager to move away from dogmatic
statements like the Westminster Confession and toward a
broader theology that might act as a solvent to interminable
religious disputes. But both Cudworth's *The True Intellectual
System of the Universe*[23] and More's *Enchiridion Ethicum*[24] were
rambling attempts to systematize an attitude that defied clear
exposition. The crux of their spiritual philosophy was a commitment to reasonable religion, a rationalistic conception of God
and man, and a practical morality. Their preference for reasonable beliefs caused them to denounce the Puritan doctrines of
predestination and justification by faith and call instead for a
simpler but broader religion that precluded ignoble wrangling
over obscure theological distinctions. They suggested that the

21. Ibid., pp. 502–25 for Johnson's book list.
22. Simon Patrick in John Tulloch's *Rational Theology and Christian
Philosophy in England in the Seventeenth Century*, 2 vols. (London, 1872),
1 : 36.
23. London, 1678.
24. London, 1658.

religious essentials were contained in the Bible, where reasonable men could discover God's will without recourse to creedal pronouncements.

The Cambridge Platonists were also congenital compromisers whose penchant for moderation allowed them to serve as mediators between traditional religious enemies. They advised the Anglicans committed to Laudian policies to consider Christian morality before episcopal polity. They advised the English Puritans to forsake the doctrines of Westminster for a rational reading of Scripture. They reminded both parties that any genuine religious movement should allow each man to discover a way of affirming divine truth as he saw it. And they were certain that men who examined their consciences and acted accordingly would discover a spiritual heritage all could share.

Finally, these Cambridge Platonists encouraged all religious men to discard the scholastic categories that froze religious discussion into prefabricated terms and thereby facilitated sectarian disputes. Cudworth counseled an appreciation for current philosophical discoveries—what Johnson called the New Learning—and "a philosophy of religion confirmed and established by philosophical reasons in an age so philosophical." [25] He and his compatriots called for a fusion of essential Christianity with the insights of modern philosophy. They were confident that established religious doctrines would be infused with new life when exposed to more vital intellectual propositions.

The ideas of the Cambridge Platonists appealed to Johnson because they confirmed his own suspicions. In Cudworth and More he discovered two prominent thinkers who verified his theological predilections. He too had concluded that God dealt with men as rational creatures. He too believed that devout persons should pay more attention to the morality of their actions than the telltale signs of grace in their souls. And these theological similarities reflected a temperamental affinity for the broad, inclusive thrust of their religious message. Moreover, these Cambridge scholars, like Johnson, recognized the need to refurbish religion with elements of the New Learning. Although

25. Ralph Cudworth, *The True Intellectual System of the Universe*, preface.

many of them predated Locke and Newton, and therefore did not perceive the specific changes wrought by the new science, they were aware that scholasticism was antiquated. They encouraged religious men to be receptive to fresh ideas. And, like Johnson, their main goal was to harness the insights of enlightened scholarship to a renovated conception of religion.[26]

Johnson was simultaneously investigating the writings of a second group of English latitudinarians, many of whom had studied under the Cambridge Platonists and shared both the moderate temper and the intellectual predisposition of Cudworth and More. But Edward Stillingfleet, Simon Patrick, John Tillotson, and Daniel Whitby were not Puritan academicians; they were Anglican churchmen who rose to prominence during the Restoration. Subsequently, the name "latitudinarian" changed from a term of abuse to one of respect. Despite their involvement in the ecclesiastical problems of the Restoration, the latitudinarians inherited from their Cambridge teachers a desire "not to increase the Controversies of the times, nor to ferment the differences that are among us." [27] They exercised a restraining influence over vitriolic Anglicans who were eager to persecute Puritans after the accession of Charles II.[28]

The latitudinarians also welcomed discoveries in philosophy and science. They applauded the establishment of the Royal Society, recognized the importance of Boyle and Newton, were familiar with Locke's *Essay*, and urged the assimilation of enlightened philosophy into contemporary theology. They were reasonable men, who asked their readers to recognize that the proper exercise of the rational faculties necessitated the reform of scholastic learning and an end to sectarian enthusiasm. They were careful to mention that faith and the Scriptures provided the ultimate avenues to religious truth, but they tended to show

26. G. R. Cragg, *From Puritanism to the Age of Reason* (Cambridge, 1950), pp. 37–60, for the best short account of the Cambridge Platonists. F. J. Powicke, *The Cambridge Platonists* (London, 1926), and W. R. Inge, *The Platonic Tradition in English Religious Thought* (London, 1917), are old but useful.

27. Edward Stillingfleet, *Irenicum: A Weapon Salve for the Churches Wounds* . . . (London, 1662), A–2.

28. G. R. Cragg, *The Church and the Age of Reason* (New York, 1961), pp. 70–73, and *Puritanism in the Period of the Great Persecutions, 1660–1688* (Cambridge, 1957), pp. 246–47.

how articles of faith were reasonable probabilities; and they insisted that Scripture be studied from a rational perspective. Stillingfleet summarized the latitudinarian movement as a noble attempt "to give a Statement of Christianity more satisfying to the present temper of the age." [29] Since that age was fraught with conflict between Anglicans and Puritans, religion and science, Scripture and reason, the latitudinarians often found themselves occupying the middle ground between hostile factions and historical forces. At times Stillingfleet's attempts to mediate controversies avoided conflict at the price of ambivalent nonsense; and Tillotson's sermons often degenerated into a heterogeneous collection of inconsistencies. This was a natural consequence of their effort to adjust Christian ideas to the fast-changing intellectual environment without fully understanding where the Enlightenment was headed. Johnson found the latitudinarians instructive because he too was searching for philosophic stability during a transitional phase of western intellectual history. Lacking the insight and secularism of a philosophe, Johnson found that he shared the uncertainty and religious concern of the latitudinarians.[30]

Church polity was another matter. The polity issues to which the latitudinarians addressed themselves were shaped by the historical situation in England created by the Restoration. The return of Anglicans to positions of power had resulted in a new Act of Uniformity (1662) and sporadic persecutions of Puritan clergy and laity. The more moderate Puritan clergy, led by Richard Baxter, attempted to distinguish between fundamental issues of belief and secondary issues that were capable of compromise. Stillingfleet headed the moderate wing of episcopacy that opposed persecution and attempted to reach an agreement with Baxter and his followers.[31]

29. Edward Stillingfleet, *Origines Sacrae* (London, 1666), preface.

30. Tulloch's *Rational Theology* provides a survey of the chief latitudinarians; see also John Hunt, *Religious Thought in England,* 3 vols. (London, 1870–72), vol. 2; Cragg, *From Puritanism to the Age of Reason,* pp. 61–86; and Martin Griffin, "Latitudinarianism in the Seventeenth-Century Church of England" (Ph.D. diss., Yale University, 1962).

31. Cragg, *Puritanism in the Period of the Great Persecution,* pp. 4–29; Stillingfleet, *Irenicum,* p. xiii.

Out of the mass of ecclesiastical writing generated by this situation, two issues attracted Johnson's attention. The first concerned the status of Puritan ministers ordained during the Interregnum. Was ordination at the hands of Puritan ministers valid? Should Puritan ministers submit to reordination by Anglican bishops? At the nub of this controversy lay disagreement over the nature and origin of the ministerial office. In *Irenicum,* Stillingfleet endeavored to lay this argument to rest by admitting that scriptural evidence could be used to sanction ordination by ministers as well as bishops. Less moderate Anglicans refused to make this concession and pressed for the exclusion of Puritan ministers who would not submit to reordination.[32]

The second source of ecclesiastical controversy that interested Johnson concerned the question of religious uniformity. At what point did the Puritan refusal to conform to episcopal polity constitute a schism? How could the conscientious beliefs of Puritans be tolerated without endangering the religious unity of the nation? Here Stillingfleet and Whitby supported the long-standing idea that an established church was the religious expression of national solidarity, that the corporate life of the community required uniform religious practices, that the established church of England was episcopacy. Although the latitudinarians prided themselves on their moderation and rationality—characteristics that made insistence on conformity very difficult—they retained the medieval idea that religious uniformity was essential for the survival of an orderly society. The latitudinarian support for reasonable religion contributed to the eventual acceptance of the idea of toleration, but few latitudinarians were willing to accept the social implications of their liberal philosophy. They favored the inclusion of Puritans in the national religious establishment rather than the recognition of legalized dissenting sects.[33]

---

32. John Humphrey, *The Question of Re-ordination* . . . (London, 1661), pp. 18–32; G[iles] F[irmin], *Presbyterian Ordination Vindicated* (London, 1660), pp. 21–25.

33. Edward Stillingfleet, *The Apostolic Institution of Episcopacy Demonstrated* (London, 1675), pp. 321–22; Daniel Whitby, *The Evidences of Christianity* (London, 1671), p. 134.

Johnson was aware that the ecclesiastical controversies of the Restoration had entered a new phase after the religious settlement of 1689. Still, the question raised by the latitudinarians prior to the passage of the Act of Toleration stuck in his mind. The credibility of the polity views of Stillingfleet and Tillotson was enhanced by their support for the same New Learning that Johnson was in the process of discovering; and the English latitudinarians combined religion and philosophy in a way that Johnson found attractive. But intellectual and temperamental compatibility merely supplemented a more basic commonality. As Johnson read them, the problems faced by the latitudinarians in England in the 1660s were unsettlingly similar to the ecclesiastical problems of the New England churches in 1720; and the more Johnson thought about the similarity, the more unsettled he became.

New Englanders were not accustomed to looking across the ocean for ecclesiastical guidance. The original Puritan settlers believed that Englishmen would regard the Massachusetts Bay Colony as a "Citty Upon a Hill," a new model for church organization as well as communal sanctity. While Englishmen ignored the colonial experiment in favor of civil war and Cromwell's military vision of the New Model, an entire generation of colonial Puritans was reared in awe of their founding fathers. Men like Cotton, Hooker, and Shepard were enshrined as the religious exemplars of the Puritan tradition. The Cambridge Platform was regarded as the ecclesiastical legacy of those first-generation demigods.[34]

By the beginning of the eighteenth century Solomon Stoddard was eager to call a halt to this cult of ancestor worship. Stoddard condemned the "inordinate Veneration" of the founders because it encouraged current leaders to mimic the past and conform to dated ecclesiastical practices, "as if it were a transgression to call them into question." Stoddard's view was less nostalgic and more realistic: "The first Planters drew up a Platform of Church Discipline, before they had much time to weigh those things; . . .

34. Walker, *Creeds and Platforms*, pp. 185–88.

and some of their Posterity are mightily devoted to it, as if the Platform were the Pattern on the Mount, and all deviations from it, are looked upon as a degree of Apostasy." [35]

At issue was the most fundamental of all ecclesiastical questions: what is a church? Stoddard's denigration of the Cambridge Platform called attention to the discrepancies between the congregational polity of the first generation and the semi-presbyterian practices of 1718. Under the Saybrook Platform congregational autonomy had been replaced by a system of county consociations that claimed power over individual congregations, encouraged cooperation among the churches, and discouraged the localistic conception of the church. The consolidation of ecclesiastical authority had been necessitated by the increase in church membership, itself the product of increased population, the rejection of visible sainthood as a criterion for membership, and the admission of the unregenerate to the communion table. And these changes were accompanied by the recognition that the church was more than a gathering of divinely elected persons; it was an institution that developed converts, a function formerly left to God. The increased membership and expanded function gave the church a formal role in the regulation of community behavior. [36]

In his majestic history of seventeenth-century New England, *Magnalia Christi Americana,* Cotton Mather tried to retain respect for the architects of the Cambridge Platform at the same time as he registered approval for a more centralized church discipline. Mather rediscovered that the first generation had insisted that each congregation remain connected spiritually to the Church of England and accept "all the *Fundamentals* of *Christianity* embraced by that Church." [37] Although Mather insisted that the founders believed that the ties with episcopacy were

---

35. Solomon Stoddard, *An Examination of the Power of the Fraternity* (Boston, 1718), pp. 1–2; and *The Presence of Christ with the Ministers of the Gospel* (Boston, 1718); p. 26.

36. See above, chap. 1.

37. Cotton Mather, *Magnalia Christi Americana,* 2 vols. (London, 1702), 1 : 21; see Miller, *Orthodoxy in Massachusetts,* and Emil Oberholzer, *Delinquent Saints* (New York, 1956), for coverage of the religious practices of the first generation.

spiritual rather than organizational, he held up the non-sep-
aratist strain in New England ecclesiastical history as a precedent
for a broader, more inclusive conception of the church with
extensive powers of coercion and control.

Mather's concern for ecclesiastical order was merely part of a
widespread concern for social order. From a modern perspective
it appears that the economic dislocations produced by the Indian
wars, the currency problem, the hassles over property boundaries,
along with the ecclesiastical turmoil inherent in congregational autonomy, all made "the land of steady habits" less stable
than the name implies. But the Puritan leaders of Connecticut
still accepted the medieval notion that worldly events were
visible manifestations of their spiritual condition. They therefore regarded social discord as a symptom of a pervasive human
depravity that was raging out of control. According to this view
all social problems were ultimately religious problems.

It followed that the church had a major role in the restoration
of communal order. In 1713 John Bulkley expressed the view
that "the wisest Constitutions without this [religion], are ineffectual to bridle men's Lusts, and hold them within due
Limits." [38] Jonathan Marsh told the legislature that until "the
Heart of the People be Prepared and Disposed for it" by diligent ministers, civil rulers could not hope to preserve social
order.[39] On the other hand the clergy knew that their ministrations were dependent upon support from the magistrates, that
"Civil Government duly Administered, contributes not a little
to the Well-being, Growth & Progress of Religion in Society's." [40] For example, the consociations required civil backing
if they were to bring dissident congregations into line; clerical
salaries were paid out of taxes levied by the legislature and collected by civil officials; Yale, the training ground for future
ministers, was dependent upon civil support.

As a result, the election sermons of this period were filled
not only with an exaltation of the churches' role in restoring tran-

38. Bulkley, *The Necessity of Religion*, p. 44.
39. Jonathan Marsh, *An Essay, To Prove the Thorough Reformation of a
Sinning People is not to be Expected* . . . (New London, 1721), p. 8.
40. Bulkley, *The Necessity of Religion*, p. 3.

quility, but also with a plea for deference to civil authorities. Anthony Stoddard advised the colonists to "Murmur not against Rulers; Ben't always finding fault with their Managements; . . . Honour, Submit unto, Assist them what you can." [41] William Burnham reiterated the conservative idea that "Government is a great Blessing to this Sinful & Miserable world & if it should be destitute thereof, it should soon become a heap of Confusion." [42] Azariah Mather went even further. He asserted that "Subjects may not Rebel against lawful Authority (and indeed there is no other Authority but such)." [43]

By the second decade of the eighteenth century, then, the Puritan ministers and magistrates had forged an informal alliance in which the church played an important role as a bulwark of social stability. No longer a mere gathering of visible saints, or simply an institution that facilitated conversion, the church was also a pillar of the existent civil order. Despite the long-standing Puritan abhorrence of any union between church and state, an abhorrence shaped by persecutions at the hands of the royally supported agents of episcopacy, the governor of Connecticut from 1707 to 1724 was Gurdon Saltonstall, a Puritan minister who used his civil authority to enforce the policies of the Saybrook Synod. Under Saltonstall the traditional Puritan hostility to the union of church and state was largely ignored. The churches organized under the Saybrook Association enjoyed the same political support that episcopacy had enjoyed under Charles II. Connecticut Puritanism was more and more becoming a provincial version of the established Church of England.[44]

But infatuation with Anglicanism had its limits. One of the limits was defined by differences on the question of ordination. The early Puritan clergy had considered it an insignificant cere-

41. Anthony Stoddard, *Connecticut Election Sermon* (New London, 1716).
42. William Burnham, *God's Providence in Placing Men in their Respective Stations and Conditions* . . . (New London, 1722), p. 2.
43. Azariah Mather, *Good Rulers a Choice Blessing* . . . (New London, 1725), p. A-2.
44. Eliphalet Adams, *A Funeral Discourse* (New London, 1724), praises Saltonstall for his ability to "*maintain a steady Order & keep up the due Honour of Authority*" even when the people had "*increased in their Numbers* . . . & run almost wild with *Liberty*."

mony, merely the formal recognition of a minister's selection by the congregation. Although neighboring clergy usually performed the service, the Cambridge Platform recognized ordination by laymen as valid. Implicit in this attitude toward ordination was the assumption that Christ dispensed his spiritual powers through the church membership, that members made ministers. It was the principle of republican government applied to church polity.[45]

By the time Johnson was ordained, most New England ministers were reluctant to admit their dependence upon the will of the congregation.[46] And, once again, as the ecclesiastical legacy of the founders was found wanting, the Puritan clergy moved toward Anglican remedies. No longer could the fiction be maintained that the churches were filled with regenerate members. Puritan churches, like Anglican churches, admitted saints and sinners to the communion table. Stoddard, the man most responsible for bringing the unregenerate into the church, was one of the first to insist that the impure membership "are not fit to judge & rule in the Church." [47] How could a minister restrain the sinful if the people he was to restrain determined his admis-

45. Bushman, *Puritan to Yankee*, pp. 221–34. The religious and political literature of the period is filled with cries for more authoritarian rulers and stronger churches as a restraining influence on a population that was verging on revolution. Allowing for the exaggerations of election-day orators, the widespread sense of imminent anarchy was genuine and was, in part, a response to basic alterations in social and economic conditions. Bushman shows how competition for land, as well as unstable currency and agricultural problems, underlay this drive for order. Recent demographic studies of certain towns in colonial New England suggest that family size, patterns of marriage, generational conflict, and other basic social and psychological factors were operating in such a way as to increase anxiety. Despite contradictions among this new band of social historians, further work on the local level should clarify the long-range causes of the unrest that provoked civil and clerical concern. See John Demos, "Notes on Life in Plymouth Colony," *William and Mary Quarterly*, 3rd ser. 22 (1965): 264–86; Philip J. Greven, "Family Structure in Seventeenth-Century Andover, Massachusetts," ibid. 23 (1966): 234–56; Kenneth Lockridge, "Land, Population, and the Evolution of New England Society, 1630–1790; and an Afterthought," *Past and Present*, no. 39 (April 1968).

46. Walker, *Creeds and Platforms*, p. 195; also James L. Ainslie, *The Doctrines of Ministerial Order in the Reformed Churches of the Sixteenth and Seventeenth Centuries* (Edinburgh, 1940), p. 188.

47. Stoddard, *The Doctrine of Instituted Churches*, p. 12.

sion to the ministerial office? And if a minister did not derive his clerical power from the congregation, what was the source of his authority?

It was a question Johnson had seen debated in the exchange between Edmund Calamy and Benjamin Hoadley in England. He had also studied the accounts of less prominent Anglican spokesmen like William Sclater and John Potter.[48] The Anglicans argued that a minister was more than an elected representative of the church membership; he was a descendant of the apostles, who could trace his ministry back through a historical succession of ministers all the way to Christ himself. Hoadley, Sclater, and Potter insisted that the office of bishop was specifically instituted by Christ to preserve the historical connection among clerical descendants of the apostles; in other words, only bishops could ordain. Stillingfleet preferred to avoid the latter point, because it implied the illegitimacy of ordination by ministers and thereby excluded the Puritans from the broad religious consensus the latitudinarians wished to create.[49] But all Anglicans agreed that the ministry was a divinely ordained office with historic roots in the primitive Christian era.

In search of guarantees for their ministerial legitimacy that would be more tangible than the approval of the congregation, the New England ministers redefined their conception of the ministry. Between 1710 and 1720 a host of ministers addressed the issue in the press, but Ebenezer Pemberton put it most concisely.[50] Pemberton rejected the Anglican notion that bishops provided the only valid link with the apostles, since this implied

48. William Sclater, *Original Draught of the Primitive Church* (London, 1691); John Potter, *Discourse on Church Government* (London, 1701). Johnson mentions these authors in *Career*, 1 : 13.

49. Stillingfleet, *Irenicum*, p. 413.

50. Ebenezer Pemberton, *A Discourse on the Validity of Ordination by the Hands of Presbyters* . . . (Boston, 1718), pp. 7–12, 15. See also Joseph Morgan, *The Great Concernment of Gospel Ordinances* . . . (New York, 1709); Benjamin Colman, *A Sermon Preach'd at the Ordination of Mr. William Cooper* . . . (Boston, 1716); William Williams, *A Painful Ministry* . . . (Boston, 1716); Thomas Foxcroft, *A Practical Discourse Relating to the Gospel Ministry* (Boston, 1718); Thomas Prince, *A Sermon Delivered by Thomas Prince at His Ordination* (Boston, 1718); Stoddard, *The Presence of Christ With the Ministers of the Gospel*.

that the New England churches "*have no regular or Lawful Ministers. And we cannot pass a Judgement so rash and severe.*" But Pemberton defended the idea that ministers were "the successors of the Apostles to the end of the World." He claimed that the connection between the current generation and the apostolic era had been maintained not by bishops, but by "the Ordinary standing Ministry of the Gospel." He recalled that it was customary for neighboring ministers to attend ordinations, often preaching a sermon and conveying their blessing. Pemberton and other Puritan divines now declared that this custom was fraught with meaning. They argued that the ministers, not the laymen, had been the ordaining agents. Each minister could trace his authority through un unbroken succession of ministers, all the way back to the Church of England under the Tudors and then to the apostolic era. In sum, the emerging new rationale for clerical legitimacy abandoned the earlier Puritan belief in ordination by the congregation and replaced it with the Anglican notion of ordination by a recognized successor of the apostles.

What Pemberton did not mention, but other concerned ministers did, was that the chain of apostolic succession in New England was broken in certain key spots. If one man was ordained by laymen without the presence of ministers, he was not legitimately ordained. And any ministers he ordained were also illegitimate. Joseph Webb recalled that Israel Chauncey and Samuel Andrew (former rector of Yale!) had been ordained by laymen.[51] Two of Yale's trustees mentioned this matter to Cotton Mather, then asked Mather and themselves "whether an uninterrupted succession from the apostles' days be not absolutely necessary to the validity of a minister's ordination?" If the answer was yes, many respected New England clergymen were not legitimate ministers. And since so many of the seventeenth-century ordinations were not recorded accurately, it would be very difficult to distinguish a minister from an unknowing pretender.[52]

It is equally difficult for us to appreciate the genuine con-

51. Webb to Cotton Mather, 18 January 1723, *Conn. Episcopacy*, 1 : 64.

52. John Davenport and Steven Buckingham to Increase and Cotton Mather, 25 September 1722, *Conn. Episcopacy*, 1 : 69.

cern the ordination issue aroused among the Puritan clergy,
including Samuel Johnson. He read and reread histories of the
early Christian church, compared these histories with scriptural
accounts, studied the Anglican distinction between bishops and
ministers and reviewed the evolving Puritan conception of the
ministry. The empiricism of Locke and Newton had not altered
the religious caste of his mind. He retained the conviction—
a conviction rooted in medieval scholasticism and supported
by the Platonism of Ames and Puritan metaphysics—that there
were final, universal answers to his important queries. There was
a prescribed form for the church. There was a proper way to
become a minister. Johnson was intellectually incapable of regarding the development of New England church polity as a
justifiable response to altered social conditions. The archetypes
could not change with time. In his mind reason was not a faculty
that permitted a historical understanding of a shifting religious
truth. It was a tool that men must use to discover the permanent
truths buried in the Bible and the primitive Christian Era.

And so the care with which Johnson scrutinized the biblical
accounts of the early church and studied the convoluted ecclesiastical literature that dealt with the origin of the ministry must
be understood as an attempt to decipher the archetypes, an attempt unencumbered by the secular insights inherent in the
New Learning. Over and above the specific polity details, Johnson's keen interest in Anglicanism was part of an emerging appreciation of English institutions and attitudes that was sweeping through New England.[53] Many of the political and religious
leaders of Connecticut became committed to a rejection of the
customary patterns of life that had evolved in the seventeenth
century. Civil rulers were demanding the same arbitrary power
that Charles I and the royalists had used against English Puritans. The Connecticut clergy not only supported these demands,

53. In *The Character of the Good Ruler: Puritan Political Ideas in New
England 1630–1730*, pp. 203–39, T. H. Breen discusses the emergence of a
"court persuasion" in New England, and a permanent class of political leaders
that looked to England for their ideas and style. See also the forth coming
book by John M. Murrin, *Anglicizing an American Colony: The Transformation of Provincial Massachusetts*, for an analysis of the colonial imitation of
English traditions in politics, law, and religion.

they also encouraged civil enforcement of the clerical policies formulated by the consociations, thereby creating a religious establishment which detractors compared with Laudian Anglicanism. These same clergy derived their ministerial authority from an apostolic tradition independent of popular support, a tradition that Puritans had formerly associated with the corrupt episcopal pastors who claimed immunity from criticism on the basis of their membership in the apostolic family. In fact, the overwhelming concern for church order and ministerial legitimacy fastened attention on procedural issues and relegated substantative religious matters to the background. In an effort to restructure the church so that it could meet the needs of an increasingly diverse population, the Connecticut ministers were not only looking toward England for polity guidelines, they were also obfuscating the spiritual truths New England had been founded to affirm.

What was going through Johnson's mind during the period from 1719 to 1722? The fullest account of those years is in his autobiography, written fifty years later and colored by a lifetime of bitter experiences at the hands of an anti-Anglican populace. He recalled that his conversion to Anglicanism, like his conversion to the New Learning, was an immediately and wholly rational decision: he studied the ecclesiastical arguments and his prejudices against the Church of England "vanish[ed] like smoke." [54] His notebook for 1719 does contain an entry in which he declared that he "would with full approbation and complacency of mind and with the greatest delight and satisfaction submit to the order of it [episcopacy]." [55] But such bold statements were never uttered in public. He continued to perform his duties as Puritan pastor at West Haven without incident. He had yet to distill his appreciation for episcopal polity, his rejection of New England scholasticism, his fascination with English scholarship, including Locke, Newton, and the latitudinarians, into a meaningful directive.

54. *Career*, 1 : 11.
55. Ibid., 3 : 6.

Moreover, his notebook reveals that he was racked with self-doubt, that his rational convictions were complicated by emotional uncertainty. On 3 June 1722 he wrote "Oh that I could either gain satisfaction that I may lawfully proceed in the execution of the ministerial function or that Providence would make my way plain for obtaining Episcopal orders; what course I shall take I know not." [56] Practical considerations were weighing heavily on his mind. If he turned against Puritanism in favor of the Church of England, he reasoned, his ministerial career would be ruined, Yale would disown him, and his mother would be terribly offended.[57]

Like most New Englanders, he had been raised in an anti-Anglican atmosphere in which, as one episcopal agent reported, "the people are not only not of the Church, but have been trained up with all the care imaginable, to be its enemies." [58] Anglican missionaries who ventured into Connecticut concurred that "it was as much as a man's life was worth even to talk of 'the Church' in Connecticut without the means of self-defense." [59] Johnson was sufficiently aware of this Anglophobia to think twice before announcing his desertion to the enemy. Perhaps God wanted him to use his influence to push the colonial churches closer to Anglican policies. Perhaps he should join with those Puritan ministers who were endeavoring to solidify the religious establishment in Connecticut. Perhaps the minister who ordained him had been ordained by a minister who had received his clerical authority from a bishop. Had not Stillingfleet admitted that the Bible did not clearly distinguish between the offices of bishop and minister in the primitive church? As

---

56. Ibid., 1 : 61.
57. Ibid., 3 : 8.
58. Caleb Heathcote to Secretary, 9 November 1705, *Conn. Episcopacy,* 1 : 11. See also Trumbull, *History of Conn.,* 1 : 477–91; Evarts B. Greene, "The Anglican Outlook on the American Colonies in the Early Eighteenth Century," *American Historical Review* 20 (1914): 64–85; M. Louise Greene, *The Development of Religious Liberty in Connecticut* (Boston, 1905); I. S. Seymour, "The Beginnings of the Episcopal Church in Connecticut," *Publications of the Tercentenary Commission of Connecticut,* no. 30 (New Haven, 1934), all for early Anglican missionary activity in Connecticut.
59. Caleb Heathcote to Secretary, 9 November 1705, *Conn. Episcopacy,* 1 : 14.

surely as he knew there were divinely prescribed forms for the church and the ministry, Johnson also knew that the frailty of his rational faculty would frustrate his search for the truth. For three years he wrestled with the dilemma, exploring the attractions of Anglicanism with his friends, listing the pros and cons of conversion to episcopacy, never finding satisfaction, holding open all his options.

In June of 1722 Johnson believed that God gave him the answers to his questions. A man named George Pigot had recently been sent by the Society for the Propagation of the Gospel in Foreign Parts (S.P.G.) to Stratford to minister to the thirty Anglican families residing in the area.[60] Johnson went to Pigot with a host of questions about Anglican polity, as well as some practical questions about the role of episcopacy in Connecticut, and Pigot immediately wrote home to the secretary of the S.P.G. to announce his "great expectations of a glorious revolution of the ecclesiastics of this colony, because the most distinguished gentlemen among them are resolvedly bent to promote her welfare and embrace her baptism and discipline, and, if the leaders fall in, there is no doubt to be made of her people." [61]

Pigot counseled Johnson and his six friends throughout the summer. He tactfully reinforced their own doubts about the validity of the Puritan ordination procedure, assured them that the Church of England would accept their ministerial credentials once they had been ordained by a bishop, and suggested that the S.P.G. would finance a voyage to London to make Anglican ordination possible. His prodding eventually proved decisive. By the end of the summer, Johnson and his six friends were convinced that conversion to episcopacy was worth the popular abuse and ridicule they knew it would generate. They decided to make their decision public on the commencement day of Yale College.[62]

60. Aeneas Mackenzie to Secretary, n.d., S.P.G. MSS, A, 9 : 243, 248, and 10 : 212–14; *Career*, 1 : 13.
61. Pigot to Secretary, 20 August 1722, *Conn. Episcopacy*, 1 : 56–57.
62. *Career*, 1 : 14.

The Yale trustees had heard rumors about conferences between a certain Anglican missionary and Rector Cutler, former tutor of Johnson, and other distinguished leaders of the community. They had said nothing, probably thinking that if anyone was going to be converted, it would be the missionary. When the commencement ceremonies began on September 12, the trustees watched proudly as degrees were conferred, valedictories given, and theses defended. Everything went smoothly and solemnly until the end. As the trustees rose to leave, Rector Cutler concluded the commencement with the words, "And let all the people say Amen." This was a specifically Anglican prayer, designed to attract the attention of the trustees, which it did. The trustees immediately requested that Messrs. Cutler, Johnson, Brown, Hart, Wetmore, Whittlesey, and Eliot gather at the college library the next day and explain themselves.[63]

It was a short meeting. When the trustees demanded to know what Johnson, Cutler, and the others were doing with the Reverend Pigot, each member of the group calmly pronounced himself a convert to Anglicanism. The trustees had not come prepared to debate the merits of episcopacy. They asked the self-confessed Anglicans to reconsider and adjourned. Word quickly spread that seven of the most respected leaders of Connecticut "have made an open declaration in favor of the Church of England." [64]

All New England exploded. Brown reported that the announcement "raises no small stir among the people of all ranks." Joseph Webb informed Cotton Mather that "the axe is hereby laid to the root of our civil and sacred enjoyments, and a doleful gap opened for trouble and confusion in our churches." [65] Two of the Yale trustees bemoaned the fate of their college and asked Increase and Cotton Mather "who would have conjectured . . . it [Yale] should groan out Ichabod in about three years and a half under its second tutor?" [66]

63. Brown to ?, 21 September 1722, *Career*, 1 : 73; also Oviatt, *The Beginnings of Yale*, chap. 2, and E. E. Beardsley, *The History of the Episcopal Church in Connecticut*, 2 vols. (New York, 1865), 1 : 35–39.
64. *Career*, 1 : 73.
65. Quoted from Beardsley, *Episcopal Church*, 1 : 39.
66. Dexter, *Doc. Hist.*, p. 227.

Benjamin Franklin reported that in Boston "all the Pepel are runnin mad." He advised all readers of the *New England Courant* to salvage something practical from the chaos by allowing henpecked husbands to renounce their marriage vows on the grounds that the ministers who performed the ceremony were not properly ordained.[67] The commotion even spilled over to England, where Jeremiah Dummer, the colonial agent responsible for sending the books that Johnson and his fellow apostates had read, denied that he had "fill'd the library with every book for the Church and not one of the Other Side" and claimed "there never was an Eminent Dissenter & Author whose works are not in the Collection." [68] Governor Saltonstall was determined to maintain a cool head in the midst of the disaster and, hopefully, to undo some of the damage. He ordered the trustees and the self-proclaimed Anglican converts to debate the issues in his presence immediately prior to the fall session of the Connecticut legislature.

Since his friends had selected him as spokesman for their side in the debate, Johnson felt an obligation to review the ecclesiastical arguments in favor of episcopacy. In effect, he prepared a brief for the defense of Anglican polity, complete with biblical citations and references to the history of the early Christian church. But the elaborate structure of his argument was more a means of girding up his own cautious instincts than an indication of self-confidence. His main worry was not the logic or validity of his arguments as much as the depth of his conviction. Up to October 13, three days before the debate, he expressed doubts about going through with it.[69] Finally, he told himself in his diary that neither "the frowns or applauses, the pleasures or profits of the world have any prevailing influence in the affair," and reiterated his belief that "If this be therefore a divine or at least Apostolic Institution (as I am fully persuaded it is) fear of breaking peace should not shut up my mouth in a matter of so much consequence." [70]

67. *The New England Courant*, 1–8, 22–29 October 1722.
68. Dummer to Trustees, 3 June 1723, in Dexter, *Doc. Hist.*, pp. 240–41.
69. Citation for 13 October 1722, *Career*, 1 : 63, which lists his arguments for episcopacy and his doubts.
70. *Career*, 1 : 64.

On 16 October 1722, Johnson got his chance to speak. What he or the trustees said has not survived, although a few general features of the session appear clear. First, the debate involved only ecclesiastical issues; the trustees did not discuss the question of Arminianism or theological heresy. In Johnson's account and in the reports of the Boston newspapers, there was the recognition that both sides admitted that church polity, not theology, was the basis of controversy.[71]

It is also clear that Johnson's account of the debate is not completely reliable. Johnson made it seem that the trustees were unfamiliar with the points at issue, "that the subject was in great measure new to the gentlemen [trustees]." [72] But the confrontation in the Yale Library after commencement had alerted the trustees to the nature of the polity questions; moreover, the New England ministry had argued among themselves for years about the church, the form of the early church, the basis of ministerial authority, and ordination procedure. What made the conversion of Johnson and his friends so alarming to orthodox Puritans was the realization that the converts were troubled by these same ecclesiastical problems and that the answers that the converts had agreed upon—Anglican answers—were logical extensions of the answers that Puritan ministers had reached in recent years. The central issue in the debate between the Anglican converts and the trustees was the validity of Puritan ordination, an issue that emerged directly out of an ecclesiastical context in which other New England ministers were searching for more formal guarantees of their clerical authority. The vehemence with which the trustees denounced the converts was not due to the trustees' inability to grasp the rationale for Anglicanism, but to their sudden realization that the New England churches had drifted perilously close to the same apostasy.

Whatever the reasons, the trustees did react vehemently. The intimidation which Johnson had feared began when "an old minister got up and made a harangue against them in a declara-

71. Ibid., pp. 14–15; *The Boston News-letter*, 22–29 October 1722; *The New England Courant*, 29 October–5 November 1722 and 4 March 1723.
72. *Career*, 1 : 15, 62–64.

tory way." [73] Eliot, Harte, Whittlesey, and Wetmore failed to survive the denunciations. They admitted their doubts about episcopacy and agreed to delay a final decision. Johnson, Brown, and Cutler held their ground until Saltonstall put an end to the proceedings. Within a few days, the three were on their way to Boston. On 5 November 1722 they sailed for England.[74]

73. Ibid., p. 16.
74. A contemporary narrative of the entire apostasy by a militant but nameless Puritan is in *Conn. Episcopacy*, 1 : 72–75.

5

From London to Stratford

The voyage took thirty-nine days, from November 5 to December 15.[1] Johnson used the time to read; he had finished ten books before he sighted the Isle of Wight, landed at Ramsgate, and proceeded to Canterbury.[2] There was an awkward moment as he, Cutler, and Brown disembarked to find no coach or transportation available and no welcoming committee to tell them what to do or where to go. Had Pigot failed to alert the proper Anglican authorities? Fearing that they might be unannounced guests, they wondered how and where to proceed. Eventually they made their way to Canterbury, where they were treated to a royal welcome by Dean Stanhope and a gathering of Anglican officials who had only recently read about the Yale apostates in the London newspapers. Stanhope sensed their discomfort and did his best to put them at ease in the strange surroundings. He assured them that England and the English church were home.[3]

The first thing Johnson noticed was the architecture. During his stay at Canterbury, he marveled at "the ancient magnificence of the Cathedral," counted its steps, measured its height, and attended the services at every opportunity.[4] After he and his friends moved on to London, he was very much impressed by St. Paul's, where he "took a view of that stupendous fabric, ascended

1. Journal, p. 5. Johnson kept a "journal of his voyage to, abode at, and return from England." Beardsley, *Johnson*, pp. 23–50, prints selections from the Journal, which is in the Johnson MSS.
2. *Career*, 1 : 510–11, for the books read on the voyage.
3. Journal, p. 6.
4. Ibid., p. 7.

to the top of the dome by five hundred and fifty steps, which with the Cupola and Cross made four hundred feet in height. . . . It is perhaps one of the finest buildings in the world—an amazing mass of stones!" [5] Johnson visited Lambeth Palace, Westminster Abbey, the Tower, and various estates around London, always noting their size, the elaborate interior decorations, gardens, statues, and other "glorious things" which served as the external symbols of a rich and ancient culture.[6]

There was the theater at Drury Lane, "where we had a Tragedy," the New England coffee house, the Half-Moon coffee house, St. Paul's coffee house, "the theater at Lincoln's Inn, where we had a Comedy," a charitable trip to Bedlam, a tour of "the Antiquarian and Picture Galleries," and even a visit "to Tyburn to see Counselor Layer hanged." [7] Along the way Johnson saw "a wonderous clock that performed all sorts of music," "a remarkable gun that went off eleven times in a minute" and the "skeletons, mummies, medals, jewels, [and] antiquities" of the various museums.[8]

The people as well as the places kept changing. On January 3 Johnson and his friends were joined by John Checkley, an Oxford graduate "noted for the ugliness of his countenance," who had recently defended episcopacy in Massachusetts.[9] The Boston presses were presently turning out two inflammatory pamphlets in which Checkley launched a full-scale assault on the ministers, churches, and governments of New England.[10] More extreme and passionate in his religious and political views than Johnson, Checkley nevertheless shared with him a desire for episcopal ordination and a colonist's affection for English culture. His Oxford degree provided him with the credentials of an English

5. Ibid., pp. 20–21.
6. Ibid., pp. 6, 7, 33, 34.
7. Ibid., pp. 20, 22, 32, 35.
8. Ibid., pp. 25, 43. Pagination ends on 14 May 1723, with p. 40. References after p. 40 will be given by date. The museum tour was on 24 May 1723.
9. Journal, pp. 11–12. The description of Checkley is from Henry W. Foote, *Annals of King's Chapel*, 2 vols. (Boston, 1882–96), 1 : 285.
10. John Checkley, *A Modest Proof of the Order and Government Settled by Christ and His Apostles in the Church* (Boston, 1724); *A Defence of a Book Lately Reprinted at Boston* (Boston, 1724). Also see his *Choice Dialogues . . . Concerning Election and Predestination* (Boston, 1720).

gentleman, and he sometimes flaunted his diploma as a badge of a kind of civilized intellectualism that he felt was impossible at Harvard or Yale. Even his friends regarded him as "too much of a wag for intimate acquaintance," but he was an excellent companion to have on a tour through the monuments of English history. Like the cathedrals and statues of London, he blended in with the English landscape.[11]

Checkley accompanied Johnson on a tour of Oxford, where Johnson registered his favorable impression of the architecture, listened to lectures, discussed mathematics and philosophy with prominent professors, browsed in the libraries, and examined some of the scientific equipment, "including the curiosities of the air-pump and other engines." [12] On a trip to Cambridge a week later Johnson discovered the same highly charged intellectual climate. There he met "Mr. Saunderson, the Blind Mathematical Professor—a prodigy," had tea with the college masters, and, as at Oxford, was awarded an honorary Master of Arts degree.[13] At both universities he recognized an academic intensity and scholarly sophistication that were impossible in a colonial setting and that added an intellectual dimension to what he had come to regard as his cultural home.

Johnson's experience in England reinforced his instinctive respect for civilized society and high culture. It provided him with a group of like-minded English friends with whom he maintained contact long after he returned to America. They, in turn, arranged introductions with other prominent Englishmen soon to visit the colonies, like William Burnet and George Berkeley. Visits to Oxford and Cambridge fed his intellectual pretensions and gave him a vision of academic utopia that he carried back to Connecticut and nurtured for the remainder of his life. He later admitted that "I can scarce speak of Oxon without raptures, for I must allow that throughout the whole course of my life, I never spent ten days with half the pleasure which I had during the

11. A short biography of Checkley is in William Sprague, *Annals of the American Pulpit*, 6 vols. (New York, 1857–60), 5 : 109–11. See *Harvard Graduates*, 5 : 47, 53, 55, 57, 155, for this phase of Checkley's career. See also *The New England Courant*, 4–11 March 1723, for a poem on Checkley.

12. Journal, 20–31 May 1723.

13. Journal, 7–15 June 1723.

little time I was there." [14] Even his fascination with the elaborate architecture of English churches lingered on. As late as 1743, after he had established himself as the nearest thing to a bishop in Connecticut, he made every effort to erect in Stratford a colonial version of Canterbury Cathedral with "large arched sash windows and a handsome spire," an imported organ, and an enormous bell.[15]

It is important to notice the depth of Johnson's love affair with English culture because it stimulated and amplified his attraction to episcopacy. He had repudiated the intellectual authorities of New England, including Ramus and Ames, and discovered a more compelling scholarly tradition in English latitudinarianism. He had come to value good conversation, intellectual stimulation, and knowledge of what was in vogue. The visit to England verified what Johnson had already suspected, that Connecticut was merely a frontier outpost of the empire, the center of which, culturally as well as commercially, was London. His conversion to episcopacy was not just a rational decision based on biblical evidence. It was a complex transferral of allegiance. The decision to seek episcopal ordination was only the final stage of a cultural and psychological reorientation that had begun when he first read the Dummer books. Johnson was one of the first in what was to become a long line of New England intellectuals who recoiled from the sterility of American culture and found personal salvation, as well as urbanity and intellectual sophistication, in the old world rather than the new.

But Johnson's motives were also different from those of later expatriates like Henry James. As a man of the early eighteenth rather than the late nineteenth century, Johnson expressed his personal preferences in the religious terms appropriate to his age. He recalled that his great-grandfather had joined the Puritan migration to New England almost a century earlier in order to escape the religious and political persecutions of the Laudians

14. Johnson to [?] of Queens, Oxford, 25 January 1724, *Career*, 3 : 221.
15. A. B. Hart, *The Itinerarium of Dr. Alexander Hamilton* (St. Louis, 1907), p. 204. References to the Stratford church and to Johnson's concern for the architectural details are in Beardsley, *Episcopal Church*, 1 : 138; George Croce, *William Samuel Johnson, A Maker of the Constitution* (New York, 1937), p. 37; William Wilcoxson, *History of Stratford* (Stratford, 1939).

and to establish a haven for the ideals of "pure Christianity" that were under attack in England. Now, in 1723, he could see that his Puritan ancestors, though men of conviction who "deserve the honest charity of every good man," had made a serious mistake.[16] New England was racked with ecclesiastical problems; the civil and religious leaders admitted that the ideal of the godly community had not been realized. Meanwhile, God had blessed England with an end to the Civil War, the return of a stable Anglican establishment governed by latitudinarian rather than Laudian leaders, the development of an exciting new philosophy and science, and the ascension of London as cultural capital of the world. The divine will was clear. It was "apparent from the whole face of Ecclesiastical History, that not Episcopacy, but opposition to it and Rebellion against it, and usurpation over it have been the Cause of these horrid Conculsions [convulsions?]."[17] History had made it clear that New England was not only a colonial outpost, but also that Puritanism was a sectarian aberration.

The question that bothered Johnson the most while he was in England was how far to push his denunciation of New England Puritanism. He was convinced of the superiority of the Church of England, but unsure of how this affected the New England churches. If the churches of New England did not have bishops and therefore could not maintain the apostolic succession, were all Puritan ordinations invalid? If so, were all Puritan church services worthless? If one believed that the Church of England was a true church, did that mean that the New England churches were and always had been untrue? Beneath these ecclesiastical questions lay the more fundamental issue: to what extent did God expect men to insist on a strict allegiance to biblical precedents? How much honest disagreement could be tolerated short of hypocrisy?

These were the same kinds of questions that had troubled Johnson in New England. Once in England, the answers seemed obvious. On 31 March 1723 "at 6 in the morning, Sunday, at the

16. *Career*, 3 : 4.
17. From an undated letter by Johnson, included in his *Eleutherius Enervatus* . . . (New York, 1733).

Church of St. Martin-in-the-Fields, at the continued appointment and desire of William, Lord Abp. of Canterbury, and John, Lord Bishop of London, we [Johnson, Brown and Cutler] were ordained Priests most gravely by the Right Revd Thomas, Lord Bp. of Norwich." [18] Johnson did not claim that his ordination was conditional, a ceremony that guaranteed his ministerial legitimacy in case his Puritan ordination was ineffectual. He, along with Checkley and Cutler, affirmed their belief in the "nullity and invalidity" of the Puritan ministry. They called Puritan ministers "invaders of the sacred services" and reiterated that only Anglican clergy who were ordained by bishops "are to be acknowledged true ministers of the Gospel." [19]

A few days earlier, on March 9, Johnson had confessed that he was "having grave doubts whether Baptism received among the Presbyterians is valid." [20] He requested rebaptism, apparently reasoning that his baptism at the hands of a Puritan minister was as invalid as his ordination. Johnson had carried the notion of a pure or true church to its logical conclusion. He repudiated all churches that did not subscribe to his standards of church purity. It was an unequivocal position, the kind of position Johnson usually tried to avoid. But it followed logically from his belief that episcopacy was divinely prescribed in the Bible. If it was hard on devout Puritans, it was at least consistent. And the flourishing condition of English culture, in contrast to the sterility of New England, seemed like a divine sanction for episcopal religion.

One tragic event distorted this impression. In early April Brown came down with what appeared to be a cold. Cutler had been ill a month earlier, but had recovered and joined the group in time for ordination. Still, Johnson was worried about his best friend and reluctant to leave his bedside. Checkley and Cutler eventually persuaded him to depart London for a week at Greenwich. When he returned to London on April 13, Brown was dead. What had been diagnosed as a cold had turned out to be small-

18. Journal, p. 34. Checkley was not ordained at this time, because Edmund Gibson, Bishop of London, disapproved of the high church views he had expressed in his publications.

19. John Nichols, *Illustrations of the Literary History of the Eighteenth Century*, 8 vols. (1817–58), 4 : 279–300; Checkley, *A Modest Proof*, preface.

20. Journal, pp. 27–28.

pox. For two weeks Johnson went into seclusion, appearing in public only to attend church services.[21]

Johnson blamed Brown's death on London. A few days before the symptoms of illness appeared he and Brown had toured one of the worst sections of a London slum area. Clearly, that was where Brown had contracted the disease. Admiration for the high culture of London gave way to ambivalence. On the day of Brown's funeral at St. Dunstan's, Johnson commented in his journal on the contrast between the splendor of the funeral procession and the squalor of urban London. He then resolved to stop his brooding and "be silent and shut my mouth." [22] Nevertheless, for the rest of his life Johnson was of two minds about London. His recollection of the disease-ridden city was revived each time he sent Anglican recruits over to London for ordination and saw one out of every five die of smallpox. Despite his affection for cosmopolitan culture, he never returned to England himself. And he turned down missionary jobs in Providence and Boston because he preferred the security of rural Connecticut. Even when he became president of King's College in New York, he refused to remain in the city during epidemics.[23]

The summer of 1723 brought hot weather and an increased vulnerability to smallpox contagion. Johnson was anxious to leave London and eager to settle into Stratford, Connecticut, where he was to replace Pigot as Anglican pastor. In July he sailed for New England, where he would be forced to match his idea of the pure and true Anglican church against Puritan critics and the conditions of colonial Connecticut. On September 22, after a seven-week voyage, he landed at Piscataqua. He traveled overland to Stratford in the rain.[24]

If Johnson had been the kind of man whose energies were proportional to the challenge, Stratford would have elicited a

21. Ibid., pp. 28–36.
22. Ibid., pp. 36–38.
23. The death rate of the missionaries who returned to London for ordination is discussed in chap. 7. Johnson's fear of urban diseases is expressed throughout his correspondence. See especially *Career*, 4 : 8, 51, 62, 94.
24. Journal, 28 July to 22 September 1723. Johnson's landing was reported in the *Boston News-Letter*, 26 September 1723, and by Samuel Sewall in his diary, *Collections of the Mass. Historical Society*, 3 : 326.

superhuman effort. The old parish of Cutler and Pigot had about three hundred families, of which a fifth were Anglicans. There were also approximately two hundred Indians and twenty black slaves in the town.[25] Since Johnson was the only Anglican minister in the entire colony, he was expected to punctuate his regular ministrations in Stratford with periodic forays into neighboring towns and counties. Pigot had tried to alert him to the problems of the Stratford mission, but he had not foreseen the expectations that Johnson would bring back from England. All of the intellectual vitality and conviviality that sustained one culturally in England were missing in Stratford. Johnson experienced the same kind of apprehension that has troubled missionaries in all ages; convinced that he had something valuable to offer the local populace—namely, the true church and cultural uplift—he quickly discovered that the vast majority of people felt no need for what he was selling. In his first letter to Anglican officials in England, he reported that he was "laughed at and looked awry upon." [26] The Puritan settlers would not listen to what he had to say. They were so "trained up in prejudice against the Episcopal Church" that they could not perceive the superiority of his arguments in favor of the Church of England.[27] He felt "entirely alone in a large Colony." Apprehension soon gave way to despair. He feared that he "must give up the cause, and our Church must sink and come to nothing." [28]

It was not simply that Johnson was getting the cold shoulder, a reception that should not have surprised a man familiar with the Anglophobia of the local populace. His former ministerial colleagues regarded him as something more than an Anglican missionary. He was also a traitor, a Puritan who had sold out to the enemy and had the audacity to return and expect cooperation. The passion and vehemence of the pamphlet attacks that greeted Johnson's arrival at Stratford might seem more than one lonely missionary warranted, but the Puritan ministers were expressing their contempt for a turncoat who dared to challenge the legitimacy of the New England churches. Thomas Foxcroft, minister of

25. Johnson to Bishop of London, 4 November 1723, Johnson MSS.
26. Johnson to Berriman, 1 January 1725, *Career*, 3 : 218–19.
27. Johnson to Secretary, 16 September 1724, S.P.G. MSS, A, 19 : 453.
28. Johnson to Secretary, 10 February 1724, *Conn. Episcopacy*, 1 : 113.

the First Church of Boston, tried to explain to Johnson that any Puritan minister who felt "the absolute necessity of prelatical ordination" so strongly that he went to England for orders had spit in the face of all Puritan clergy. By his actions he had expressed a belief in the "utter invalidity of the Presbyterian ministry." [29] The prodigal son had returned, but only to entice his family into some Anglican odyssey.

The Puritans' antipathy to Johnson was also the result of their own insecurity. His denunciation of Puritan ordination played on the doubts they themselves had about the status of the ministry. His conversion to episcopacy had been no aberration; it was part of an ecclesiastical milieu in which many Puritan ministers were searching for tangible evidence of their clerical power. His return to Connecticut threatened to exacerbate the wounds that Puritan ministers had inflicted on one another in earlier ecclesiastical struggles. The new Stratford missionary represented an unacceptable but dangerously appealing alternative to a set of common ecclesiastical problems that worried them deeply. Ironically, Johnson's presence produced not just frenzied character assaults, but a consensus about polity that had not been possible prior to his conversion. Johnson became an embodiment of an Anglican challenge that demanded a unified response. Puritan divines who had been unable to agree on ecclesiastical questions found themselves denouncing Johnson in unison. All that had been lacking in those earlier years of polity turmoil was a visible, common enemy, a man to resurrect the Laudian specter that had once before produced a Puritan consensus. The devil, in the person of Samuel Johnson, had returned to Connecticut.

During the early years of Johnson's Stratford mission the Puritan ministers carved out their position on the question of clerical authority in terms that countered the formal arguments employed by Johnson, while also providing the established Puritan clergy with a defense they would use against itinerant preachers who appeared during the Great Awakening and rejected all formal justifications of ministerial power. Jonathan Dickinson, a Yale graduate and pastor at Elizabethtown, New

29. Foxcroft to Johnson, 12 August 1726, Career, 3 : 10.

Jersey, published *A Defence of Presbyterian Ordination* the year
after Johnson returned from London and defined the problem
in terms that united Johnson's enemies for the next thirty years.
Dickinson said that the essential question was "Whether *Bishops*
are by *Divine Right,* superior to Presbyters, and have by virtue
of that Superiority, the sole power of *Ordination* and *Jurisdiction?*" [30] And all the pamphlets on the Puritan side followed
Dickinson's lead in arguing that an inspection of Scripture
showed no distinction between a bishop and a minister. Thomas
Foxcroft agreed that "THERE is no special Mark put upon any
single Person among them, as having a Prerogative above the
Rest. . . . They were a Company of Congregational Bishops,
acting in an Equality." [31] Nathaniel Eells also contended that all
the early bishops were ministers and all the early ministers were
bishops; both words referred to a clergyman who occupied "the
pastoral office of a single Church." [32] Noah Hobart summarized
the Puritan position when he said that "all Christ left in Commission as officers in the Gospel Church, at the time of his
Ascension into Heaven, were equal in office and power." [33]

It followed logically, and the Puritan clergy used their Ramist
categories to demonstrate the point, that present-day ministers
were "the successors of the apostles." Dickinson again led the
way, reasoning that "the power of Ordination and Jurisdiction"
descended from early Christian pastors, none of whom was referred to as a bishop.[34] John Graham rejoiced at the "unanswer-
able Arguments . . . to prove the Presbyterian Government
truly apostolic." [35] Eells also expressed confidence that the apos-

30. Jonathan Dickinson, *A Defence of Presbyterian Ordination* (Boston,
1724), p. 1.
31. Thomas Foxcroft, *A Vindication of the Appendix to the Sober Remarks*
. . . (Boston, 1725), p. 58.
32. Nathaniel Eells, *The Evangelical Bishop* . . . (New London, 1734),
p. 10.
33. Noah Hobart, *A Serious Address to the Members of the Episcopal
Separation in New England* (Boston, 1748), p. 80. See also, by an anonymous
author, *A Brief Account of the Ceremony Pomp and State of the Bishops*
. . . (Boston, 1725); Jonathan Dickinson, *The Scripture Bishop* (Boston, 1732).
34. Dickinson, *A Defence of Presbyterian Ordination,* p. 13.
35. John Graham, *Some Remarks Upon a Late Pamphlet* . . . (Boston,
1733), p. 7.

tolic succession transferred power in ordination "by ordinary Ministers." [36]

In none of the pamphlets directed at Johnson or other Connecticut Anglicans was there any attempt to defend the view that the people of the congregation had a role in directing church affairs. The Puritan pamphleteers agreed that bishops did not make ministers, but they also agreed that the members had no ordaining power either. Ministers transferred power among themselves. What emerged on the Puritan side of the pamphlet war was not only unanimity in the arguments against episcopal ordination, but also a coherent defense of the ecclesiastical practices initiated by the Saybrook Synod. Like Johnson, the Puritan clergy required assurance for their ministerial authority. Like Johnson, they discovered such assurance in the scriptural account of the primitive church. But, unlike Johnson, they interpreted Scripture to mean that all ministers were bishops, then used the Anglican arguments for bishops to sanction New England polity.

While his Puritan antagonists coopted the Anglican conception of apostolic succession for their own use, Johnson refused to defend the Anglican doctrines he had traveled all the way to London to embrace. For a considerable time he refused to take part in the polity debate at all. He claimed that he was too busy; he was tending to his pastoral duties in Stratford and the outlying towns of Fairfield, Norwalk, Newton, Ripton, and West Haven.[37]

And then there was his work with the students at nearby Yale, where Cutler surmised that "nothing keeps the brightest of our youth from coming into the Church but courage enough to starve." [38] If Johnson had been completely honest with himself, he would have admitted that he was not very good at pastoral work. He was friendly, charitable, genuinely concerned about his parishioners, yet he had a way that set him apart from the local

36. Eells, *The Evangelical Bishop*, p. 3. See also Noah Hobart, *Ministers of the Gospel Considered as Fellow-Labourers* (Boston, 1747), pp. 16–17; Solomon Paine, *A Short View of the Differences Between the Church of Christ, and the Established Churches of Connecticut* (Newport, 1752).

37. For a survey of Johnson's parish duties, see Pigot to Secretary, 7 June 1723, S.P.G. MSS, A, 17 : 385; also Beardsley, *Episcopal Church*, p. 52.

38. Cutler to Grey, 4 September 1732, *Mass. Episcopacy*, 3 : 672.

Anglican converts. He was not an overbearing snob. He did not regard his parishioners as underlings. But he lacked the ability to communicate with them on their own terms. He was perceptive enough to sense his limitations and by 1732 had decided to channel his productive energies toward a goal that suited his temperament. He convinced himself that

> there is not any One thing wherein I can do more service to the Interest of Religion and Learning in these parts than in the Influence . . . I have on the College at New Haven, in putting the Young Men Bred there upon reading of Good Books, in directing their studies and leading them into a good affection to our Excellent Church.[39]

His work with the Yale students had already begun to bear fruit in 1726, when Henry Caner decided to study theology with him in the hope of eventually obtaining episcopal orders. Caner was followed by John Beach, and Beach by Ebenezer Punderson. And these were only the first of over forty Yale graduates converted by Johnson, who went overseas for ordination, then returned to Connecticut as Anglican missionaries. It was soon apparent that Johnson worked more effectively with the shepherds than the sheep. No matter who occupied his time, he claimed there was not enough of it to indulge in polemical battles with the local polity experts.[40]

On top of it all, Johnson was occupied with the affairs of a new family. In 1725 he had married Charity Nicoll, widow of Benjamin Nicoll and daughter of Colonel Richard Floyd. She was a prize catch who brought to the marriage a substantial dowry and important connections with leading New York families, as well as two sons and a daughter by her former marriage. In the next six years she gave birth to two more sons, William Samuel in 1727 and William in 1731. Since she and Johnson were

39. Johnson to Secretary, 25 March 1732, S.P.G. MSS, A, 24 : 123.

40. Reports on Caner, Beach, and Punderson are in the following: Johnson to Secretary, 20 September 1724, Conn. Episcopacy, 1 : 117; Johnson to Secretary, 25 October 1730, ibid., p. 145; Johnson to Secretary, 30 March 1734, S.P.G. MSS, A, 25 : 136–38. Statistics on the Yale graduates who were trained by Johnson are in Hector Kinloch, "Anglican Clergy in Connecticut, 1701–1785" (Ph.D. diss., Yale University, 1959).

seldom separated, they had few occasions to correspond and, therefore, left to posterity little evidence of their relationship. Charity was five years older than her new husband, and Johnson's stepsons were old enough to begin preparation for college. Johnson worked hard with them on Latin and Greek, sending the older boy off to Yale in 1730.[41]

It was three years later before he put pen to paper in a public defense of the Anglican doctrines he had espoused in 1722. Granted, pastoral work, supervising the recruits from Yale, and the new family all took time; but were these legitimate reasons for his lengthy silence on the polity questions that separated him from the Puritan ministers? Or were they excuses that allowed Johnson to evade publication of ecclesiastical views that he knew would alienate him even more from his former Puritan colleagues? In 1733 he set down his views in a pamphlet entitled *Eleutherius Enervatus*,[42] which was followed by *A Letter . . . to his Dissenting Parishioners* and *A Second Letter*.[43] These pamphlets made it clear that Johnson felt obliged to temper his zeal for Anglicanism with a realistic appraisal of his isolated situation in New England. Whether or not he still believed the doctrines of Anglican supremacy which had propelled him to England and which he had embraced while there, he refused to defend the idea of a "pure church" that had once seemed so compelling.

First, he was unwilling to repudiate either the churches or the ministers of New England. He insisted that a belief in episcopacy did not necessitate a denial of Puritan polity. When Hezekiah Gold, a Puritan minister in Stratford, accused him of calling the New England clergy "usurpers, invaders and blind guides," Johnson denied that he had "ever used those expressions or any others that savored of uncharitableness." Although he admitted to the belief that the Church of England was a true church, Gold and other Puritan ministers were wrong to infer that he regarded all nonepiscopal churches as untrue. Puritan ministers who were satisfied with their ordination, he claimed, did not deserve cen-

---

41. *Career*, 1 : 20; William R. Cutter, *Genealogical and Family History of the State of Connecticut*, 2 vols. (New York, 1911), 1 : 209–10.
42. Boston, 1734.
43. *Career*, 3 : 19–118.

sure. On questions of church polity "they and every man have a right to think for themselves and judge and choose for themselves."[44] According to this view the distinguishing marks of the true church were sufficiently obscure to allow honest men to disagree.

Johnson carried the same tolerant attitude into his discussion of the legal status of Anglicanism in the colonies. Some of his Anglican compatriots, including his friend James Wetmore, argued that the Act of Uniformity established episcopacy as the official religion of all British colonies.[45] But Johnson maintained that "there is no regular establishment of any national or provincial church in these plantations." Both the Anglican and Puritan churches had a legal right to exist "side by side," Johnson insisted.[46] John Beach, a disciple of Johnson's, argued the same line.[47] When Noah Hobart responded to Wetmore's attack on the legal status of the Puritan churches, he quoted Johnson against Wetmore.[48]

Instead of emphasizing the ecclesiastical differences between Anglicanism and Puritanism, Johnson preferred to point to the religious doctrines they held in common. He repeatedly asserted that the Church of England and the New England churches "have the same religion, the same Gospel, and the same hope."[49] To harp on the ecclesiastical differences was silly, because "outward rites and observances are indifferent in their nature [and] only required for external order and decency."[50] He agreed with James Honyman, Anglican minister at Newport, that overzealous members of both camps were "racking some Unguarded Expressions of [Church] Fathers, and Dragging them to speak the sense of each side According to the Fancies and Notions of Criticks."[51]

44. Gold to Johnson, 21 July 1741, and Johnson to Gold, 16 July 1741, ibid. 138–41.

45. James Wetmore, *A Letter From a Minister* . . . (New York, 1730), pp. 7–13.

46. *Career*, 3 : 41, 68.

47. John Beach, *A Calm and Dispassionate Vindication* . . . (Boston, 1749), p. vi.

48. Noah Hobart, *A Serious Address*, p. 17.

49. *Career*, 3 : 38.

50. Ibid., p. 22.

51. Honyman to Johnson, 3 May 1727, Johnson MSS.

All such wrangling depended on biblical accounts of the primitive church that were terribly imprecise, "because the Church was then in her Embryo and first Rudiments; and therefore nothing can be so absolutely concluded from thence." [52]

The Puritan ministers were suspicious of Johnson's excessive tolerance. John Graham, the pastor at Southbury, accused Johnson of harping on "the Essentials, and Fundamentals of Religion" in order to avoid a confrontation over ecclesiastical matters that, in his heart of hearts, Johnson believed were important.[53] If he regarded polity details as so inconsequential, then why had he gone to the trouble of becoming a convert to Anglicanism in the first place? And how could he justify his status as an Anglican missionary if he sincerely believed the Puritan churches were legitimate houses of worship? These were searching and relevant questions, but Johnson did not answer them. Instead he repeated his disdain for polity arguments and reminded the disputants that "outward performances without an inward change of heart and a good life are of no account with God." [54] How could the Puritans disagree, especially since New England had been founded as a refuge for the same idea?

Graham's suspicion that Johnson's efforts at conciliation masked a fundamental hypocrisy was not unwarranted. One of the reasons why Dickinson, Foxcroft, Graham, and Hobart continued to churn out pamphlets attacking episcopal polity was their conviction that Johnson was only trying to lull them to sleep with promises of friendship while he awaited the opportunity for a complete Anglican take-over. And if the Puritan writers had been able to read Johnson's correspondence with Anglican officials in London, they would have seen that Johnson did have hopes for the anglicization of Connecticut. In his dealings with fellow Anglican missionaries, Johnson implied that the charity he displayed toward New England clerics was more a strategic ploy than a sincere modification of his belief in Puritan illegitimacy. He told Matthew Graves, one of the foreign-born Anglican missionaries, that "the truth is we can do little or no good to people

52. Johnson, *Eleutherius Enervatus*, p. 60.
53. John Graham, *Some Remarks Upon a Late Pamphlet*, p. 32.
54. *Career*, 3 : 62.

here unless we do all we can to keep them in good humor . . . ;
otherwise we can neither do nor get any good from them. So that
we are obliged to treat them with great temper and tenderness
especially in the present condition of things." [55] Ironically, Graves
also accused Johnson of misrepresenting the Anglican position.
But Johnson was adamant in his insistence that there was no dis-
honesty involved in his effort to "make Allowance for the
Temper & Prejudices of the Country." [56]

And Johnson was not just offering a lame excuse. Part of his
initial attraction to Anglicanism was based on an affection for
Stillingfleet and Tillotson and the open-minded philosophy that
underlay their analysis of episcopal polity. Like these latitudinarians, he was instinctively disposed to search for some common
ground on which antagonists could come together. By his own
admission a man of excessive "Caution and tenderness," he found
himself unable to take part in an extended polity fight that
"breathe[d] nothing of the English Spirit." [57] He was tempera-
mentally equipped to serve as an arbiter between dissident religious factions or as the gracious leader of an entrenched religious establishment. As head of an embattled minority of
Anglican missionaries, he was badly miscast.

In 1743 Johnson was awarded an honorary Doctor of Divinity
degree from Oxford in recognition of his missionary activities.
Thereafter, friends and associates referred to him as "Dr. Johnson." [58] His academic title, along with his aristocratic wife, the
handsome spire and stained glass windows of Stratford's Christ
Church, and an occasional letter from a London friend, all served
as reminders of his continued affection for the urbane world beyond the borders of his Stratford parish. None of the local Puritan
clergy, however, regarded him as a fop or an excessively genteel
parson. Of course, he was an Anglican and, therefore, not to be
trusted. But he preached a moderate brand of Anglicanism, devoid of any outright condemnation of the New England churches.
Clearly, he wished to coexist peacefully with his Puritan neigh-

55. Johnson to Graves, 27 June 1748, *Career,* 1 : 133–34.
56. Johnson to Secretary, 3 December 1743, S.P.G. MSS, B, 11 : 37.
57. *Career,* 3 : 36.
58. Chandler, *Life of Johnson,* p. 71.

bors. The cultural aspirations of his youth and his zealous advocacy of episcopal purity had been scaled down to a size that
fitted a provincial parish. The idealistic quest for the pure church
of primitive Christianity had given way to the mundane considerations necessary for Christ Church's survival. A piece of
advice that Thomas Burnet, governor of New York, had given
him in 1727 had proven prophetic: "So much a better school is
adversity than prosperity in every stage and profession of life." [59]

59. Burnet to Johnson, 14 August 1727, *Career*, 1 : 78.

6

The Conversion of the Missionary

The family undoubtedly received a great deal of Johnson's attention during the years at Stratford. Charity and her three children needed his affection and counsel. And his own children needed tutoring. One observer surmised that, by the time he was thirteen, William Samuel was not only ready for Yale, but had "read more of the Latin and Greek classics, than had been read by any boys in the country." When his elder son wrote that the Yale course work was rather easy, Johnson sent him copies of the works of Shakespeare and Epictetus to study. He did not oppose the boy's preference for a legal rather than a ministerial career and even helped him through a bout with that "human frailty which is called *Love.*" When William Samuel, in a fit of excessive modesty, wrote that he was "not worth a farthing," his father remarked, "It is true . . . but . . . I can spare you 2000 pounds worth of lands." Billy followed his older brother to Yale in 1744, was also swamped with extra reading from home, and pleased his father enormously by deciding to prepare for the Anglican ministry.[1]

While his wife and children were receiving considerable attention, Johnson was trying to attract some notice from the S.P.G. officials in England. Unfortunately, the Anglican officials were less dutiful in managing the colonial missionaries than Johnson was in running a family. In 1725 Edmund Gibson, the newly appointed Bishop of London, had to apologize for not being aware previously that the colony of Connecticut even existed.

1. S. Johnson to W. S. Johnson, 5 July 1743, 23 April 1744, 7 July 1747, *Career*, 1 : 117–19, 127–29; Thomas Bradbury Chandler, *The Life of Samuel Johnson, D.D.* (New York, 1805), pp. 79–84.

Gibson had "consider'd all New England as one government" and asked the colonial governor "to pardon the omission." Even the Board of Trade, whose business it was to keep track of colonial affairs, confessed "we are very little informed of what is done," because Connecticut was not "under any obligation . . . to return authentic copies of their Laws to the Crown for Approbation or Disallowance or to give any account of their Proceedings." From 1723 to 1752, Johnson endeavored to make his ecclesiastical superiors more knowledgeable about colonial affairs and to inform the political authorities at Whitehall about the highly irregular policies of the Connecticut government.[2]

The irony of the Anglicans' situation, Johnson explained, lay in the fact that they constituted a minority sect. In Connecticut the Puritan churches were established; the Puritan clergy enjoyed the support of the colony's political leaders. Not only did the Puritan clergy employ Anglican arguments for a religious establishment against colonial Anglicans, they compounded the irony of the colonial situation by calling the Anglican missionaries "dissenters" and defining their right to dissent according to the English Toleration Act of 1689. In drafting the Connecticut Toleration Act of 1708, for example, the colonial legislature had adopted the terminology of the English law, but reversed the position of the religious groups to which the law applied. In Connecticut, Puritanism was the religion "which is by law established"; the Anglicans were required to register their unorthodox opinions at the county court, take an oath of fidelity to the government, and pay taxes toward the salary of the resident Puritan minister. The terms and limits of religious discrimination were taken directly from an English law designed to favor Anglicans.[3]

From the time he first arrived in Stratford, Johnson criticized

2. Bishop of London to Joseph Talcott, 3 June 1725, in The Talcott Papers, 1724–1741, *Collections of the Connecticut Historical Society* (Hartford, 1892–96), 4 : 53; Representation of the Board of Trade to Lords, etc., 15 June 1733, ibid., p. 447.

3. *Conn. Recs.*, 5 : 50. See M. Louise Greene, *The Development of Religious Liberty in Connecticut*, pp. 154–92, and P. W. Coons, "The Achievement of Religious Liberty in Connecticut," *Publications of the Tercentenary Commission of Connecticut* 60 : 12–17.

"those who have, to our misfortune and oppression, the civil power here, and have made that a handle to usurp the ecclesiastical." [4] The big complaint concerned taxation. In June 1724, when the Anglican converts at Newton and Fairfield refused to pay taxes to the Puritan minister, the governor jailed them. Johnson reported the incident to Gibson, explaining that "sundry people of both sexes, have been unmercifully imprisoned" because they refused to contribute to "the support of the Independent teachers." Johnson's letters to the secretary of the Society for the Propagation of the Gospel and the Bishop of London recounted the injustices done to Anglican clergy and laity and soon aroused Gibson to intervene in their behalf with Joseph Talcott, governor of Connecticut.[5] Talcott took it upon himself to set Gibson straight. Those few souls who had been converted to episcopacy, he wrote, "cannot well be judged to act from any other motive than to appear singular, or to be freed from a small tax." Talcott made it clear that the tax was there to stay, as were the established colonial churches: "all our towns and ecclesiastical societies are supplied with orthodox ministers. We have no vacancies at present. When the death of an incumbent happens, they are quickly supplied by persons of our own communion, educated in our public schools of learning." [6]

According to the Connecticut charter, the only legal requirement that the colonial government had to meet was a negative one; it could pass no laws repugnant to the laws of England.[7] Johnson insisted that the charter did not give the colonial legislators "*any* authority about *ecclesiastical* affairs, or in any manner enable them to establish any way of religion . . . which, by their laws, they have done; which, therefore seem to me to be repugnant to the laws of England." [8] He sent to England copies of the

4. Members of the Church of England at Ripton, All Saints' Day, 1722, *Conn. Episcopacy*, 1 : 81.
5. Johnson to Secretary, 10 January 1724 and 11 June 1724; Johnson to Bishop of London, 23 June 1724, ibid., pp. 94–95, 100–101; Johnson to Secretary, 12 June 1724, S.P.G. MSS, A, 19 : 224.
6. Talcott to Bishop of London, 1 December 1725, Talcott Papers, 4 : 65.
7. *Conn. Recs.*, 2 : 1–11 for the charter.
8. Johnson to Bishop of London, 4 November 1725, *Conn. Episcopacy*, 1 : 103.

Connecticut laws that he deemed offensive, passionately reported
the abuses which Anglicans were suffering at the hands of the
Puritans, and maintained that the "charter is indeed the foundation of all their insolence and happy would it be for the Church
if it were taken away." [9] The English response remained one of
sympathetic silence.

But Governor Talcott and the members of the Assembly were
aware of Johnson's attempt to obtain a new charter, and they
feared that his influence in England might bring down the entire
colonial government. When the Assembly convened at Hartford
in May of 1727, the representatives were in a conciliatory mood,
willing to sacrifice a portion of their ecclesiastical control for
security against future English intervention. Whether or not
their charter was in danger, Johnson's public outcries had them
worried. In an effort to forestall a possible investigation of their
charter and quiet Johnson's cries of discrimination, the Assembly
passed an act allowing any person who regularly attended
Anglican services to have his church taxes paid to the Anglican
minister. Anglicans who lived within the parish of a minister
of the Church of England were thereby excused from paying
taxes to the Puritan pastor. In 1729 Baptists and Quakers demanded and received the same privileges that had been extended
to the Anglicans.[10] In this confrontration between Anglicanism
and Connecticut orthodoxy, the Anglicans found themselves in
the unfamiliar posture of religious and civil libertarians, while
the colonial legislators found it necessary to broaden the base
of their narrow community in order to provide room for Anglicans, then Baptists, and then Quakers. It was a liberalizing experience for both sides.

Johnson soon learned that Connecticut laws, no matter how
generous they seemed, were enforced by men who hated Anglicans. In 1728 the Anglicans of Fairfield petitioned the Connecticut Assembly requesting the return of taxes collected from
them and used to support the Puritan minister. When the

9. Johnson to Gibson, 26 September 1727, *Career*, 3 : 222. Johnson to Bishop
of London, 10 February 1727, *Conn. Episcopacy*, 1 : 107–09.
10. *Conn. Recs.*, 7 : 107, 237, 257.

Assembly refused to comply, the churchwardens and vestry demanded clarification of the act of 1727, claiming to be parishioners of Richard and Henry Caner.[11] The Assembly replied that, in the opinion of the local tax-collector, none of the people of Fairfield lived close enough to an Anglican minister to qualify for exemption from the tax. The act itself was ambiguous, stipulating that it applied to those who could "conveniently attend" Anglican services. Without taking a definitive stand on what "conveniently" meant, the Assembly gave the local tax-collector full power to interpret the phrase as he saw fit.[12] Henry Caner, one of the Anglican missionaries, dashed off enraged letters to the Bishop of London and the secretary of the S.P.G. in which he complained that the colonial practice was to tax all Anglicans who lived more than a mile from an episcopal minister. Caner suggested that the Society alter his instructions to allow him to reside in several locations in order that all Anglicans, for the purpose of the law, might be said to live within a mile of him. When the secretary refused Caner's request, the bulk of his parishioners were required to contribute to the support of the Puritan pastor.[13]

Complaints began to pour into the Assembly from all over the colony. An Anglican group living in Wallingford was denied tax exemption in 1729 on the highly ironic grounds that their pastor, Samuel Seabury, had not yet been properly ordained in the Church of England. Governor Talcott listened impatiently to their persistent requests, then ordered the justice of the peace "to enlarge the gaol and fill it with them."[14] Johnson affirmed that Anglicans on the outskirts of Stratford, who were being forced to support the Puritan church, had begun to flee to New York as early as 1730.[15] In 1736 Ebenezer Punderson, the fifth episcopal minister in Connecticut after Johnson, Beach, Caner, and Sea-

11. Petition of Churchwardens and Vestry of Fairfield to Connecticut Legislature, 15 March 1727, *Conn. Episcopacy*, 1 : 124.

12. Petition to General Assembly, 9 May 1728, ibid., p. 129.

13. Caner to Secretary, 10 October 1728; Minutes of the Society, 18 July 1729; Caner to Secretary, 13 March 1728, ibid., pp. 132–36, 126.

14. Churchwardens, etc., of Wallingford to Bishop of London, 1729 [?]; Inhabitants of New London to Secretary, 13 April 1730; Johnson to Bishop of London, 2 April 1728, *Conn. Episcopacy*, 1 : 138–40, 126–27.

15. Johnson to Secretary, 5 May 1730, S.P.G. MSS, A, 23 : 113–14.

bury, told Talcott that two of his parishioners at North Groton had attended services regularly, but had been jailed when they refused to contribute to the Puritan church. Although Talcott admitted, "I don't think the Colector you mention hath any Rite to demand their money on this Rate," he would not supersede the authority of the local officials. He referred Punderson to the county court, where, he believed, "justice will be done in the Case." Punderson then appealed to the county court and lost.[16] Although Johnson supported numerous pleas for tax exemptions under the law and amendments to clarify the act of 1727, no amendments were adopted by the Assembly. Enforcement of the tax laws continued to vary according to the discretion of town and local officials.[17]

A second incident which taught the Anglicans the same painful lesson had to do with public lands. The Connecticut Assembly voted to open seven townships of public land for sale in 1737. Instead of putting the £70,000 profit that resulted into the colonial treasury, the Assembly voted to "divide the proceeds proportionally to each town according to their estates, for the support of dissenting [Puritan] ministers." [18] Johnson disputed this arrangement, arguing that the land was "the common right of the whole community," and that citizens who happened to be Anglicans had a right to their fair share of the profits.[19] In May of 1738 Johnson sent a petition to that effect to the Assembly, supplemented with the signatures of approximately 650 Anglican males over the age of sixteen. Ignoring the petition, the Assembly reminded the Anglicans of a law passed in 1737, which allowed the towns to use money received from public sources as "their majority vote in any of their meetings regularly assembled" saw fit. By referring decisions about the allotment of funds to the town governments, the Assembly had discreetly eliminated any chance of Anglican inclusion in the profit-taking, while avoiding a direct refutation of Anglican rights to such profit. The result

16. Punderson to Talcott, 15 November 1736; Talcott to Punderson, 18 November 1736, Talcott Papers, 5 : 9–13.
17. The events are summarized in The Episcopal Clergy of Connecticut to the Archbishop of Canterbury, 15 November 1738, Career, 1 : 94–98.
18. Johnson to Berkeley, 14 May 1739, Career, 1 : 98.
19. Johnson to Secretary, 3 November 1738, Career, 3 : 224.

was the same. "According to their sense of the law," wrote Johnson, "we of the Church of England are excluded from any benefit of that sale." [20]

The letters Johnson sent to Anglican leaders in England painted a bleak but accurate picture of the episcopal predicament in Connecticut. It was the predicament of an embattled minority at the mercy of a colonial legislature that accurately reflected the Anglophobia of the bulk of the voters. In matters not defined by the legislature, the local town meetings assumed authority and acted in accordance with the majority vote of the selectmen. Until the Anglicans could muster a significant number of converts with votes in the town meetings, they would be unable to block discriminatory legislation. And the persecution of Anglicans by means of extra tax loads effectively discouraged converts and thereby assured their minority status. The Anglicans in Connecticut, Johnson explained, were caught in a vicious circle that could only be broken by powerful allies in the Church in England. He concluded "that it is the design of this government not only to prevent the growth of the Church in this Colony, but even utterly to destroy it in its infancy, which we fear they will be able to accomplish if they have no check from a superior authority at home." [21]

Although it took Johnson some time to realize it, the religious authorities in England were themselves enmeshed in a web of political constraints that deprived them of effective control over the colonial church. Convocation, the legislature of the Church of England, rarely met. Parliament had assumed control over new canons and clerical taxes. The twenty-six bishops who sat in the House of Lords usually voted according to the instructions of the ministry. In return for faithful service an aspiring cleric could expect to be elevated to more lucrative bishoprics, perhaps to Canterbury itself. The ecclesiastical office that Johnson considered a legacy of the apostolic era had become a political pawn in

20. Connecticut State Library, Ecclesiastical Papers (1659–1789), 2nd ser. 5 : 56, a, b, c, d; *Conn. Recs.*, 8 : 123, 234; Johnson to Secretary, 5 April 1740, *Career*, 3 : 225.

21. Episcopal Clergy of Connecticut to Archbishop of Canterbury, 15 November 1738, *Career*, 1 : 97.

eighteenth-century England. Certain Anglican bishops were devout and well-intentioned men; Gibson was one such man. But he was powerless to alter colonial religious policies when the ministry wanted them to remain static.[22]

Not knowing this, Johnson sent a barrage of letters to the Bishop of London suggesting changes in colonial episcopacy. The point he repeated for over forty years was simply that there should be an Anglican bishop resident in the colonies. The Bishop of London, Johnson insisted, could not ordain, discipline, and suspend Anglican ministers in the colonies. London was too far removed from the scene of his jurisdiction. At the end of the seventeenth century, the Anglicans had instituted the office of commissary, which was empowered with certain disciplinary functions that might be exercised if the bishop was too far away to perform his duties properly. But Johnson thought that commissaries were insufficient. His belief in the sovereign power of bishops had motivated his own conversion to episcopacy. In the absence of a resident Anglican bishop Johnson discovered that the church he had admired for its orderliness was plagued by domestic infighting that could not be settled by anyone on the scene.[23]

Most of the disciplinary problems were minor. A minister at Brookhaven was said to be lavishing attention on his youngest and prettiest female convert. Or the missionary at West Haven refused to make the long ride to conduct services during the illness of the regular Anglican pastor at Groton.[24] But there were

---

22. Three books by Norman Sykes are excellent: *Church and State in England in the XVIIIth Century* (Hamden, 1962), pp. 92–147; *Edmund Gibson* (London, 1926), esp. pp. 333–76; *From Sheldon to Secker* (Cambridge, 1959).

23. The powers of the Bishop of London are best summarized in Arthur Lyon Cross, *The Anglican Episcopate and the American Colonies* (Hamden, 1964), pp. 3–18. Carl Bridenbaugh's *Mitre and Sceptre* (New York, 1962) is the best account of the Anglican quest for a resident bishop and it does not exhaust the topic. Work needs to be done in English sources, especially the Newcastle Papers, to discover the various reasons for ministerial opposition to the appointment of American bishops. My intention here is to describe Johnson's position on bishops and place it in the context of his overall strategy for anglicizing New England.

24. Johnson to Secretary, 19 April 1733, S.P.G. MSS, A, 24 : 403; Johnson to Secretary, 20 November 1729, ibid., 22 : 180; Johnson to Secretary, 17 November 1738, S.P.G. MSS, B, 7 : 45–51.

also serious fights, like the one for the pastorship of King's Chapel at Boston, in which Johnson surmised that the unrelieved hassles did "more mischief to the Church than the Dissenters themselves." [25] The most unique problem was posed by the foreign-born missionaries; they simply did not get along with the colonial Anglicans. Theophilus Morris, an Irishman who arrived in New Haven in 1740, criticized the deportment of his Anglican brethren and admitted that Connecticut "does not so well suite my complexion." [26] His replacement was James Lyons, another Irishman, who gained a reputation for drunkenness, dirty clothes, foul language, and a persecution complex. Lyons was convinced that the the local Anglicans planned "to get rid of missionaries that are not country borne." Johnson was glad to see him leave in 1745.[27] Matthew Graves was another foreigner who referred to one of the native-born missionaries as "a covetous man, a farmer, an apothecary, a merchant, and a usurer." He too requested transfer to greener pastures, "where I hope to give them more satisfaction than its possible any European can in New-England." [28] In all these cases the absence of a resident bishop entrusted with clerical discipline prevented the resolution of local squabbles as they arose.

A resident bishop was also needed to ordain new Anglican ministers. Under the existing arrangement, all ministerial candidates were required to journey to England for orders. During Johnson's first thirty years at Stratford, six of the twenty-nine potential missionaries who made the trip did not survive it.[29] Johnson reported that "a considerable number of promising young gentlemen" were cognizant of the dangers of "the seas and the distempers" and had decided to decline the ministry and "go into secular business" rather than risk their lives for Anglican orders. The justifiable fear of the voyage acted as a solvent to dilute the zeal of "sundry other very worthy young gentlemen"

25. Johnson to Bishop of London, 10 October 1724, *Conn. Episcopacy,* 1 : 97.
26. Morris to Secretary, 13 September 1740, ibid., 1 : 172.
27. Lyons to Secretary, 8 May 1744, ibid., 1 : 209.
28. Graves to Secretary, 20 January 1751, and 22 September 1752, ibid., 1 : 273–74, 295–96.
29. Johnson to Berriman, 30 October 1752, *Career,* 1 : 159–60.

who preferred to "wait with great impatience or hopes that, possibly, Providence may send us a Bishop." [30] Instead, providence continued to take the life of one out of every five who decided not to wait.

The round trip to England took time, usually over a year. Ministerial candidates were not only unable to fight for souls during that period, but their absence also provided the local Puritan ministers with the opportunity to reclaim the parishes to which the missionaries hoped to return. More importantly, the surplus of Puritan clergy and the comparative ease of their ordination made it possible for them to fill pastoral vacancies as soon as they appeared. In 1725 the people of Newton and Ripton, despite what Johnson described as a "promising disposition among them to the Church," became "impatient for the want of ministrations of religion" and accepted a Puritan minister who was willing to take "advantage of the want of a Bishop to supply them immediately." [31] While Anglican missionaries took their chances on the Atlantic, Johnson saw the Puritans "take the advantage of immediately fixing teachers wherever they please, in opposition to the Church and defy us to our faces." [32]

Johnson's pleas for an American bishopric proved to be a vain and delusive hope, nothing more. In 1736 the Bishop of Gloucester tried to explain to Johnson that "the United interest of the Bishops here is not powerful enough to affect so reasonable and right a thing as the sending some bishops into America." [33] When Thomas Sherlock succeeded Gibson in 1749, Johnson renewed his request, only to be told again that "others who have more power and influence, do not see the light that we do." [34] The quest for a resident American bishop was one of the blind alleys down which Johnson carried New England Anglicanism.

A related proposal seemed to have more promise. When Johnson beseeched his superiors for an American bishopric, he periodically included a request for the revocation of the Connecticut

30. Johnson to Bishop of London, 18 January 1724, Career, 3 : 217.
31. Johnson to Secretary, 14 August 1725, Conn. Episcopacy, 1 : 105–06.
32. Johnson to Secretary, 16 September 1726, S.P.G. MSS, A, 19 : 451–52.
33. Hutton to Johnson, 9 March 1736, Career, 1 : 86.
34. Sherlock to Johnson, 21 April 1752, Career, 3 : 246; see also ibid., pp. 237, 244–45.

charter. The two ideas were intimately related in his own thinking for, taken together, they envisaged the replacement of the elected colonial governor by an appointee of the crown and the destruction of the Puritan religious monopoly by a bishop responsible to Canterbury. In 1732, for example, he wrote Gibson that "it would be much happier for the Church, especially unless we had a Bishop, if the charters were taken away; and most people begin to think, since they have got into such a wretched, mobbish way of management, that it would be best for the people themselves." [35]

This, of course, was a gross distortion of colonial popular opinion. Most colonists cherished their charter government and opposed the notion of a royal governor. Most Puritan ministers also suspected that Johnson was not only misrepresenting the colonial situation to authorities in England, but also concealing his genuine desire for an Anglican establishment when he talked with local ministers. The suspicion that Johnson was two-faced was not unfounded. At the same time that he was assuring the Puritan ministers of his modest goal of coexistence, he was writing the Archbishop of Canterbury

> that the most effectual method to secure our dependence on the Crown of Great Britain would be to render our constitution here both in church and state, as near as possible conformable to that of our mother country, and consequently to send us wise and good bishops to be at the head of our ecclesiastical affairs, as well as governors (and I could wish a Viceroy) to represent his most Sacred Majesty in the affairs of civil government.[36]

The publication of this proposal would have verified the local contention that Johnson was a liar and a hypocrite who preached religious toleration and equity under the law while he conspired to subject Puritans to Anglican political and religious hegemony.

The fact of the matter was that Johnson probably did not know what he wanted. It is difficult to know whether he was a hypocrite or just a confused Anglican pastor who made inconsistent requests

35. *Conn. Episcopacy*, 1 : 154.
36. Johnson to Archbishop of Canterbury, 3 May 1737, *Career*, 1 : 88.

to his superiors. At one time he could ask Gibson for a colonial episcopate "in its full vigor as at home." [37] At another he could write the same official and disavow "any severity towards the Dissenters," only desiring to be "upon a level with the Dissenters and free from any oppressions from them." [38] In fact, few of the letters he sent to England during his first thirty years at Stratford contained any political suggestions at all. And the majority of them complained of the legal discrimination against Anglicans that made it impossible to "live upon a par . . . with our brethren that dissent from us." [39] The common thread running through his correspondence during these years was the desire to enlist English assistance in order to safeguard the rights of colonists who "are persuaded in their consciences that it is safer to retire unto the unity of the Church" and to protect the Anglican minority from being "overruled by a majority." [40] The longer he stayed in Stratford, however, the more frustrated and cynical he grew; and the more convinced he became that the Anglophobia of the citizens could only be controlled by a government more responsive to England than to Connecticut.[41]

Johnson's hope that the Anglicans might be rescued by the politicians at Whitehall, like his hope for an American bishopric, never materialized. He could use his hypothetical influence with English officials as a threat against excessive Puritan encroachments, since colonial leaders never knew how hypothetical his influence was. But Johnson knew that the empty threats were of limited value. He also knew that colonial Anglicans could not afford to sit back and wait for outside assistance. He resolved

37. Johnson to Secretary, Fall 1750, *Career*, 3 : 242.

38. Johnson to Bishop of London, 26 September 1726, ibid., p. 223.

39. Johnson to Law, 20 February 1744, *Career*, 1 : 115.

40. Johnson to Bishop of London, 4 November 1725, *Conn. Episcopacy*, 1 : 103.

41. Bridenbaugh, *Mitre and Sceptre*, pp. 92–98, discusses the attempts by colonial Anglicans to beseech Sherlock for an American episcopate from 1749 to 1752. Material not presented by Bridenbaugh, dealing with the activity of colonial agents to foil the Anglican plan, is in The Law Papers, *Collections of the Connecticut Historical Society*, 15 : 298, 323–25, 340–41, 429. See below, chap. 11 for Johnson's evolving conviction that Anglican persecution could only end with political aid from the ministry.

to modify the more cumbersome features of Anglican missionary activity in Connecticut in the hope of making it more capable of surviving this "starving time." Johnson began to streamline ecclesiastical procedures and make the Anglican operation more responsive to "the vastly different circumstances" presented by New England.

First, he tried to organize the clergy. All of the Anglican missionaries were officially responsible to the Bishop of London until 1730, when Roger Price was appointed commissary for New England. Even before 1730, however, in 1725 and 1727, there had been unofficial meetings of the Anglican clergy in Boston and Newport, which had informally attempted to settle the dispute between the Anglicans at King's Chapel and establish guidelines for clerical discipline.[42] Johnson attended these meetings, as well as later ones in 1738 and 1740, after Price became commissary. But the affairs of Connecticut received little attention at the meetings. As long as Johnson was the sole missionary in the colony, this was excusable. By 1734, however, there were five American ministers in Connecticut, yet Price had never made a visitation. For all practical purposes, Price was the commissary only of the Boston area.[43]

Johnson responded to this negligence by organizing separate meetings of the Connecticut clergy in 1734, 1740, 1742, and 1747. Like the earlier meetings at Boston and Newport, these gatherings were informal and had no official ecclesiastical authority. But they did bring the Connecticut missionaries together, and once together, they discussed their common problems.[44] As Henry Caner thought back on these attempts at colony-wide organization, he wished they had been more regular and had had the

42. New England Clergy to Bishop of London, 21 July 1725, and New England Clergy to Secretary, 20 July 1727, in William S. Perry, ed., *Historical Collections Relating to the American Colonial Church*, 5 vols. (Hartford, 1870–78), 3 : 175–76, 224–27. Johnson signed the proposals adopted at these conferences.

43. Clergy of New England to Secretary, 4 May 1740, *Conn. Episcopacy*, 1 : 170–71.

44. Clergy of Connecticut to Bishop of London, 14 March 1734; Clergy of New England to Secretary, 4 May 1740; Clergy of Connecticut to Bishop of London, 24 August 1742, *Conn. Episcopacy*, 1 : 157–58, 170–71, 181–82; Episcopal Clergy of Connecticut to Secretary, 17 March 1747, *Career*, 3 : 233–37.

power to make policy for the colonial church on the local level. He remembered the meetings as "a rope of Sand" with "no union, no authority among us," while the colonial clergy were able to "summon a Convention for united Counsell and advice" complete with "Monthly, Quarterly and Annual Associations." [45] In addition to facilitating communication among the various Connecticut missions, the Anglican meetings usually recommended candidates for ordination to the Bishop of London and, in 1747, passed joint resolutions opposing the taxing practices of the Connecticut government. Matthew Graves, one of the English missionaries, regarded such joint action as a violation of proper Anglican ecclesiastical procedure and an infringement of the authority of the Bishop of London. He not only refused to sign the proposals approved by the meetings, but also reported to the Bishop of London that the Connecticut Anglicans were conspiring to "reduce us into a Presbyterian, servile dependence." After Graves called the resolution of the meeting "a spurious address," Johnson and the other clergy "thought it best to drop the whole affair." The meeting of 1747 had been victimized by the organizational problem it was intended to solve. Yet the very existence of such meetings indicated the willingness of Johnson and the other Anglican clergy to assume some of the powers exercised by Puritan ministers in the associations established under the Saybrook Platform of 1708, powers which could not be easily exercised from London. [46]

Johnson also made ecclesiastical modifications in a second way: he established the practice of lay preaching. It had always been customary for a graduate of Yale who was considering a career in the ministry to preach before different congregations while he prepared for his ordination. Frequently, one of the churches would then select the aspiring minister as its pastor on the basis of his performance as a lay preacher. Johnson, for example, had been chosen minister of West Haven after he had delivered sermons there while tutoring at Yale.

45. Caner to Archbishop of Canterbury, 1763, *Conn. Episcopacy*, 2 : 125.
46. Graves to Bishop of London, 20 July 1750, *Conn. Episcopacy*, 1 : 226, for the quotation from Graves. The meeting's proposals are in *Career*, 3 : 223–37. Johnson's reaction to Graves is in Johnson to Secretary, 5 October 1750, ibid., pp. 238–39.

As Johnson recruited ministerial candidates, he discerned that the most convenient way to manage his potential missionaries was to assign each of them to a neighboring parish which had expressed some sympathy for Anglicanism. There the candidates could "conduct services and improve themselves in the study of Divinity till they are qualified for higher business." If possible, Johnson obtained a teaching position for each candidate at the local grammar school, with a small salary provided by the S.P.G. The salary gave the ministerial candidates a source of income that was especially welcome after they had been "rejected from all business by the Dissenters, on account of their being reconciled to the Church of England." When Johnson was satisfied that a candidate had undergone sufficient theological training, he was sent to England for ordination. And he usually returned as a missionary to the same parish at which he had been a lay reader. It was the old Connecticut ministerial pattern supplemented by a trip to England.[47]

During the eighteen-year period 1723 to 1741, six Anglican recruits, all of them graduates of Yale, went through all or part of this program of lay preaching.[48] Johnson found it "highly useful in keeping up a sense of religion" and, he might have added, for strategic reasons as well.[49] In addition to providing the candidate with money and experience, it also facilitated conversions, supplied a parish with an Anglican rather than a Puritan pastor, and fulfilled the terms of the law of 1727 by which Anglican parishioners were absolved from paying taxes to the neighboring Puritan minister.

Johnson recognized that lay preaching posed ecclesiastical problems, but he wrote to the Bishop of London in 1731 that it was "excusable by reason of the necessities of the country." In his next letter to the bishop, in 1732, Johnson felt it necessary to

47. Johnson outlined his strategy in letters to the Secretary, 20 September 1727, *Con. Episcopacy*, 1 : 117–18, and to the Bishop of London, 14 June 1731, ibid., p. 148. More than half of his letters to the Society contain requests for positions or salary increases for candidates.

48. The recruits were Jonathan Arnold, John Beach, Isaac Browne, Henry Caner, Richard Caner, and John Pierson. A description of each is in Dexter, *Biographical Sketches*, 1 : 273–77, 239–43, 380–82, 296–99, 557, 394, respectively.

49. Johnson to Bishop of London, 14 June 1731, *Conn. Episcopacy*, 1 : 148.

defend lay preaching again, arguing that he had never dared to "vary from the establishment in the least instance, unless there was an evident necessity for it." [50] A final letter to Gibson in the same year provided further clarification of Johnson's pragmatic position:

> It will perhaps be impossible to procure a general reconciliation, especially among the populace, to all the ceremonies and constitutions of our Church . . . ; it is, therefore, humbly submitted, whether it would be necessary or expedient to insist or be much intent upon the external and confessedly circumstantial matters . . . and [instead may] some things [be] a little altered to suit the present circumstances, and other things, which are of less importance and most objected against, only recommended? [51]

Johnson was firmly convinced that lay preaching was necessary for strategic reasons. Without a resident bishop to ordain candidates in the colonies, lay preaching was the most efficient way to employ those converts who intended to become missionaries. It imitated a tradition of the New England churches, a tradition familiar to all the Yale converts. Ultimately, it was the most effective way to increase converts and hasten the growth of episcopacy in Connecticut. Johnson did not have to be reminded that ordination at the hands of a bishop was necessary before a man could conduct episcopal services. He always stipulated that the lay preachers were only delivering sermons and reading prayers to their congregations; he insisted that they were "omitting everything that is properly sacerdotal" or "everything that is proper to the priest's office." [52] In 1743, however, Theophilus Morris complained that the ministerial candidates thought they were full-fledged ministers and conducted themselves as such. [53] Precisely what was going on at the parish level is unclear. James

50. Johnson to Bishop of London, 5 April 1732, ibid., pp. 151–52.
51. "Proposals relating to some method for the more successful reformation and propagation of religion in America," Johnson to Bishop of London, 1732, ibid., pp. 153–54.
52. Johnson to Secretary, 16 September 1726, S.P.G. MSS, A, 19 : 451–52.
53. Johnson to Secretary, 3 December 1743, S.P.G. MSS, B, 11 : 37.

MacSparran, the English-born missionary at Narragansett, Rhode Island, opposed lay preaching of any sort. He thought it his "Duty to bear Testimony against Lay-reading," both because it was unscriptural and because it "may prove perilous to Country Parishes and ignorant people." [54]

Although such criticism worried Johnson enough to oblige him to defend lay preaching in his letters to the Society, he always maintained that the lay preaching program was a minor ecclesiastical adjustment. Englishmen like Morris and MacSparran who were unfamiliar with the problems of the colonial Anglicans tended to demand strict obedience to the formal ecclesiastical standards of episcopacy. If the Anglican cause were to have any chance of survival, Johnson argued, its proponents would have to sacrifice "circumstantial matters" for expediency. The secretary of the Society did suggest that Johnson give "a Caution to the Young Readers," but the isolation of the colony assured that Johnson's minor adjustments would not come in for careful scrutiny. [55]

In a third area, the power of the vestries, Johnson also encouraged alterations in the accepted Anglican pattern. And again, a strong New England ecclesiastical tradition served as the model. Whereas in England the vestry had always been a weak and parochial institution with little power, in New England the individual congregations had traditionally exercised considerable control over the selection and discipline of ministers, as well as over ministerial salaries. Under the semi-presbyterian type of church government instituted in the Saybrook Platform, the clergy had assumed much of the power previously exercised by the church members, but ministers still found it difficult to make decisions without taking the desires of the church members into account. Especially in New Haven County, the heritage of congregational control was very much alive. If the Anglican clergy followed the lead of the Connecticut clergy in organizing clerical meetings, the Anglican laity followed the lead of their New

---

54. Daniel Goodwin, ed., *The MacSparran Diary* . . . (Boston, 1899), pp. 46–49.

55. Secretary to Johnson, 21 October 1750, S.P.G. MSS, B, 18 : 212; also Secretary to Johnson, 25 April 1743, *Conn. Episcopacy*, 1 : 185–86.

England ancestors in assuming greater power for the church members.[56]

One measure of the extent of lay control among the Anglican churches in Connecticut was the reaction of the foreign-born missionaries. Matthew Graves reported a debate with his parishioners in which he was told that

> the minister has nothing to do in parish affairs, only to read and preach, that the Church is vested in lay patrons . . . ; that the Vestry and Churchwardens are the minister's directors, and could place and displace him at their pleasure; that no minister can or shall do any duty in this Church . . . without the knowledge and consent of the Vestry.[57]

Graves believed that such demands were part of a general plan to deprive ministers of power and "shake the foundation of these infant Churches, by casting us absolutely upon the mercy of the populace." [58] James Lyons also had trouble with the members of his parish who "asserted that they have no occasion to consult me, nor make me privy to their purposes." But Lyons did not feel that the laymen were trying to take over the churches for themselves; rather that the vestries were "so fond of thir countrymen" that they were working in combination with them "to get rid of missionaries that are not country born." [59]

Although the foreign-born missionaries were the only ones to complain about the exaggerated power of the vestries, the right of the laymen to have a minister of their own choosing affected foreign and New England missionaries alike. Since the Society usually assigned its newly ordained ministers to parishes that had already requested them, the question of who had control over appointments, the Society or the vestry, did not arise frequently. In at least three instances, however—at Brookhaven in 1731, at New London in 1743, and at Norwalk in 1749—the vestries did not approve of the man sent to them by the Society. And in each

56. Borden W. Painter, Jr., "The Anglican Vestry in Colonial America" (Ph.D. diss., Yale University, 1965).
57. Graves to Secretary, 2 September 1752, *Conn. Episcopacy*, 1 : 295–96.
58. Graves to Secretary, 24 March 1750, ibid., p. 266.
59. Lyons to Secretary, 8 May 1744, ibid., pp. 208–09.

case the vestry was able to get a new pastor.[60] In 1747, when
Henry Caner left his parish at Fairfield for a post at King's
Chapel, he recommended that the Society appoint Joseph Lamson
as his successor, both because the people wanted him and because
"A custom of being indulged this way had made it a matter of
consequence in this part of the world, that the people should, as
much as possible, be gratified in the choice of their ministers."[61]
Four years earlier Johnson had also advised the Archbishop of
Canterbury that, when vacancies appeared in the colony, "the
people may have leave before they are filled to recommend some
young gentleman." As with lay preaching, Johnson was on the
side of New England tradition.[62]

The Society always remained in official control of ministerial
appointments. In the 1740s, however, it began to surrender this
power to the vestries in return for financial compensation. In
1744 the secretary sent a letter to Johnson ordering him not to
dispatch any more candidates to England until a parish could
guarantee the man a decent house or glebe of land.[63] By 1750 the
Society had adopted the policy of accepting all candidates for
orders who "shall appear duly qualified and bring with them a
security in Land" from the churches which they planned to serve.
Since the vestry reserved the right to give the land to the missionary they wanted, the Society's policy effectively transferred
the power of ministerial selection to the local level.[64]

The increased power of the vestries, like lay preaching and
Anglican clerical organization, was an ecclesiastical modification
Johnson inaugurated or encouraged in order to make Anglicanism
responsive to colonial conditions. In October of 1740 those conditions changed drastically. And from Johnson's point of view the

60. Johnson to Secretary, 2 June 1731, S.P.G. MSS, A, 23 : 247–50; Johnson
to Secretary, 3 December 1743, S.P.G. MSS, B, 11 : 37; Secretary to Johnson, 21
October 1750, S.P.G. MSS, B, 18 : 212.
61. Caner to Secretary, 12 February 1747, Conn. Episcopacy, 1 : 230–31.
62. Johnson to Archbishop of Canterbury, 22 May 1743, S.P.G. MSS, B,
11 : 33.
63. Secretary to Johnson, 30 May 1744 and 27 September 1744, S.P.G. MSS,
B, 13 : 20, 30. Johnson's reply is in a letter to the Secretary, 12 February 1745,
Conn. Episcopacy, 1 : 212.
64. Secretary to Johnson, 1 March 1750, S.P.G. MSS, B, 17 : 201; also
Painter, "Anglican Vestry," p. 194.

change verified his analysis of the New England churches. The agent of change was a twenty-five-year-old Anglican minister named George Whitefield, who had just come from preaching engagements in Boston and Northampton, where his revivalistic services had produced an unprecedented release of religious energy. In his wake, however, he left exposed the fissures and ecclesiastical divisions that Johnson had claimed were inherent in Puritanism. Here, Johnson believed, was the providential opportunity for which he had been preparing his Anglican missionaries. When the dust cleared, Johnson predicted that the Puritan churches would be racked with "endless divisions and separations." And the Anglicans would take "a very considerable advantage" of the confusion.[65]

None of the Anglican missionaries invited Whitefield into their parishes, but they had a good view of the results that he and two other prominent itinerant preachers, Gilbert Tennant and James Davenport, were able to provoke. Johnson went to hear both Whitefield and Davenport and reported that they propagated "the most horrid notions both of God and Gospel." He concluded that their preaching style consisted of saying "in the most affecting tones . . . the most frightful things they could think of about the devil, hell and damnation, so as to scare people out of their wits, in order to bring them to what they called conversion." [66] Ebenezer Punderson watched Davenport perform at New London and produce "screechings, faintings, convulsions, visions, [and] apparent death for twenty or thirty hours." [67] Henry Caner at Fairfield likened the religious frenzy to an "epidemical sickness." All of the Anglican missionaries opposed the enthusiasm, while expecting to benefit from its excesses.

Johnson made the general observation that "the madness of the times . . . does remarkably engage people's attention to our preaching and administrations." [68] Henry Caner was more specific:

65. On Whitefield, see John Gillies, *Memoirs of Rev. George Whitefield,* 2 vols. (New York, 1877); see also Edwin L. Gaustad, *The Great Awakening in New England* (New York, 1957); Alan Heimert, *Religion and the American Mind* (Cambridge, Mass., 1966); and Bushman, *Puritan to Yankee,* pp. 183–220.
66. *Career,* 1 : 28.
67. Punderson to Bishop of London, 12 December 1741, *Conn. Episcopacy,* 1 : 174.
68. Johnson to Secretary, 25 March 1742, *Career,* 3 : 230.

Where the late spirit of enthusiasm has most abounded, the Church has received the largest accession. Many of those deluded people, having lost themselves in the midst of error, wearied in the pursuit, as their passions subsided, sought for rest in the bosom and communion of the Church; and others reflecting upon the weakness of their present disorders, have likewise thought proper to take shelter under the wings of the Church.[69]

Whitefield and his New Light disciples had taught that there could be no buffer between the awesome power of God and dependent and helpless man. The first step toward genuine religious conviction, said Whitefield, was the terror and depression that accompanied a man's awareness of this basic fact. For those who found the terror unbearable, for those who professed to believe that God could be devoutly worshiped within a highly structured church, Anglicanism represented an "ark of safety" in the middle of a revivalistic deluge.[70] Within the towns that already had Anglican missionaries, conversions to episcopacy went up dramatically. Johnson reported that twelve families in Stratford came over to his church in one year. Punderson, Beach, Caner, and Seabury noted similar increases in their parishes. More importantly, between 1740 and 1750 eleven Connecticut towns previously unoccupied by Anglicans requested that an episcopal minister establish a mission within their boundaries. One of the towns explained that "the insufferable enthusiastic whims and extemporaneous jargon" of the Great Awakening had made citizens aware of "the weakness of the pretended condition of the Churches . . . in this land." [71]

In the end, however, the Anglicans failed. It was a frustrating failure, because Johnson's diagnosis of the chronic instability of the new England churches had proven accurate. Puritan polity

69. Caner to Secretary, 30, November 1743, *Conn. Episcopacy*, 1 : 201.
70. *Career*, 1 : 29.
71. For Stratford see *Notitia Parochialis*, 1 October 1741, *Conn. Episcopacy*, 1 : 299, and 5 October 1742, ibid., p. 233. See the survey of Connecticut parishes in Clergy of Connecticut to Bishop of London, 24 August 1742, ibid., pp. 181–82. The requests from the towns are in ibid., pp. 18, 185, 197, 202, 206, 210–11, 218, 233, 235, 238, 247–48. The quotation is taken from the Northbury request of 28 May 1744.

had shown itself incapable of controlling the centrifugal tendencies of the congregations. The familiar dilemma of determining what qualified a man to be a minister—the dilemma Johnson had wrestled with and resolved twenty years earlier—appeared again when Whitefield and Tennant accused the bulk of the New England clergy of being unregenerate. The established clergy replied that regeneration was not what distinguished a minister from a layman; and then repeated the defense of the Puritan ministry they had used against Johnson and the Anglicans. Arguments over the ministry, preaching styles, and the signs of grace divided the colony into two camps, called Old Lights and New Lights, but the Anglicans were unable to exploit the divisions adequately.[72]

In part, the Anglicans were hampered by the confusion they sought to exploit. Rather than take advantage of the conflict between Old and New Lights, they sometimes got caught in the crossfire. When Johnson went to Ripton to dedicate a new mission in 1743, he encountered a New Light minister who "insisted there was no more holiness in the Church than under an oak tree" and then spread horse manure over the walls of the Anglican mission. Samuel Seabury reported that a group of New Lights had raided his house, burned some religious books, and tried to burn the episcopal vestments.[73] From the Old Lights, who controlled the government, there came legal persecution. In 1743 the legislature passed a law nullifying the Toleration Act of 1708 and requiring all dissenters to register their unorthodox opinions at one of the semiannual meetings of the Assembly rather than at the county court. Although the act was aimed at the New Lights, it also hit the Anglicans and discouraged converts far removed from the place of registration.[74]

---

72. Key publications include Gilbert Tennant, *The Danger of An Unconverted Ministry* (Philadelphia, 1740); Charles Chauncy, *Seasonable Thoughts on the State of Religion in New England* (Boston, 1743); Jonathan Edwards, *The Distinguishing Marks of the Work of the Spirit* (Boston, 1743).

73. Johnson to Secretary, 30 September 1743, and Seabury to Secretary, 25 March 1743, *Conn. Episcopacy*, 1 : 189–90, 197.

74. *Conn. Recs.*, 8 : 521–22 gives the law of 1743. In the same year the Assembly forbade the establishment of schools that varied from Old Light doctrines. In 1746 the Assembly denied the franchise in town meetings to all persons who did not pay taxes to the Puritan (Old Light) minister. Ibid., p. 502; 9 : 218–19.

But Anglican failure was ultimately due to the paucity of missionaries, itself the product of the inflexibility of Anglican ordination procedure. Of the seven Anglican missionaries in Connecticut in 1740, only Johnson remained in the colony a decade later. Seabury and Henry Caner had gone off to different colonies, Lyons and Morris had returned to England, Jonathan Arnold had been dismissed for excessive drinking, and Richard Caner had died. New men like Ebenezer Dibble, William Gibbs, and Richard Mansfield had been recruited from Yale, served as lay readers, and returned to fill the vacant positions, but they were not enough. At precisely the moment that whole parishes were beseeching the Society for ministers, the Anglicans found themselves shorthanded.[75] Johnson continued to plead for a resident bishop and to churn as many candidates through his lay-reading program as possible, but it was not enough. In 1750 he wrote the secretary that "the little hope that we have, Sir, of having candidates or destitute places provided for even so slenderly, and *for a long time,* is a very great damp to the Church in these parts."[76]

Johnson continued to write the Bishop of London that the church was on the verge of mass conversions. Ashbel Woodbridge, the Connecticut minister who delivered the election sermon in 1753, even envisaged the "unhappy day" when there would be more Anglicans than Puritans in the colony.[77] But the facts proved Johnson's hopes delusive and Woodbridge's warning unnecessary. Between 1740 and 1750 the Connecticut Anglicans showed a net gain of two missionaries and five parishes. At Stratford, Johnson could claim approximately one-third of the population for his church, only a 10 percent increase for the ten-year period. Noah Hobart, in fact, singled out Stratford as the symbol of Anglican failure. In 1748 Hobart recalled that "the Society

75. Johnson narrated the ministerial losses in a letter to the Secretary, 28 April 1747, *Conn. Episcopacy,* 1 : 236–38. Corroboration is supplied by Roger Price, in Ernest Hawkins, *Historical Notices of the Missions of the Church of England in North America* (London, 1845), pp. 216–17. See also Kinloch, "Anglican Clergy in Connecticut," pp. 54–110, 232–33.
76. Johnson to Secretary, 30 March 1750, *Conn. Episcopacy,* 1 : 258.
77. Ashbel Woodbridge, *A Sermon Delivered Before the General Assembly . . . May 14, 1753* (New London, 1753).

have maintained a minister there for almost *thirty years.*" Then he asked, "What good Effect has it produced at Stratford?" [78]

Johnson did not try to answer Hobart or explain the colony-wide failure. In 1763 Johnson's elder son surmised that the Anglicans had failed because they had remained "quiet and easy and have given neither party any disturbance." [79] What William Samuel did not say was that his father had charted a course of moderation because it suited his temperament and because he was content to make strategic compromises while awaiting assistance from London and Whitehall. The absence of such assistance left the Anglicans stranded, incapable of exploiting the religious divisions produced by the Great Awakening. In the end, and by a curious irony, the ecclesiastical structure that had attracted Johnson to Anglicanism prevented him from carrying the message to others. And to further compound the irony, Johnson found it necessary to adopt Anglican procedures that he considered archetypal principles of apostolic origin to the colonial locale. As leader of an embattled minority sect, he found it expedient to borrow a few principles from the Puritans.

78. Kinloch, "Anglican Clergy in Connecticut," p. 232; Beardsley, *Episcopal Church*, 1 : 161–64. At Stratford the number of Anglicans went from 73 out of 400 to 143 out of 500. See *Notitia Parochialis*, 10 September 1739 and 14 October 1751, *Career*, 3 : 224–43; Noah Hobart, *A Serious Address*, p. 134.

79. Johnson to Beach, 4 January 1763, *Career*, 3 : 266.

7

A Sense of Insufficiency

Of course, the New England clergy never referred to Johnson as a Puritan. In their minds he always remained an Anglican and, because of his Anglicanism, an Arminian. In eighteenth-century New England the word "Arminian" was used in much the same way the word "latitudinarian" had been used in seventeenth-century England. Each was an imprecise term, more a slanderous accusation than an easily definable theological position. Each was associated with a cluster of beliefs that threatened the existent religious order. Each borrowed heavily from the intellectual movement that came to be called the Enlightenment. Each had proponents who survived orthodox criticism to become, in time, established leaders of a new orthodoxy.[1] But before Arminianism was accepted as the semi-official religion of Boston's more respected citizens, it had to change its name to Unitarianism, partly because the older word still carried vestiges of impropriety. In Johnson's day it was an epithet used to refer to a theological deviant. John Beach thought that the word had degenerated into an empty piece of rhetoric, "a strange Word made up of eight letters, that wonderfully inflames them [the Puritans] and transports them, and sets them a raving and madding, they know not why nor wherefore."[2] Johnson thought that

1. For the development of Arminianism, see Conrad Wright, *The Beginnings of Unitarianism in America* (Boston, 1966). See G. J. Goodwin, "The Myth of 'Arminian-Calvinism' in Eighteenth-Century New England," *The New England Quarterly* 41 (1968): 213–37, for the view that Arminianism was a heresy the Puritans understood, not a rhetorical slander.
2. John Beach, *An Appeal to the Unprejudiced* . . . (Boston, 1737), p. 8.

"the odious name of Arminianism" had lost whatever substantive meaning it once possessed and had become "a cry . . . from those little minds that are affected with sound more than sense." [3]

This had not always been the case. Arminianism had once been a clearly definable set of religious tenets enunciated by the Dutchman Jacobus Arminius (1560–1609) and declared heretical by the Synod of Dort in 1619. At the center of the Arminian position was the notion that divine grace was conditional or, to put it differently, that grace was not irresistible. An Arminian was one who believed that the efficacy of God's grace depended on man's ability to accept or reject it. He tended to emphasize the human role in the regenerative process, making election dependent on man's ability to earn God's grace. An Arminian could not subscribe to the confession of faith adopted at Westminster and later renewed by the synod at Savoy, because these doctrinal statements reasserted the orthodox belief that grace was irresistible and unconditional; election did not depend on any human capacity; it was solely a function of God's arbitrary will.[4]

In the first half of the eighteenth century very few, if any, New England ministers embraced this formal version of Arminianism. Cotton Mather was probably referring to this kind of Arminianism when, in 1726, he wrote, "I cannot learn, that among all the Pastors of Two Hundred Churches, there is one Arminian." [5] Whether or not there were any dyed-in-the-wool Arminians among the Puritan clergy, there was a good deal of talk about Arminianism. Jonathan Edwards remembered that about 1734 there was a "great noise in this part of the country, about Arminianism, which seemed to appear with a very threatening aspect upon the interest of religion here." [6] During the 1730s three Puritan ministers were ejected from their pulpits

3. *Career*, 3 : 161.

4. Walker, *Creeds and Platforms*, pp. 189–95, 284; Wright, *Unitarianism*, pp. 1–8.

5. Quoted in Williston Walker, *A History of the Congregational Churches in the United States* (New York, 1894), p. 216; also in Wright, *Unitarianism*, p. 9.

6. Jonathan Edwards, ed., *The Works of President Edwards*, 4 vols. (New York, 1843), 3 : 233.

for what was labeled Arminianism. A fourth, Robert Breck, survived censure only because he renounced his previous Arminian statements; a fifth, Jonathan Parsons, admitted that he had once been under the influence of "Arminian Principles." In none of these admittedly isolated incidents was there a thorough discussion of the theological points at issue; but in each case what disturbed the orthodox ministers was a laxity of doctrine that exalted human capabilities at the expense of divine sovereignty. The Puritan clergy recognized this laxity as a distortion of Ames and Wollebius, a corruption of the theological principles on which New England had been founded and something akin to the Dortian definition of Arminianism. The name stuck and became a catchword to describe a theological malaise that, they warned, threatened to infect all the churches of New England.[7]

When the Puritan clergy of Connecticut cast about to discover the source of their troubles, they quickly fastened their attention on the Anglicans. When Johnson and Cutler defected to the Church of England, the Puritan ministers regarded "Arminian books" as the cause of the mischief and the Yale trustees immediately established a "*Confession* of Faith . . . in opposition to *Arminian* and Prelatical Corruptions." It was easier to believe that their theological problems had been imported from England than that they had been manufactured at home. The leaders of the Church of England were blatantly Arminian and, although it was difficult to determine what doctrines the English Arminians held, it was readily acknowledged that they held the best bishoprics and deaneries in England. Clearly, Anglican polity and Arminian theology were seen as part of the same package, a package that had been smuggled into New England under the covers of the Dummer books and had corrupted young Samuel Johnson. When Johnson returned to Connecticut from

7. A good summary of the specific episodes is in Thomas Prince, Jr., ed., *The Christian History*, 2 vols. (Boston 1744–45), 1 : 93–106; also John White, *New England's Lamentations* (Boston, 1734). The Breck episode is summarized in *Harvard Graduates*, 8 : 611–80. Two conflicting secondary accounts are F. A. Christie, "The Beginnings of Arminianism in New England," American Society of Church History, *Papers*, 2nd ser. 3 (1912): 153–71, and Wright, *Unitarianism*, pp. 9–27.

England and began to recruit missionaries at Yale, the orthodox clergy feared that he was the harbinger of theological heresy as well as ecclesiastical error. The outbreak of Arminianism in the 1730s only confirmed their worst fears.[8]

But it is important to recognize, and Johnson continually made this point, that the warnings issued by Puritan ministers revealed as much about their own theological ambivalence as about the supposed heresy of others. Despite a common reliance on Ames, Wollebius, and the covenant theologians of the Reformation, New England divines never codified their theology as they did their polity. The result was a certain lack of coherence in which Puritan theologians claimed allegiance to a variety of apparently contradictory ideas. Clarification of the conveniently blurred Puritan position tended to occur when someone like Anne Hutchinson pushed an orthodox notion, in her case the notion of divine sovereignty, so far that it destroyed a parallel doctrine, the idea that men were responsible for their actions. But when some preacher, perhaps reacting to Hutchinson's heresy (which was called Antimonianism), pressed too hard on the idea that men must strive to merit salvation, he was flirting with Arminianism. And if he continued to neglect divine sovereignty, orthodox ministers would attack him for heresy. In theology as well as polity, then, the New Englanders defined the parameter of Puritan orthodoxy in conflict with recognizable enemies. The suspected Arminianism of Johnson was the kind of whetstone on which they could sharpen their double-edged theological instruments.[9]

It was in this context that Johnson preached and shaped his own theological views and only within this highly charged atmos-

8. *Yale Biographies*, 1 : 260. Jonathan Dickinson claimed that he and his fellow ministers "heartily consent to their [Anglican] Doctrinal articles; and would rejoice to find that all the Ministers of the Church of England did so too. But . . . the generality of their clergy are professedly Arminians." See Dickinson, *The Vanity of Human Institutions in the Worship of God* (New York, 1736), p. v.

9. For the most recent synthesis of the extensive literature on Puritan theology, see David Hall, "Understanding the Puritans," in Stanley Katz, ed., *Colonial America: Essays on Politics and Social Development* (Boston, 1970), pp. 31–50.

phere that they can be understood. He was continually on the defensive, trying to convince all who would listen that

> We hold no doctrines now but what were held and taught in our Church long before Arminius was heard of. . . . And if *Arminius* happened to agree with them in some of his notions, I know no reason why we should be called after his name. In short, we have no business with *Arminius,* he was a Dutch Presbyterian, and we are none of his followers.[10]

Johnson tried to rid himself of the Arminian stigma. He constantly encouraged his enemies to rise above their name-calling and examine objectively those notions about God and man that lay behind the label they had affixed to him. In the end he failed, but in the process of pleading with the Puritan clergy, he worked out a sophisticated system of theology that defied any single-minded categorization and shed a good deal of light on the theological confusion which surrounded the term "Arminianism." Along the way, he showed his Puritan detractors that the doctrines he espoused were not Anglican or English in origin, but merely extensions of doctrines identified with the covenant theology of New England. If he was preaching heresy, the heresy was home grown, not imported. And it was a heresy that certain Puritan ministers were beginning to find increasingly attractive.

Johnson willingly and enthusiastically defended his beliefs in a series of three pamphlets entitled *Letters to His Dissenting Parishioners* (1733–37). A decade later he took on his old antagonist, Jonathan Dickinson, in a theological debate which Johnson entitled *Aristocles to Authades* (1745–47). These publications provided the outline for his battle-plan against what he called the "necessitating doctrine" of New England orthodoxy; in his weekly sermons at Stratford he preached the same message, but added supplementary details that he never managed to squeeze into print. Since some of his ideas changed as he got older and since each of his arguments was designed to counter

10. Johnson, "A Letter From A Minister of the Church of England to His Dissenting Parishioners," *Career,* 3 : 26.

a specific accusation, whatever coherence his theological system did have was obscured by the eclectic and fragmentary manner in which it was presented. But if there was a logical beginning to his theology, it was his conception of God.

When trying to describe God, Johnson strung together long lists of adjectives, including good, holy, wise, merciful, generous, rational, charitable, and just.[11] These were characteristics of such universal admiration that few men could quarrel with them, but they did not exhaust all the possibilities. Most importantly, Johnson's God was not uncontrollable or unpredictable. Johnson did not talk about a Jehovah, a God of anger or intemperance. God was "a moral governor . . . proceeding according to equity." He was "not a hard master," but "a righteous judge of the behavior of his creatures." [12] Johnson's God, in other words, was a projection of those moderate values that he himself tried to exemplify. He was not a God who would sanction the way in which the Puritan clergy had treated the Anglicans in Connecticut.

Johnson's God was more than just the sum total of those human attributes that most impressed the leading episcopal missionary in Connecticut. He was also a God of distinctly different characteristics from the one preached by some Puritan ministers. According to Johnson, "the God which some people have of late described in this country . . . is not the God of Israel, nor the God of Christians." [13] He was addressing this remark specifically to Jonathan Dickinson, but he made similar comments in reference to George Whitefield and the revivalistic preachers who swept through New England during the early 1740s. Dickinson undoubtedly resented being bracketed with Whitefield, who represented the kind of evangelical and enthusiastic approach to religion that Dickinson despised. But Johnson's point was that Dickinson shared in the guilt for "the sad havoc

---

11. Full-blown descriptions of the deity are in *Career*, 3 : 162, 164, 176; *A Letter to Jonathan Dickinson*, ibid., p. 204; *A Discourse Concerning the Nature of God*, ibid., pp. 482–500.

12. Ibid., pp. 166, 177.

13. Johnson, *A Letter to Jonathan Dickinson*, ibid., p. 192.

that Mr. Whitefield has made of Christianity," because he preached the narrow and arbitrary conception of God which made a phenomenon like Whitefield possible.[14] The problem centered around the use of the word "arbitrary" when describing God. Johnson was willing to admit that the Bible contained "some obscure texts [that] dictate arbitrary judgment . . . , yet methinks we should be strongly inclined, for God's sake as well as our own, to get over them."[15] What Johnson wanted to get over was the notion of God that emphasized sovereignty or uncontrolled power. An arbitrary God was a God who could not be counted on. He might decimate a whole community without reason or abandon a colony of people who were devoutly striving to obey his dictates. He was a God who obeyed no laws and was governed by no restrictions. He was the kind of God that George Whitefield preached; an unfathomable deity who might parcel out his graces in emotional packages that were awarded indiscriminately and that left the recipients rolling in the dust, a God who was just as likely to appear at a wild revival as at a solemn church service. He was not a God who exemplified the judicious attitude that Johnson prized so dearly.

When Jonathan Dickinson confronted Johnson with a God who was "*sovereign* and *arbitrary,*" Johnson reminded him that such a God could provoke and sanction the evangelical excesses that Dickinson opposed. The theological tracts that Johnson published in the 1740s, especially *Aristocles to Authades,* differed from his preceding publications in one important way: they took delight in citing the chaotic events of the Great Awakening as the product of a misguided conception of the Lord. Johnson preferred to believe that the revivals were not the work of God at all, for they were evidence of "manifest double dealing in the sovereign toward them [the people]," and Johnson could not accept an image of God which "seems plainly inconsistent with the very notion of his being a moral governor of the world."[16]

14. Ibid., p. 177.
15. Ibid., p. 164.
16. Jonathan Dickinson, *A Vindication of God's Sovereign Free Grace* . . . (Boston, 1746), p. 74; Johnson to Samuel Brown, 1 January 1738, *Career,* 3 : 149; Johnson, *A Letter to Jonathan Dickinson,* ibid., p. 194.

Instead of accepting a version of the deity that made him a rule unto himself, Johnson insisted that God embodied certain values which were both recognizable and comprehensible to human beings. Otherwise, he could not serve as a model for his creatures. Moreover, if God was an inconsistent and indiscriminate sovereign who dealt with men without rhyme or reason, then how could men be expected to order their lives in preparation for his grace? How would they know what to do? If God did not willingly agree to conduct himself according to certain prescribed rules that men could understand, he would tend "at once to destroy all religion and morality, and all civil and family government, and render them unmeaning and ridiculous things." [17] Throughout his life, Johnson asserted that such an insensitive and unapproachable God was morally indefensible and socially disastrous. Johnson continued to preach that "tho God is not accountable to his creatures for any of his proceedings, yet we must conceive, that his infinite wisdom, holiness, justice, and goodness must be a law to him from which he cannot vary." [18]

Under constant attack from Dickinson for seriously limiting and overly humanizing God's personality, Johnson was prepared to make a concession and another distinction. He admitted that God had not completely abdicated his sovereign powers. In fact, God continually exercised his sovereignty in the act of creating men with diverse capabilities and talents. The variety of the human species was, in this sense, an accurate reflection of God's sovereign will. However, he ceased to conduct himself arbitrarily once the act of creation was completed. As a creator, God was both sovereign and arbitrary, but "As a judge deciding the eternal condition of men, God never once represents himself as arbitrary, but everywhere as proceeding according to equity . . . in exact proportion to their own conduct in the use of talents committed to their trust.[19]

Dickinson read this statement and chose to reply with a question: "What Reason can possibly be assigned, why God has not

17. *Career,* 3 : 200.
18. *Ibid.,* p. 167.
19. Ibid., p. 176.

a Right to act with the same *Sovereignty* in the Donation of saving Grace, as in the Distribution of those Favours and Privileges, upon which eternal Salvation is so dependent?" [20] Johnson's answer was quick and simple; God could do anything he pleased, but because he was—and then there followed the familiar list of attributes—he pleased to do what was just and fair.[21]

Both Dickinson and John Graham called such motions about God Arminian. Johnson claimed that they were part of the traditional doctrine of the covenant and had long been recognized as part of the orthodox position in New England and England. The God defined in the *Medulla* of William Ames, taught at Yale, and adopted as orthodox at the Westminster Synod, was, in fact, an infinite God who had entered into a covenant with his chosen people, whereby he agreed to act in the matter of their salvation according to rules they could understand. In this sense, Johnson was right. New England Puritanism had always been rooted in the federal or covenant school of reformed theology, which taught that God voluntarily restricted himself to act in a predictable fashion. When attacked by Dickinson on this point, Johnson referred him to the covenant tradition and asked whether Dickinson's doctrine of a completely arbitrary God "does not, by unavoidable consequence, destroy the Covenant of Grace?" [22]

Dickinson replied that Johnson's characterization of God was too humanistic, predictable, and limited. There must always be room for the mysterious and the unexpected; one must always be aware of the awesome power that underlay voluntary restrictions. God had indeed been charitable enough to bind himself into a covenant, but he bound himself only to those persons whom he had arbitrarily destined for salvation in the first place. Dickinson justifiably argued that Johnson had seriously distorted the theology of the founders by placing an undue em-

---

20. Jonathan Dickinson, *A Vindication of God's Sovereign Free Grace*, p. 66.
21. Johnson, *A Letter to Jonathan Dickinson, Career*, 3 : 204.
22. *Career*, 3 : 201. Johnson had made the same point earlier, when he told Dickinson, "If you deny the being of any promises consistent with the sovereignty of God, you do in effect, destroy the very being of the New Covenant, and by consequence, the whole design and purport of revealed religion." Ibid., p. 177.

phasis on those soft features of the divine personality that were originally intended to provide hope but not security. It was perfectly orthodox to say, as Johnson did say, "that he [God] will, for his Sake, give his Holy Spirit to everyone that seriously asks him," [23] as long as one remembered that a sovereign God had decided beforehand who would be able to do any serious asking. The covenant theology was, then, a finely tuned instrument that had to be employed carefully, as the founders had done, and had only been intended for use by those already marked for salvation. By preaching only a God of justice and compassion, Dickinson argued, Johnson had undermined divine sovereignty and perverted the meaning of the covenant in such a way as to imply that God would offer his grace to everyone. According to Dickinson, such an idea reeked of Arminianism.[24]

Even if Johnson had admitted that Dickinson was right, which he never did, Dickinson's arguments effectively destroyed the contention that Arminianism was a heresy imported from England by the forces of episcopacy. The covenant theology of New England had always contained within itself the seeds of Arminianism. Although Arminianism in the Dortian sense was primarily a heresy which was condemned because it elevated human capabilities, the same dilution of doctrine which it achieved could be effected by lowering the divine agent more closely to the human level. By adopting a device which obliged God to deal with his creatures in a comprehensible fashion, the covenant theologians had unwittingly taken the first steps toward this form of Arminianism. Johnson had proceeded further along the same path, but they had pointed the way.

Finally, Johnson never made an effort to eliminate all the mysterious and inscrutable features of the deity. He believed that God conducted himself with justice and intelligence when

23. Ibid., p. 162.
24. Jonathan Dickinson, *A Vindication of God's Sovereign Free Grace,* esp. pp. 66–67, 74. The debate continued with Dickinson's *A Second Vindication of God's Sovereign Free Grace* (Boston, 1748), which was finished by Moses Dickinson when Jonathan died before its completion. John Beach replied in *An Answer to A Second Vindication of God's Sovereign Free Grace . . .* (Boston, 1748). Moses Dickinson had the last word in *An Inquiry Into the Consequences of Calvinistic and Arminian Principles . . .* (Boston, 1750).

dealing with men, but this did not mean that men could ever understand him in the same sense that they understood themselves. God was ultimately a spirit, part of a realm which human beings could never fully experience until they died. Men could make only metaphoric gestures at comprehending a being who defied the categories of human discourse. They could say that God was "like" the sun or "like" a mountain, but the comparison was always an imperfect one which only approximated the characteristics beyond human perception. Johnson liked to think of God as light, though he was quick to add

> that when it is said that God is light, it cannot be spoken in a direct and literal sense, light being nothing else but an impression of sense made of Him upon our minds, by means of an inconceivably fine subtle ether. . . . As therefore, we learn to think and speak of things spiritual by means of things sensible, it must be in a translated or figurative way of speaking that God is called light.[25]

Johnson consistently asserted that the infinitely wide gap between "things spiritual" and "things sensible" could only be bridged with divine assistance, a belief that had major significance for his purely philosophical thinking and served as the focal point for his theological estimate of man.

The public disputations over Arminianism should have settled down to a discussion of differing conceptions of human nature at some point, but they did not. When the Puritan clergy detected Arminian doctrines among their own in the 1730s, they insisted that Benjamin Kent, one of the accused, had "denied an absolute Election, and asserted a conditional one on the foresight of good works' and had claimed "that infants come into the world free and clear of original guilt."[26] Another of the suspected Arminian heretics, Samuel Osborn, admitted his belief that "men can do that upon the doing of which they will

25. Johnson, "A Discourse Concerning the Nature of God," *Career*, 3 : 484; also "The Spiritual Discerning of Spiritual Things," ibid., pp. 447–57, and The Allsufficiency of God, dated 2 September 1744, in Johnson MSS.
26. Quoted in Wright, *Unitarianism*, p. 23.

certainly be saved," for which he was dismissed from his parish at Eastham.[27] John Bass was one of the few Connecticut clergy accused of Arminianism; he was eventually relieved of his parish for suspected laxity on the question of human depravity.[28] These Arminian outbreaks only verified what the orthodox clergy already knew, that one's estimate of human nature stood at the center of the entire Arminian problem. Johnson and his critics were content to circle around the periphery of this troublesome issue, perhaps because it was so obviously loaded with explosive implications.

The Anglicans were as evasive as the Puritans. John Beach conceded that every infant that came into the world "brings along with it the Guilt of *Adam's* Sin," yet also carried along a counterbalancing amount of grace as a result of "the benefit of Christ's meritorious death." [29] Johnson outraged his Puritan opponents by insisting that human beings do not sin as a natural result of their innate depravity, for that was tantamount to making God the author of sin; they sin because they choose to sin. He accused his detractors of "hardening some in their evil Ways, & discouraging others from any attempts to reform their wicked Lives" by preaching a doctrine of absolute predestination which left no room for freedom of choice or moral action.[30] Moses Dickinson, younger brother of Jonathan, came to Stratford to inform Johnson and the residents that men were responsible for their sins even though their actions were predetermined by God.[31] Johnson confessed that this kind of reasoning was beyond his comprehension. He preferred to believe that every man possessed a moral sense and "a self-assertive power." [32] At a gathering of the Anglican clergy at Newport in 1731, he even waxed

27. Samuel Osborn, *The Case and Complaint of Mr. Samuel Osborn . . .* (Boston, 1743), p. 5.

28. John Bass, *A True Narrative of an Unhappy Contention in the Church at Ashford* (Boston, 1751).

29. John Beach, *An Appeal to the Unprejudiced*, p. 8.

30. Johnson, Encouragement for all men to seek salvation, n.d., p. 39, in Johnson MSS; also *A Letter to Jonathan Dickinson, Career*, 3 : 201.

31. Moses Dickinson, *A Discourse Showing that the Consideration of God's Sovereignty . . . is a most powerful Motive to Quicken their Endeavors. Preached at Stratford in the Colony of Connecticut* (Boston, 1742).

32. Johnson, *A Letter to Jonathan Dickinson, Career*, 3 : 203–04.

eloquent on "our exalted powers of reasoning and understanding" and equated a life of reason with a life of sanctity.[33]

These were only snippets of the Anglican doctrine about human nature, phrases lifted out of pamphlets and sermons. Nevertheless, to those Puritans who were looking for evidence to substantiate their opinion that the Anglicans were Arminian heretics, such phrases were more than enough. Beach seemed clearly to deny the doctrine of innate depravity; Johnson denied predestination, affirmed that men possessed a free will, and elevated the rational faculty at the expense of revelation. Reason, free will, good works, moralism—such was the stuff of which Arminians were made. The Anglicans had convicted themselves.

Only in his sermons, few of which were published, did Johnson attempt an extended exposition of his view of the human species. He began with man at birth. Instead of discovering a group of lovable infants, he found creatures "trained up under the government of sense and passion . . . and the gratification of their bodily appetites is all they aim at."[34] Johnson touched on this theme of innate depravity throughout his career at Stratford. In 1725 he reminded his congregation that men come into the world "blind & dark . . . , naturally altogether polluted, Sinful, Guilty & Filthy Creatures."[35] He preached the same message over the years and was still convinced of its applicability in 1753, when he called newborn babies "children of wrath . . . full of Anger, malice & Revenge & under the power of furious & diabolical passion."[36]

Johnson regarded the sinful tendencies of men as an inheritance passed down to the sons of Adam. Original sin was, for Johnson, a genetic legacy for "the original rebellion and apostasy of our first parents," a legacy which had resulted in "the deplorable pollution, guilt and corruption of the whole human race."[37] Johnson took care to specify what his conception of

33. Johnson, "True Philosophy, or the Wisdom of Religion and Virtue," ibid., p. 397.

34. Johnson, "The Necessity of Revealed Religion," ibid., p. 373.

35. Johnson, Concerning the Nature of Repentance, p. 7, 14 March 1725, in Johnson MSS.

36. Johnson, Of our Salvation by Grace through Faith, the Gift of God, p. 3, June 1753, in Johnson MSS.

37. Johnson to Jedediah Mills, 23 November 1741, Career, 3 : 147.

original sin meant. It did not mean "a voluntary opposition of
our wills to the divine will of God, of which infants are evi-
dently incapable." [38] An infant was not "guilty" of sin; he could
not help but sin. A child's sinful act was as natural and necessary
as any biological function. The poor creatures came into the
world "prepossessed with sensual habits . . . , habitually sen-
sualized . . . with an habitual prepossession against religion." [39]
They were the prisoners of their own perverse instincts, incapable
of regarding their actions with any moral scrutiny, totally dominated by reflexes that had been conditioned since the time of
Adam. When Johnson referred to the inheritance of original
sin, he was using the term literally. Adam's sin was more than
just a symbol. He was the father of man in the strict physical
sense and his posterity shared the sinful characteristics that were
the fruit of natural generation.

Johnson consistently maintained that men were inherently
depraved at birth and he also insisted that only an act of God
could shake a man out of this corrupt condition. A man "can't
repent and turn to God . . . without God's help." [40] From the
very beginning of his tenure at Stratford, Johnson taught that
the first burst of grace to enter the human soul was neither
earned nor deserved; it was a gift of God.[41] He frequently
preached on "the Entire Dependence of the Creature Upon God"
and emphasized that any genuinely holy endeavor that the human agent performed was "in consequence of its being as-
sisted." [42] Johnson's version of the morphology of conversion
was entirely orthodox. Justification came before sanctification;
grace came before works; God acted on man before man was
capable of worthwhile actions on his own.

But Johnson was neither orthodox nor consistent in describing how this initial influx of grace occurred. Any systematic

38. From Johnson's preface to Beach's *A Second Vindication*, ibid., p. 210.
39. Johnson, "The Necessity of Revealed Religion," ibid., p. 373.
40. Johnson, "The Entire Dependence of the Creature Upon God," *Career*,
3 : 540.
41. Johnson, The True Scripture Notion of Faith and Justification Stated,
10 October 1723, Concerning the Nature of Repentance, 14 March 1725,
Of the Nature of Sanctification and Christian Obedience Under the New
Covenant, February 1726, all in Johnson MSS.
42. Johnson, "Of the New Creature," *Career*, 3 : 414.

attempt to discover the source of Johnson's Arminianism should have begun at this point. His arguments were hazy, but the main thrust of his position was that God dispensed his graces liberally and that every man received grace sometime in his life, usually at an early age. God was too considerate a being to withhold divine grace for a long time. Johnson's conception of the deity forced him to conclude that "God has promised to hear and help him [man] by his blessed Spirit, if he earnestly prays and strives in such a manner as may be expected for such a frail creature as he is." [43]

Johnson did not believe that every person who received grace was saved. What this initial flow of grace did achieve was to dilute man's sinful habits. It weakened the hold of original sin, and gave man a fighting chance against the evil instincts inherited from Adam. It did not eliminate the last vestiges of Adam's legacy, but it did make man capable of moral or immoral action.[44]

More specifically, grace activated two human faculties which had lain dormant prior to God's intervention. The first was reason. As Johnson used the word, it did not refer to any logical or analytical faculty but to a "spiritual sense" which enabled man to "look through things seen and temporal to the things which are unseen and eternal." [45] Without reason man "knows no other good but that of eating and drinking, and carnal pleasure. . . . Let him have his dainties, his cups and his mistresses and he wants nothing more." [46] With reason he pursues "things of an eternal and unchangeable duration" and reduces his sensual habits "to the obedience of those pure and heavenly laws." [47] Grace brought this faculty of reason to life and thereby provided man a brief and imperfect glimpse into what the world should be and what heaven would be.

Johnson sometimes used the word "reason" in a more con-

43. Ibid., p. 179.
44. Johnson, preface to Beach's *A Vindication,* ibid., p. 211. Of the Nature of Santification and Christian Obedience Under the New Covenant, February 1726, in Johnson MSS.
45. Johnson, "A Sermon Concerning the Intellectual World," *Career,* 3 : 502.
46. Johnson, "A Sermon of the Spiritual Discerning of Spiritual Things," ibid., pp. 449–51.
47. Johnson, "Of the New Creature," ibid., p. 407.

ventional sense, as the ability to understand or comprehend difficult problems, but he did not think that men could reach religious truth by using this kind of analytical faculty. In 1727, after an extended exchange of correspondence with William Burnet, Anglican governor of New York, Johnson concluded that certain mysteries were incapable of being broken down logically and reduced to comprehensible components.[48] Man could never hope to get any closer to God by speculating on the Trinity or pondering the Incarnation. In religious matters, men had to learn *"to live by faith and not by sight."* The faculty of reason, in this analytical sense, was a convenient tool, but its applicability did not extend to the spiritual realm, where Scripture was the surest guide.[49]

The second faculty which grace activated was the will. Once the hold of original sin had been loosened by divine intervention, Johnson believed that human beings were free to choose between different courses of action. Men became "free, moral agents" in the sense that their "spiritual discerning powers" or reason let them know what was morally right and their will empowered them to act on what they knew. This doctrine had roots and extensions which Johnson dealt with more fully in his formal philosophical treatises. In his theological sermons and pamphlets he was concerned to show that the human will was the mechanism which resolved the tension between the sinful portion of human nature that Adam had transmitted to all his descendants and the spiritual part of man that had come into being with the entrance of grace. The will monitored reception from the sensual and spiritual elements of the human being and thereby affected an immoral or moral choice.[50]

48. Ibid., 1 : 21–23.
49. The quotation is from "The Necessity of Revealed Religion," *Career*, 3 : 369–80. Johnson's conception of reason was quite similar to Samuel Clarke's (1675–1729). For references to Clarke in Johnson's writings, see *Career*, 1 : 506, 507, 514 and 3 : 171, 176. Johnson read Clarke's Arminian tract *A Demonstration of the Being and Attributes of God . . .* (London, 1725) in September 1728, February 1729, and December 1734.
50. *Career*, 3 : 189–90, 209–10. See Daniel Whitby's *A Discourse Concerning [the Five Points]* (London, 1735) for a similar account of the will. Johnson read Whitby in preparation for *Aristocles to Authades*. For references to Whitby's theology in Johnson's work, see *Career*, 3 : 164, 171, 173, 186.

Johnson's acceptance of free will solved one persistent theological problem and produced another. He did not have to hedge or perform any logical hocus-pocus to explain the existence of sin. Sin was "the sole object of our perverse wills, nor can it be the object of his will, who is of purer eyes than to behold iniquity." [51]

But Jonathan Dickinson was quick to jump on Johnson's free will doctrine as a denial of God's sovereignty. If men are free to make moral choices on their own, said Dickinson, then they are not dependent on God for their every thought and action.[52] Johnson tried to counter Dickinson by distinguishing between God's knowledge and his will. All our actions are contingent on God, not because he wills them, but because he knows what we will do before we do it. "But his certain knowledge of them alters not their nature any more than our certain knowledge of them after they are facts . . . ; for he knows them as being what they are, *i.e.*, as depending on the voluntary, self-exerting nature which he hath given men." [53]

The publication of Jonathan Edwards' *Freedom of the Will* in 1754 raised several profound and serious doubts about the ability of man to decide things for himself and provoked a protracted debate which forced Johnson to reconsider his own arguments. During the 1730s, when he worked out the notion of human freedom in his sermons, and ten years later, when he made his views public in *Aristocles to Authades,* Johnson did not have to face the searching criticism of an Edwards. He could defend his acceptance of free will by telling Jonathan Dickinson that the doctrine was nothing more than the formalization of common sense; "it must be so merely because you cannot conceive how it should be otherwise." [54]

Free will was the capstone of a theological structure which Johnson put together in a piecemeal fashion, but which did manage to hang together logically. The practical lesson which

51. Johnson, *Letter to Jonathan Dickinson, Career,* 3 : 62.
52. Jonathan Dickinson, *A Vindication of God's Sovereign Free Grace,* pp. 71, 74–80.
53. Johnson, *Letter to Jonathan Dickinson, Career,* 3 : 190.
54. Ibid., p. 190.

emerged out of all the theological speculation was a simple life of
Christian morality. Although human beings came into the world
totally depraved, the assistance of a gracious God created what
Johnson came to call the "New Creature," who was neither completely sinful nor completely holy. Life was a contest between
two warring factions, the spiritual or good and the physical or
bad elements of man. The transformation of character by which
men were made fit candidates for eternal life was no easy or
automatic process, but the product of the conflict between the
antithetical forces within each personality. If a human being
exerted his will in an effort to overcome the remnants of original
sin, he could be assured that God would provide the additional
grace necessary to carry on the struggle, but Johnson realistically
refused to minimize the difficulties and argued that eventual
triumph over human weakness only ended with death.

In the end, then, Johnson's theology was Arminian, but not
of a simple kind. The source of his Arminianism was the belief
that God made grace accessible to all men. But in several important ways Johnson retained orthodox Puritan doctrines. He
did not have an enlightened view of man, but rather the lowest
estimate of unassisted human capabilities. He did not believe
that sanctification came before grace, but instead that grace made
efficacious action possible. He did not advocate a lax and easy
attitude toward salvation, as some Puritan clergy accused him
of doing, but insisted that a moral life was a never-ending war
against one's baser instincts. Even the source of Johnson's Arminianism—belief in divine benevolence—emerged out of a
New England theological context, for it was an extension (albeit
a heretical extension) of the traditional Puritan belief that God
obeyed prescribed rules when he dealt with man. The publication of Charles Chauncy's *Seasonable Thoughts* in 1744 and of
Jonathan Mayhew's *Seven Sermons* five years later signaled the
appearance of a strong and outspoken Arminian faction within
New England's orthodoxy. And Chauncy and Mayhew, both of
whom hated Johnson and the Anglicans, also reached Arminian
conclusions by pressing doctrines of the covenant theology be-

yond the limits of orthodoxy.[55] If it is clear that Johnson were
a heretic, it is equally clear that, like Chauncy and Mayhew, he
did not derive his heretical views solely from England or Anglicanism, but also from the New England Puritanism in which he
had been reared.

Moreover, by focusing on the theological differences between
Johnson's Arminianism and New England orthodoxy, it is
easy to ignore the similar psychological tensions they had in
common. There was a tremendous theoretical difference between
a man who was struggling within himself to discover if God
had ordained his election from eternity and a man who was
struggling to overcome a sinful disposition in the belief that
divine reward would be bestowed in direct proportion to his
effort, but both sides placed this internal struggle at the center
of their theology and of their lives. The fragments from Johnson's diary that survive indicate that, like his Puritan ancestors
and his orthodox opponents, he was obsessed with resolving the
constant conflict between the forces that festered in his soul.

> Fbr. 19, 1723   Having this day both in public and private con-
> fessed my sins and humbled myself before God may I ever
> have such a bitter sense of them as may sufficiently antidote
> one against them, and engage me steadfastly to watch against
> all temptation, effectually to mortify all my lusts, and sin-
> cerely to serve God in newness of life all my days.
>
> Nov. 1 [1724]   I hope I have been sincere in the renewal of
> my covenant with God in Christ. But alas, I have the same
> treacherous and unconstant heart as ever.
>
> July 4, 1725   O Lord I abhor and detest those remainders of
> my sin which alas, too much cling to me and by which I am
> too apt to be overcome. Make me so much in earnest I be-
> seech thee, in opposition to sin and temptation, that I may
> not be surprised into it, or enslaved. . . . Thou hast done

---

55. Wright, *Unitarianism*, chapters 3–7, for the best secondary account of
Chauncy and Mayhew. A good sketch of Chauncy is in *Harvard Graduates*,
6 : 439–67. Alden Bradford, *The Memoir of the Life and Writings of Rev.
Jonathan Mayhew, D.D.* (Boston, 1838).

righteously but I have done wickedly, and I am still punished far less than I deserve. Awake me to a sense of my sins
and a godly sorrow and thorough repentance of them. . . .
Ash Wednesday, 1726   I have been setting myself seriously to
renew my repentance. Oh God how weak are my attempts!
how unsteady my thoughts! how faint are my affections toward goodness . . . forgive the infirmities of my repentance,
as well as all the sins, I have laboured to repent of. . . .
Oct. 14, 1738 [Johnson's birthday]   Thus my life passeth away
like a Shadow. . . . How slippery a thing is time and how
many changes and alterations does it bring along with it.
32 years are past and gone and what are they but a dream,
a little while. . . . What multitudes in this little time become a prey to all devouring death. . . . O that I could
find I had made better proficiency in the mortification of
my sin. . . . O may I have a better account to give of
myself another year.[56]

Johnson's diary reveals a man racked with self-doubt and obsessed with the question of his own depravity. Like the diaries
of prominent New England Puritans, from John Winthrop to
Jonathan Edwards, it is concerned almost exclusively with the
inner life and the search for self-assurance.[57] It also shows that
Johnson, like the orthodox Puritans, regarded salvation as a long
process. He did not believe that grace was a lightning bolt that
transformed the soul in a sudden flash. William Perkins, a seventeenth-century English Puritan, provided the most articulate
presentation of the orthodox belief that salvation was gradual.[58]
Johnson did not, as did Perkins, break the experience of grace
into ten stages, nor did he agree with the orthodox contention
that the outcome of the internal struggle was predestined from
eternity. But he did believe that it was the influx of grace that
made resistance to sin possible. The persistence of the inner

56. Only early selections from the diary survive. The above were taken
from *Career*, 1 : 65–67, 69.
57. See *Winthrop Papers* (Boston, 1929–47), 3 : 338–44; Edwards, *Works*,
1 : 6–13.
58. William Perkins, *Workes*, 3 vols. (London, 1608–31), 1 : 353–420.

struggle was, in this sense, some assurance that the individual was on the right road. As Perkins put it, "to be grieved, therefore, is the grace itself." [59] For both Johnson and Perkins the combat within one's self lasted throughout life. The point of the inner battle was not victory over sin, for that was impossible, but the continuance of the fight.

Johnson also concurred with Perkins and the Puritans that there was some connection between visible action and one's internal disposition. He told his parishioners to "consider this visible world chiefly in this view, as an emblem of things invisible." [60] Like most Puritans, he was unwilling to argue that the relationship between the internal and the external, the invisible and the visible, was precise. Actions were only "external Marks or Badges" that had no "rational efficacy in themselves." [61] But he was prone to regard the success or failure of his Anglican mission as a reflection of his own spiritual condition. As Johnson's mother and father died, his students died en route to England, his mission at Stratford refused to grow, and the number of Anglicans in Connecticut began to level off and then decrease, he came to fear that these disasters were all signs of his moral laxity. By 1750 his sermons had become increasingly pessimistic. He referred to the human struggle against the remnants of original sin as a fight which few men could hope to win, for "the generality of mankind are so stupid, so immersed in sensual pleasures and so attached to this present world, and multitudes are so alienated from God and enslaved to their lusts and under the dominion and guilty of sin, that it seems indispensably necessary that God . . . awaken them and rouse them up." [62]

An earthquake in 1755 and the French successes against the British army the same year provoked nothing less than an old fashioned Puritan jeremiad, exhorting the people to reform their sinful ways. But the apparent failure of episcopacy in Connecti-

59. Ibid., 1 : 641.
60. Johnson, "A Sermon Concerning the Spiritual World," *Career*, 3 : 506.
61. Johnson, The Essentials of a True Church, May and June 1753, Johnson MSS.
62. Johnson, "The Duty of Trusting in God in Time of War," *Career*, 3 : 548.

cut he blamed on himself and his own moral inadequacy. He confessed that "the longer I live, the more abasing sense I have of my own weakness and insufficiency." [63] The continual demise of Anglican hopes worked on his Puritan disposition to guarantee that this sense of insufficiency would continue to grow.

63. Johnson, "A Sermon on the Entire Dependence of the Creature Upon God," ibid., p. 544.

8

Ideas and Archetypes

In 1752 Johnson published a treatise on formal philosophy entitled *Elementa Philosophica.* Benjamin Franklin, who printed the book in Philadelphia, reported to Johnson that he had "heard of no exceptions yet made to your great work, nor do I expect any, unless to those parts that savor of what is called *Berkeleyanism,* which is not well understood here."[1] The tactful Franklin did not report that the book was selling quite slowly and that the lack of criticism was, in great part, due to the fact that no one was reading it. And since *Elementa Philosophica* was not only dedicated to George Berkeley, but also intended as an explication of philosophical tenets that were rooted in Berkeley's metaphysics, Franklin's comments indicated that those people who had bothered to purchase the book had either objected to or failed to comprehend the main thrust of its message.

Although *Elementa Philosophica* was not a critical success, it does have a certain historical significance.[2] It was the first textbook in philosophy published in America and became a part of

1. Franklin to Johnson, 2 July 1752, *Career,* 2 : 328.
2. On Johnson's place in colonial philosophy, see I. W. Riley, *American Philosophy: The Early Schools* (New York, 1907), pp. 43–125; Herbert Schneider, *A History of American Philosophy* (New York, 1963), pp. 7–13, 21–26; Herbert Schneider, "The Mind of Samuel Johnson," *Career,* 2 : 1–22; Vincent Burranelli, "Colonial Philosophy," *William and Mary Quarterly,* 3rd ser. 16 (1959): 359. Professor Murray Murphey is currently at work on a new history of American philosophy which promises to supplant the dated accounts of Riley and Schneider and revise the accepted scholarly impression of colonial philosophy. I am particularly indebted to Professor Murphey for allowing me to read his chapter on Johnson's philosophy while it was still in manuscript.

the curriculum at the College in Philadelphia and later at King's College in New York. But the most intriguing fact about *Elementa Philosophica* was that it existed at all. How and why had Johnson attempted to construct a complete network of metaphysical and ethical principles? He admitted that his duties as an Anglican missionary at Stratford occupied most of his time and made him feel "not altogether dissimilar to . . . the Great Apostle, particularly in being in journeyings often and in peril among false brethren." [3] Yet, at the same time that he was traveling about Connecticut conducting services for small groups of Anglican communicants, recruiting fellow missionaries from Yale, defending Anglican polity in published pamphlets and modifying that same polity to maximize its efficiency—at the same time that he was heading up the episcopal forces in Connecticut—he had determined to set down a systematic statement of his own world view.

Not that *Elementa Philosophica* emerged unexpectedly from the colonial wilderness, some quick concoction of a harried missionary. Johnson apparently set aside a portion of each day for reading, guarded his study time jealously, and devoted considerable energy to philosophy and theology. From 1722 to 1752 he averaged about a book a week. His reading included such literary classics as Shakespeare, Milton's *Paradise Lost,* Defoe's *Robinson Crusoe,* and Swift's *Gulliver's Travels,* as well as Raleigh's *History of the World,* Spratt's *History of the Royal Society,* and Claremont's *History of the Rebellion.*[4] Such literary and historical works kept him in touch with the cultural sources of cosmopolitan England and allayed the fear that the provincial environment of rural Connecticut would sap his intellectual vitality. But his specifically philosophical studies represented an attempt to transcend all cultural categories. He was searching for the overarching principles that united colonists and Londoners with Europeans and Asiatics. Since 1731 Johnson had been turning out short philosophical pieces for publication, all of which were supposedly synthesized in the book that Franklin had

3. Johnson to Colden, 7 June 1747, *Career,* 2 : 298.
4. Johnson's reading list is in ibid., 1 : 502–25.

trouble selling, and all of which were intended to clarify the fundamental unity of "the society of man." [5] Although this was the kind of enlightened attitude that inspired Voltaire, Johnson's intellectual roots were embedded in New England Puritanism. The conviction that there was some cosmic unity that men could understand was a basic tenet of Ramist logic, a tenet that Johnson never abandoned. *Elementa Philosophica* was not the work of a colonial philosophe who was proclaiming the emergence of a new learning. It was an attempt to integrate the old learning with the new, fifteenth- and sixteenth-century scholasticism with eighteenth-century epistemology, the mental categories of Ames and Ramus with the empiricism of Locke and Berkeley, the philosophical assumptions of New England Puritanism with the emerging English Enlightenment. What Johnson regarded as an account of the relationship among timeless ideas was, instead, a documentation of the intellectual crosscurrents sweeping New England in the middle of the eighteenth century. [6]

5. Johnson published "An Introduction to the Study of Philosophy, exhibiting a General View of all the Arts and Sciences" in a curious London journal, *Present State of the Republic of Letters,* in 1731. In 1743 he published *An Introduction to the Study of Philosophy. . . . With a Catalogue of some of the most valuable Authors necessary to be read in order to instruct them in a thorough Knowledge of each of them. By a Gentleman Educated at Yale-College* (New London, 1743). This piece was republished in New London in the following year. In 1746 Johnson published *A New System of Morality. Ethices Elementa, or the First Principles of Moral Philosophy* (Boston, 1746) under the familiar pseudonym Aristocles. *Elementa Philosophica* (Philadelphia, 1752) was a distillation of these earlier philosophical ventures, organized under "Noetica, or Things relating to the Mind or Understanding," and "Ethica, or Things relating to the Moral Behaviour." A second edition of *Elementa Philosophica,* published in London in 1754 and edited by William Smith, is the version reprinted in *Career.*

6. A recent article by Norman O. Fiering, "President Samuel Johnson and the Circle of Knowledge," *William and Mary Quarterly,* 3rd ser. 28 (1971): 199–236, is the most sophisticated and scholarly attempt to locate Johnson's philosophy in the religio-philosophical crosscurrents of American intellectual history. Fiering emphasizes the encyclopedic tradition (i.e., Alsted, Ramus) and has some insightful comments on Johnson's peculiar blend of philosophy and religion. But he asserts that the title of metaphysician was "a much too exalted title for his [Johnson's] comparatively insignificant efforts in this area." I have tried to take Johnson's metaphysical writings seriously and to

The man most instrumental in developing Johnson's interests in a philosophy that would supplant the discredited Puritan intellectual authorities was George Berkeley. The famous philosopher and Anglican churchman arrived in Newport, Rhode Island, in 1729 and settled down for a two-year stay while he tried to iron out the details of his ill-fated scheme for a college in Bermuda. Berkeley took the opportunity provided by the serenity of his 94-acre estate to compose *Alciphron, or the Minute Philosopher,* and to share his thoughts with other colonists, preferably Anglicans, who were interested in philosophy. It was not long before Johnson was making regular visits to Newport in order "that he might converse with so extraordinary a genius and so great a scholar." Berkeley was precisely the kind of man that Johnson admired: an Englishman, an Anglican, a man with an international intellectual reputation, a serious student of philosophy who wanted to hear what Johnson was thinking. And in addition to Berkeley's personal qualities, it soon became clear to Johnson that the doctrines which Franklin would call "Berkeleyanism" had a special attraction: namely, they offered a sophisticated way to preserve the insights of revealed religion while at the same time assimilating and even extending the insights of Locke. In short, they allowed one to become an advocate of the New Learning without becoming a deist.[7]

Johnson had, in fact, been flirting with deism, the belief that man can know God solely through the use of reason without the aid of Scripture. He had probably become acquainted with the deist controversy among English theologians when he went to England for orders. Upon his return to Stratford he read Shaftesbury, Samuel Clarke, A. S. Sykes, Anthony Collins, William Wollaston, and Thomas Woolston—all English writers who rep-

---

understand them as part of the history of American philosophy. As long as Johnson was striving to lay out a formal statement of his philosophical system, to make explicit the ideas and assumptions that underlay his ethical views, he was acting as a metaphysician. Moreover, in a consideration of Johnson's formal philosophy as a flawed but serious effort to verbalize his world view, the disciplinary tools of philosophy can and should be used to clarify his place in intellectual history.

7. John Wild, *George Berkeley: A Study of His Life and Philosophy* (Cambridge, Mass., 1936), pp. 280–311; G. Dawes Hicks, *Berkeley* (London, 1932), pp. 16–18; *Career,* 1 : 24–25.

resented various shades of deism.[8] Deism has always been appealing to philosophically inclined Christians; in the eighteenth century it became a sort of halfway house for those intellectuals who had become disenchanted with dogmatic religion and fascinated by the potential of the rational faculties, yet who retained the need to believe in God. It was the fashionable religious posture in educated circles, although orthodox leaders warned that deism led inexorably toward atheism.[9]

Johnson made gestures toward deism in his sermons during the 1720s, when he invigorated his emphasis on human rationality, on those features of Scripture which were "founded not only upon plain and express revelation from God; but likewise upon the solid conclusions of reason." [10] He voiced the opinion that God was a distant deity who revealed himself most clearly in the operation of the natural world.[11] And in a letter published in the *New York Gazette,* Johnson surmised that it was "Unaccountable . . . that rational creatures should have their eyes upon this vast and stupendous fabric of heaven and earth and . . . not be struck with the strongest impressions, and most affecting, admiring, and adoring apprehensions of the deity.[12]

Like Samuel Clarke, whose theology he so much admired, Johnson argued that both reason and revelation were necessary ingredients of any religious formula. Yet Clarke's *Demonstration of the Being and Attributes of God,* while explicitly admitting that revelation was essential for salvation, did so in fifteen perfectly reasoned propositions designed to prove the rationality of Scripture. At times Johnson, like Clarke, seemed to regard the Bible as a convenient reference book to be kept available in case rational discourse broke down.

Johnson was also impressed by William Wollaston's *The Religion of Nature Delineated.* Wollaston repeated Clarke's praise

8. The book list is in *Career,* 1 : 502–08.

9. Herbert Morais, *Deism in Eighteenth Century America* (New York, 1960), provides a superficial survey of the issues. Riley, *American Philosophy,* pp. 191–322, covers the same ground with more insight. Leslie Stephen, *History of English Thought in the Eighteenth Century,* 2 vols. (New York, 1962), 1 : 74–277, is an excellent guide to the English deists.

10. *Career,* 3 : 361.

11. Johnson to Berkeley, 10 September 1729, ibid., 2 : 265.

12. Ibid., p. 255.

of divine rationality, but emphasized the fact that the most available depository of religious truth was the physical world; the scientist analyzing nature was most likely to uncover the significant divine messages. It was a view that Johnson had seen as a student at Yale, where he learned that one of the corollaries of the Ramist logic was "things are God's word in print." At Harvard, as well as Yale, Puritan boys learned that ethics was a discipline separate from theology, curricular recognition of a purely naturalistic morality.[13] Thomas Clap, scarcely a friend to either Anglicanism or deism, introduced Wollaston's *Religion of Nature* as a text at Yale without fear of heresy. After all, as orthodox a Puritan as Cotton Mather embraced the Newtonian explanation of the universe as an elucidation of the divine personality.[14] The Puritans could afford to sanction a religion of nature because they were certain that nature only confirmed the truths contained in the Bible. The danger inherent in Wollaston's efforts to naturalize God was that men would equate Jehovah with nature, forget what the Puritans remembered, and, in their rapture over the beauty and order of the Newtonian universe, identify God with a set of self-regulating laws.

The shifts in doctrine produced by moderate deists like Clarke and Wollaston were almost imperceptible. And the way in which deistic ideas built on Puritan intellectual precedents made deism appear even less intrusive to most New England intellectuals. Johnson, however, had a sensitive intellectual antenna that detected the danger deism presented at a very early stage. In 1726 he read *A Discourse on the Grounds and Reasons of the Christian Religion* by Anthony Collins, another English deist, but one less temperate in his attacks on orthodox religion.[15] Collins' treatise was an attempt to discredit the prophecies of the Old Testament, and in this effort Johnson perceived not only a defense of reasonable religion but a serious blow to all Christianity. At the same time, Johnson was engaged in a friendly theological dispute over the Trinity with Governor Burnet of

13. Miller, *The New England Mind: The Seventeenth Century*, pp. 196–97; Morison, *Harvard in the Seventeenth Century*, 1 : 250–61.

14. Mather, *The Christian Philosopher*, pp. 50–52.

15. Collins' work was published in London in 1724.

New York, in which Johnson was endeavoring to show "how the unity, God[,] could consist of father, son and spirit." [16] Gradually, over the next year, Johnson became more and more aware of how similar his approach was to that of Collins and how presumptuous both men were in attempting to explain religion in purely rational terms. He grew more conscious of the potential difficulties religious leaders might face if they counseled men to worship God by developing their minds.

Johnson announced his repentance in September of 1727 in a sermon entitled "The Necessity of Revealed Religion." He wondered how he could have believed that "Such a treacherous thing as our reason [could] be trusted in thinking upon such abstracted subjects" as God and the Trinity. Convinced now that "the improvements of the natural light could never extend very far in the reforming mankind," Johnson asserted that only "a divine and supernatural revelation" could impart to men "a just sense of God." He now saw the subversive implications of deism more clearly than before: reliance on reason in religion led inevitably to the worship of human rationality rather than divine glory; a naturalistic theology terminated in the glorification of science rather than the awareness of God's control of nature.[17]

Johnson's interest in philosophy and the inconsistencies of his metaphysical scheme must be seen against the backdrop of his religious convictions. He was eager to draw up a philosophical framework that would not be susceptible to the dangers of deism, that would not eliminate the need for God or banish him to the periphery of the universe. He wanted to construct a metaphysic that gave the deity essential and irreplaceable functions. On the other hand, this same metaphysic must incorporate the insights of the New Learning. It must be compatible with Locke's analysis of human perception and Newton's analysis of the physical world. It must, in other words, allow a man to retain his religious convictions at the same time that he abandoned the scholastic and medieval ideas on which his religion formerly depended.

16. *Career*, 1 : 22.
17. Ibid., 3 : 370–80.

Berkeley's somewhat odd philosophy proved attractive to Johnson not just because Berkeley was a flattering and accessible Anglican, but also because his philosophical system met all of Johnson's requirements. Like Jonathan Edwards, who also recognized the need to refurbish the traditional religious doctrines of New England with new philosophical principles, Johnson realized that Berkeley built his system on Lockean insights and accepted Newtonian physics, and, in addition, that his system "was attended with this vast advantage, that it not only gave men incontestible proofs of a deity, but moreover the most striking apprehensions of his constant presence with us, and of our entire dependence on him." [18] *Elementa Philosophica*, the work of a harried colonial missionary, was an attempt to employ Berkeleyan techniques to solve the dominant intellectual problem of the century: how to adjust religion to the onrush of the Enlightenment.[19]

Although George Berkeley departed New England in 1731, when it became clear that his hope for a college in Bermuda was a pipe dream, he left a permanent mark on Connecticut as well as on the mind of Samuel Johnson. Berkeley's concern for the quality of colonial education persisted after his departure and resulted in a gift of 880 books to the Yale library, vastly improving a collection already famous for its size, quality, and potential for heresy. Johnson not only encouraged Berkeley to donate the books, he also helped him transfer ownership of his Newport estate to Yale College, where the income was used to establish two scholarships for students who excelled in the classics.[20] The effect of Berkeley's philosophy was not as visible as the books or scholarship, but his idealistic doctrines were alive in Johnson's mind. There they remained for twenty-one years, while Johnson mulled them over in private and tried them out on a few of his Anglican friends. With the publication of his *Elementa*

18. Ibid., 1 : 25.
19. For a discussion of Edwards' role in the adaptation of Puritan theology to the Enlightenment, see Perry Miller, *Jonathan Edwards* (New York, 1959), esp. pp. 43–100.
20. Anne S. Pratt, *Isaac Watts and His Gift of Books to Yale* (New Haven, 1938); Hicks, *Berkeley*, p. 19.

Philosophica Johnson finally took the wraps off his philosophical speculations and revealed a metaphysical system that rested squarely on a set of simple Berkeleyan propositions.

Berkeley had the misfortune to begin his philosophy with a conception that was opposed to common sense, to the grammar of ordinary discourse, and to the epistemology of John Locke: namely, that there was no such thing as matter. When the famous English lexicographer, critic, and wit, whose name also happened to be Samuel Johnson, was first informed of this apparently absurd proposition, he believed that he had refuted Berkeley's doctrine by kicking a stone. In fact, the English Johnson only revealed that he did not understand the theory he was attempting to ridicule. For Berkeley did not say that stones, mountains, trees, and other physical objects did not exist. What he did say was that the Lockean explanation of their existence was wrong, that physical objects existed only as ideas or objects of perception.[21]

Although Locke argued that men perceive ideas, he believed that the source of these ideas was primary qualities, essences which inhered in the material object being apprehended. In the Lockean model of perception, physical objects gave off qualities that impinged on the human mind and produced ideas. And the ideas were accurate copies or representations of some material entity outside of the mind. Berkeley insisted that ideas were not copies of some material substratum. Men did not perceive matter; they perceived only ideas of matter; and it was wrong to infer that these ideas stood for anything outside the mind. Matter was simply an abstract idea, a fictitious plaything of philosophers, a distinctive name for a misleading Lockean speculation.[22]

21. A. C. Fraser, ed., *The Works of George Berkeley*, 4 vols. (Oxford, 1901), 1 : 217–20; R. A. Hoernlé, *Idealism as a Philosophical Doctrine* (London, 1924), p. 57; Hicks, *Berkeley*, pp. 73–74.

22. Although Berkeley's views changed as he grew older, many of his basic ideas are repeated throughout all his various treatises. The most systematic statement of his philosophy, however, is *A Treatise Concerning The Principles of Human Knowledge*. Unless otherwise noted, all references to Fraser's edition of his works will be to this treatise: Berkeley, *Works*, 1 : 216–20, 262, 268, 287, 297; Hicks, *Berkeley*, p. 75

Johnson defined ideas as "immediate objects of sense." [23] Anything and everything that was apprehended through the five senses was an idea. Here was the source of the verbal confusion over Berkeley's idealism. The perception of the physical world was the first premise of the system, yet, since Berkeley and Johnson insisted that perception was a mental act, they called the sense-objects ideas. There were simple ideas, such as sounds, colors, odors; then there were complex ideas, combinations of the simple ideas. The complex idea of an apple, for example, consisted of the simple ideas red, juicy, round, etc.[24] Finally, in addition to defining and distinguishing between different kinds of ideas, Johnson asserted that all ideas were passive. They did not possess a principle of self-activity. They could not cause themselves to be or force a mind to perceive them.[25] This raised a number of elementary philosophical problems, one of which was to explain where all these ideas originated.

The answer seemed obvious. Johnson reasoned that "they [ideas] must derive to us from an Almighty, intelligent active cause, exhibiting them to us, impressing our minds with them, or producing them in us." [26] God was the cause of all our ideas, but he was more than a first cause. He was the immediate cause of each and every existent idea. Whenever the human mind perceived an idea, that idea came directly from God at that instant. The human mind had "an immediate dependence upon the Deity" for every color, sound, and smell it received.[27] Moreover, God was the agent responsible for the way in which simple ideas were combined to form complex ideas. For example, Johnson did not believe "that there is any necessary connection . . . between the objects of sight and feeling; the one appears to have only the nature of a sign with regard to the other, being all alike, mere passive perception in our minds, between which there can be no relation of causality. So that the connection between them, tho' stable, is entirely arbitrary." [28] In other words, an apple

23. *Career*, 2 : 375. All philosophical references, unless otherwise noted, are to *Elementa Philosophica*, as reprinted in *Career*, vol. 2.

24. Berkeley, *Works*, 1 : 257; *Career*, 2 : 374.

25. Berkeley, *Works*, 1 : 270–71; *Career*, 2 : 375.

26. *Career*, 2 : 375.

27. Ibid., p. 374.

28. Ibid., pp. 375, 465–66.

was perceived as red and juicy because God had arbitrarily joined the simple ideas of redness and juiciness together in our minds. And finally, in addition to serving as the immediate cause of all ideas and arranging these ideas in patterns according to his will, God was the constant source of all perceived objects. He was "the continual Preserver of all His creatures, and consequently, that the moment he should cease to will the continuance of their existence, they must unavoidably cease, and drop into nothing." [29] He not only originated each idea, he also kept it alive as we perceived it, so "the existence of the whole creation is contingent and precarious, as deriving from, and dependent on, the mere will and power of God." [30]

The result was that God performed all the causal functions in Johnson's epistemology that matter performed in the Lockean perceptual scheme. The recurrent groups of sensible images came directly from the divine mind to the human mind. They were not detoured into a material substance and then passed on to us secondhand. God could not be recognized as the creator of the material world and then be denied a significant role in the operation of that world. He could not be credited with designing an elaborate universal mechanism which then ran itself. Nor was he a God who made only periodic appearances, in the form of natural interruptions like earthquakes and thunderstorms. He was not, in other words, a God who could fit easily into a deistic framework.

And in order to make it impossible for any erstwhile deist to remove God from the center of his philosophy, Johnson, following Berkeley's lead, gave God one final function. Since no ideas could exist unless they were perceived, and since certain ideas clearly existed without being perceived by human minds (i.e., the trees behind the hill), Johnson concluded that we "must infer the necessary existence of an eternal mind" to explain the continued existence of unseen physical objects.[31]

Although Johnson's enchantment with Berkeleyan idealism was due primarily to its antideistic implications, *Elementa*

29. Ibid., p. 469.
30. Ibid., p. 389. For the same doctrines in Berkeley's philosophy, see *Works*, 2 : 282, 342; also Berkeley to Johnson, 25 November 1729, *Career*, 2 : 273.
31. *Career*, 2 : 383; Berkeley, *Works*, 1 : 259.

Philosophica borrowed heavily from Berkeley's early philosophical treatises, especially *The Principles of Human Knowledge,* which had been explicitly intended as an attack on abstract ideas. Berkeley had directed his fire specifically at the idea of matter, but his insistence that perception was the sole criterion for existence cast doubt over various other philosophical speculations. Abstract ideas such as "matter" and "man" were not, Berkeley argued, ideas at all, they were only words.[32] Try as he might, Berkeley claimed that he could not have an idea of "man," only of individual men. There was nothing wrong with using the word "man" as an abstract noun, as long as one understood that it was only a word or, as Johnson defined it, "a name that shall indifferently stand for every individual of that sort."[33] This warning was aimed principally at speculative philosophers, who spun out elaborate theories about the nature of man without relating such terms to specific ideas, thereby confusing words with real things.

Berkeley's critique of abstract ideas encouraged Johnson to conclude that many of the apparent disagreements among philosophers were only the result of verbal confusion. If men could rigorously examine "what are the precise ideas or conceptions, which are combined and annexed to such a name," Johnson was certain that philosophical debates would be less acrimonious and more productive.[34] Johnson's concern for lingual clarity became so strong that in 1748 he drew up an outline which placed philology on an equal level with philosophy.[35]

There was a second empirical lesson to be drawn from Johnson's epistemology. Despite the fact that both Johnson and Berkeley denied the existence of matter, their theory was able to incorporate and clarify the discoveries of science. Johnson was unable to fathom this point at first. He was particularly afraid that Berkeley's philosophy contradicted the physical laws of Newtonian mechanics. Berkeley assured him that such was not the case.

32. Berkeley, *Works,* 1 : 7, 18, 187–89; Hicks, *Berkeley,* pp. 86–93.
33. *Career,* 2 : 401.
34. Ibid., p. 400; Johnson to Clap, 6 July 1765, ibid., pp. 343–44.
35. *Career,* 2 : 321–23.

The key was Berkeley's definition of causality. According to the Newtonian model the sun exerted a gravitational force on the earth which could be calculated by Newton's first law. When describing the process, physicists said that the mass of the sun caused the earth to move in a prescribed elliptical path. According to Berkeley, however, the sun and the motion of the earth were merely two ideas, two passive objects of the mind. When they appeared together, as they did in Newton's first law, a force was exerted on the earth, but this was only a correlation, not a causal relation. Physicists were free to posit laws which inferred one event (the orbit of the earth) from another event (the mass of the sun), as long as they remembered that their laws were purely descriptive, that real causality belonged only to God. Any scientific attempt to go beyond the sensible foundations of the natural world in order to posit cosmic explanations violated the empirical laws which science claimed to uphold and transgressed on the province of the theologians. Again, Johnson's philosophy found itself serving as a bulwark for religion.[36]

Thirdly, Johnson's acceptance of Berkeleyan epistemology had implications for education. This was a topic of particular interest to Johnson. He had observed the learning process as a tutor at Yale and was soon to become president of King's College. Moreover, he was extremely interested in the effectiveness of his own self-conscious efforts to overcome the educational disadvantages of colonial Stratford. In short, he wanted to understand how individuals learned and what learning was.

Berkeley agreed with Locke that the human mind came into the world as a tabula rasa. What it learned was what it perceived; education was simply the accumulation of ideas.[37] It followed that an individual whose mind was continually bombarded with ideas, a person who lived in an environment filled with different sights and sounds, had a distinct educational advantage over someone whose environment was less stimulating. The English Samuel Johnson was more capable of becoming a learned

36. Ibid., pp. 384–85; Berkeley, *Works*, 1 : 313–23; Hicks, *Berkeley*, p. 135; Hoernlé, *Idealism*, pp. 73–74.
37. Berkeley, *Works*, 1 : 215–19.

man than the American Samuel Johnson, because London fed his mind with a wider variety of perceptions than Stratford could ever supply. Reading was one way the American Johnson could compensate for this deficiency, since books supplied an artificial environment that intensified the influx of ideas. The value of the Berkeleyan perceptual model was that it made learning a function of environment rather than a matter of innate genius, thereby encouraging Johnson to maximize the available sources of knowledge, especially the Yale library. And this emphasis on environment increased Johnson's respect for social institutions, such as schools and families, as a means of controlling perception and inculcating mental habits that facilitated the reception of God's sensible signals.[38]

Berkeley's philosophy had the potential to become a rigorous empiricism, but that is not what either Berkeley or Johnson chose to make it. Johnson's plea for lingual precision and non-speculative science and his criticism of abstract ideas followed naturally from Berkeley's analysis of perception. But to have insisted doggedly that the perception of sensory images was all an individual could know would have led to a skeptical philosophy, much like that of David Hume, that consigned all supernatural and religious objects to some nonperceivable realm.[39] Berkeley certainly did not choose to believe that the universe was populated by a multiplicity of separate and unrelated minds, each receiving scattered impressions from an unknowable God. And neither did Johnson.

Both Berkeley and Johnson contended that an individual could be aware of the operation of his own mind. This awareness was not an idea, because one could only have ideas of objects, not of acts or processes, and because it was logically impossible for a passive idea to represent an active mind. Nevertheless, Johnson asserted that people were aware of themselves as they perceived, that these acts of self-consciousness were "of a different kind from the objects of sense and imagination, on

38. *Career*, 2 : 415, 417, 419, 423–24, 426–27.
39. Hicks, *Berkeley*, pp. 254–67.

which account I would call them notions or conceptions." [40] Berkeley had also been forced to use the word "notion" to describe knowledge of the self, although the introduction of the new term only indicated that self-knowledge did not fit into his original epistemology of sensible ideas. His admission of notions was the first evidence that Berkeley was moving away from a hard-headed empiricism toward the more speculative and abstract doctrines that he had previously criticized.[41]

Johnson moved farther and faster. He did not restrict the meaning of "notions" to self-consciousness, but expanded it to include "abstracted or spiritual objects, and the relations between our several ideas and conceptions, and the various dispositions, exertions and actions of our minds." Notions were nonsensible objects of the mind. They comprised all an individual knew of "the entire spiritual or moral world." Just as there were simple and complex ideas, Johnson distinguished between simple notions (i.e., consciousness, volition, affection) and complex notions (i.e., soul, justice, charity)." [42] The inclusion of notions in Johnson's philosophy violated the empirical standards on which his epistemology rested. Yet, while the things Johnson called notions sounded very much like abstract ideas, their presence broadened the range of experience which his philosophy could explicate. His subject matter was no longer simply the physical world. It now included nonphysical objects or spirits.

When Johnson spoke of spirits, he was not referring to angels or other ethereal residents of a supernatural world. Although much of his correspondence with Cadwallader Colden, a prominent New York Anglican, was occupied with defining the troublesome term, Colden never understood Johnson's definition.[43] In the first section of his *Elementa Philosophica*, where Johnson made his most systematic attempt to clarify his usage of the

40. *Career*, 2 : 373, 378.
41. Berkeley, *Works*, 1 : 17n, 71n, 307, 338; Hicks, *Berkeley*, pp. 145–47.
42. *Career*, 2 : 378.
43. The correspondence is in *Career*, 2 : 285–305. For Colden's philosophical position, see Riley, *American Philosophy*, pp. 329–72; also Brooke Hindle, *The Pursuit of Science in Revolutionary America* (Chapel Hill, 1956), pp. 41–50.

word, spirit is synonymous with mind. If there are perceived objects called ideas, there are beings which perceive called spirits or minds. God, the supreme mind, is one such spirit, but so are all human beings who possess a "principle of sense, intelligence and free activity, which we feel in ourselves, or feel ourselves to be." [44] This was at once a definition and a proof. According to Johnson, the distinguishing features of spirit were a "principle of sense," that is an ability to perceive, and secondly, "free activity" or the ability to act freely after one has perceived. The proof that such a thing with these characteristics existed was not physically demonstrable, since spirits were not sensible objects that could be perceived as ideas. The best evidence of their existence was personal—the feeling that each man had of their operation within himself.

Such evidence was flimsy at best. Cadwallader Colden, for example, confessed his inability to feel the operation of spirit and concluded that it did not exist. [45] Johnson had no problem in feeling the presence of spirit within himself; the difficulty arose when he tried to explain what that feeling was like to others. Critical readers of *Elementa Philosophica* who were stuck on this point had the following option: they could accept Johnson's explication of the doctrine of spirits and see where it led, or they could repudiate the doctrine and challenge the entire philosophical system of which it was a part. Those who chose to follow the thread of Johnson's argument through to the end discovered that the doctrine of spirits, like so many of Johnson's philosophical propositions, had important theological implications.

The issue at stake was freedom of the will. It was crucial to Johnson's theology, for it enabled him to argue that men were capable of making moral choices between different courses of action. The definitive statement of the deterministic position was Jonathan Edwards' *Freedom of the Will*, published in 1754. [46] While Edwards and Johnson agreed on many basic philosophical points, including the belief that God was the im-

44. *Career*, 2 : 372–73.
45. Colden to Johnson, 26 March 1744, *Career*, 2 : 287.
46. Miller, *Edwards*, pp. 235–64; Riley, *American Philosophy*, pp. 126–90.

mediate cause of every idea the human mind perceived, they disagreed over what happened as a consequence of that perception. It was at this point that Johnson broke with the Calvinistic tradition in New England theology and attempted to formulate a philosophical justification for liberal religious doctrines that had been inherent in American Puritanism from the beginning.

When God presented an idea to the human mind, Edwards contended, the mind was predisposed to perceive the idea in a certain way. Each mind might perceive the same idea differently, but each mind was conditioned to receive an idea according to what Edwards called "the state of the mind" at that moment.[47] Since Edwards believed that "the state of the mind" was determined by experience, by the forces of custom, education, and environment, he concluded that the choice and action which followed from this perception were also determined. Men were under a "moral necessity" to act in a predetermined way, just as the planets were under a natural necessity to move in predetermined orbits, because each human being was conditioned by experience to perceive ideas in a specified way, just as the planets' freedom of motion was limited by the laws of gravitation.[48]

Johnson defined freedom as "a power to act, or not to act, as we please." [49] Men were not capable of controlling what they perceived; that was a matter which lay within God's province. But men were capable of acting freely in consequence of perception; that was what Johnson meant when he said that the mind or spirit was active. It received ideas from God, but it was not preconditioned to perceive these ideas in any specific way. The "state of the mind" was the same for all persons; namely, neutrality or objectivity. The spirit was immune to all the forces of custom or habit. It was absolved from obeying all the empirical rules that governed natural bodies. When a person made a decision, he did so on the basis of the merit of the idea

---

47. Jonathan Edwards, *A Careful and Strict Enquiry into the Modern Prevailing Notions of that Freedom of the Will . . .* , ed. Ramsey (New Haven, 1957), pp. 145–48.
48. Edwards, *Freedom of the Will*, pp. 152–56; Miller, *Edwards*, pp. 254–56.
49. *Career*, 2 : 420–21.

which God provided, not on the basis of a previous inclination of the mind. Johnson was able to maintain that "in a strict philosophical sense, will and action is [sic] free and under no constraint," because he insisted that every man possessed a "self-asserting power" which he located in his spirit.[50] Although Johnson neglected to explain how the spirit was protected from all the environmental forces which, in Edwards' view, produced a perceptual bias, he was apparently willing to sacrifice philosophical clarity in order to preserve his moralistic theology.

In fact, Johnson's theological interests were best served by leaving the philosophical explication of spirits incomplete. He regarded spirits, notions, and God as nonphysical entities that could not be perceived and understood in the same fashion as ideas and the sensible world. The gap in Johnson's philosophy between these two realms of experience accurately reflected the gap Johnson believed to exist between the spiritual and physical worlds.[51] This gap was bridged in language by the use of metaphor or analogy, as when, for instance, one talked of God as light. Johnson contended that metaphorical language reflected a basic philosophical fact—men have some notion of what the nonsensible world is like because it manifests itself in sensible forms. God clothes himself in the sense data of the natural world. Human spirits reveal themselves in the activity of the physical body, or, as Johnson phrased it, "such is the law of union between our souls and our bodies, that upon our being affected and disaffected towards any object, we are sensible of certain commotions and perturbations in our blood and spirits, corresponding and in proportion to those pleasing or displeasing appearances." [52]

The tenuous nature of this philosophical connection between spiritual and physical suited a theology which maintained that good works were *some* indication of grace. In his theological tracts Johnson agreed that "all outward performances without an inward change of heart are of no account with God," but the thrust

50. Johnson's preface to John Beach's *A Second Vindication of God's Sovereign Free Grace Indeed*, in *Career*, 3 : 209; see also Colden to Johnson, 18 May 1747, ibid., 2 : 297.
51. *Career*, 2 : 382.
52. Ibid., p. 418; also pp. 402–04; Hoernlé, *Idealism*, pp. 100–01.

of his theology and philosophy encouraged men to regard worldly actions as a generally reliable index to the state of the soul. Johnson's treatment of the relationship between the spiritual and the physical merely reinforced the philosophical basis for the covenant theology of William Ames. It supported the traditional Puritan belief that a saint could demonstrate his possession of grace by visible actions of sanctity, that saints were visible. At the same time Johnson admitted that the inference from physical to spiritual could be misleading, that God and the human soul were ultimately beyond our range of comprehension, that sainthood could never be a matter of certainty.[53]

The drift away from a philosophy based on sense perception had begun with Johnson's discussion of notions; it continued through his analysis of spirits and culminated in the doctrine of archetypes. According to Johnson "there is a two-fold existence of things or ideas, one in the divine mind, and the other in created minds; the one archetypal and the other ectypal."[54] The archetype was an idea as it existed in the mind of God. The ectype was an idea as it existed in the human mind. Since God perceived everything, every idea that the human mind perceived also had an archetypal existence in the divine mind. When an idea was not being perceived by a human mind, it was being perceived in archetypal form by God, thereby maintaining its existence independent of human perception.[55] In addition, the archetype served as a model for all the ideas that comprised the sensible world. Johnson consistently defined truth as "the agreement of any thing with its standard."[56] Therefore, an idea was "said to be true with respect to the original archetype, plan or design of it, . . . so that its truth consisted in its conformity to its plan or archetype, which is its standard."[57]

53. Johnson, "A Letter to His Dissenting Parishioners," in *Career*, 3 : 22; also "A Sermon of the Spiritual Discerning of Spiritual Things," ibid., pp. 456–57; "A Discourse Concerning the Nature of God," ibid., p. 484; "A Sermon Concerning the Intellectual World," ibid., pp. 503–06; ibid., 2 : 434–35, 437–40.

54. Johnson to Berkeley, 10 September 1729, ibid., 2 : 266–67.

55. Ibid., p. 387.

56. Ibid., pp. 406–07.

57. Ibid., p. 391; see also pp. 383, 392, and "The Distinction of Truth," undated comments in ibid., pp. 248–49.

Johnson was neither consistent nor clear in his explication of archetypes. At one point in his *Elementa Philosophica* he claimed that archetypes were sensible ideas. As models for our human ideas, he reasoned, archetypes must "be ideas as well as ours; because an idea can resemble nothing but an idea." [58] This was a logical argument, but it had outrageous consequences. It meant that archetypes were theoretically capable of being perceived by the senses. It meant that somewhere out in space there existed an ideal chair, an ideal tree, and an ideal object for every idea in the world; moreover, that men could perceive these archetypes if they could ever get out far enough into the universe. At other points Johnson seemed to regard archetypes as notions rather than ideas, that is, as mental objects that were incapable of being perceived by the five senses. [59]

Most often, however, Johnson steered away from an analysis of archetypes. He seemed to believe that it was enough if men understood that archetypes were the originals, the standards against which all human ideas were measured. It was enough if men realized that their ideas resembled the archetypes in the same sense that a man was made in the image of God. Johnson handled the relationship between ideas and archetypes in the same way that he handled the relationship between the sensible and spiritual worlds; inferences could be drawn from one realm to the other, but the relationship would always remain a mystery. [60] And since archetypes comprised the content of the divine mind, it was appropriate for theological reasons that they remain beyond human comprehension.

In his later years, especially in *Siris,* Berkeley adopted an archetypal scheme similar to Johnson's. [61] As long as he remained in America, however, Berkeley discouraged Johnson's attempt to speculate on the divine mind. More specifically, he asked Johnson whether the doctrine of archetypes "doth not suppose the

58. Ibid., p. 376.
59. See above, notes 42 and 43.
60. For his strongest statement of this position, which can be found throughout *Elementa Philosophica,* see Johnson to Berkeley, 5 February 1730, ibid., p. 277.
61. The metaphysical sections of *Siris* are in *Works,* 3 : 231–99.

doctrine of abstract general ideas." [62] Berkeley consistently voiced his disapproval of Johnson's assumption that archetypes were "real things" or had any "absolute rational existence distinct from their being perceived." [63] At this stage of his philosophical career, Berkeley was still committed to strict empirical standards that ruled out those abstract concepts which were not capable of being perceived by the human mind. The doctrine of archetypes, like the doctrine of matter, was too speculative and unverifiable for him to accept. But as Berkeley grew older he gradually lowered his empirical standards and allowed himself to speculate on matters that were not susceptible to sense perception. The germ of this speculative tendency was already present in his early philosophy, most especially in his acceptance of nonsensible notions and spirits, but it was not until the publication of *Siris* in 1744 that he affirmed the existence of a transcendental realm of invisible archetypes. Although Johnson had encouraged Berkeley to accept archetypes as the capstone of Berkeleyanism many years earlier, it is impossible to know whether or not he was instrumental in causing him to adopt the position advanced in *Siris*. It is more likely that Johnson sensed what Berkeley was to discover on his own; namely, that a religious man's concern for the world of ideas led almost inevitably to speculations on the origin of these ideas in the mind of God.[64]

If Berkeley's philosophy was one source of Johnson's doctrine of archetypes, Yale College was another. The archetypal order which Johnson suggested to Berkeley in 1730 and then advocated in his *Elementa Philosophica* was identical to the scheme that he had drawn up in his *Technologia* in 1714, while he was a student at Yale College. He was disposed to read the doctrine of archetypes into Berkeley's philosophy because it was a crucial part of the Puritan intellectual tradition in which he had been raised. In his *Technologia*, Johnson had posited the existence of archetypes, which he defined as "the idea of the thing decreed

62. Berkeley to Johnson, 25 November 1729, *Career*, 2 : 274.
63. Berkeley to Johnson, 24 March 1730, ibid., p. 282.
64. For Berkeley's shift toward Platonism, see Hicks, *Berkeley*, pp. 140–41, 205–10; Wild, *George Berkeley*, pp. 66–69; J. D. Abbott, "The Place of God in Berkeley's Philosophy," *Journal of Philosophical Studies* 6 (1931): 18.

in the divine mind." [65] From William Ames, the father of Puritan theology, he had learned that these archetypes formed a pre-existent platform which was both the origin of and model for all human ideas.[66] Plato had been the first to describe the archetypal order, but it was through Ames and Puritan theology that Johnson, who later read Plato on his own, was first exposed to the Platonic tradition.[67] At Yale Johnson's mind had been trained to regard truth as contained by some ideal, existing absolutely and abstractly in cosmic space, or existing in pristine form in an earlier and uncorrupted era. In this as in other areas of his thinking, Johnson never really shook off his Puritan background.

The doctrine of archetypes gave Johnson's philosophy coherence and order. The archetypes served as fixed reference points from which to judge the accuracy and value of human ideas and transformed the potential chaos of Berkeley's world of transitory ideas into an orderly philosophical system with a stable and spiritual source. But it raised the same troublesome question that had plagued Johnson's explication of notions and spirits: how can one know anything about objects which are nonsensible? Johnson's earlier attempts to answer this question were primarily exercises in evasion, supplemented by the theological warning that such matters were best left to God. The doctrine of archetypes raised the question in its most blatant form: how could Johnson describe an archetypal order which he could not perceive with any of his senses?

It is easier to find out where Johnson got the answer to this question than to understand what the answer meant. In the neo-Platonic philosophy of Ralph Cudworth and John Norris, Johnson discovered a vision of archetypal order similar to his own. As Englishmen who represented an ill-defined philosophical school known as Cambridge Platonism, Cudworth and Norris were also beset with the problem of accounting for their awareness of spiritual, nonsensible objects. And in Malebranche and Fénelon, Johnson discovered two French philosophers who

65. *Career,* 2 : 65.
66. See above, chap. 2.
67. Johnson's early notes on Plato are in *Career,* 2 : 252–53.

had faced the same philosophical dilemma. Johnson read all four men in search of a solution. He borrowed most heavily from Norris and Fénelon, but the idea that he found most intriguing and most useful was present in the philosophy of all four. It was called the intellectual light.[68] Johnson described the intellectual light as a capacity "common to all intelligent beings . . . , a Chinese or Japanese, as well as an European or American, and an angel as well as a man: by which all at once see the same thing to be true or right in all places at the same time, and alike invariably in all times, past, present, and to come." [69] The intellectual light provided men with the ability to transcend the perception of a sense object and to "directly apply ourselves to the consideration of it [the object], both in itself, its properties and powers, and as it stands related to all other things." In terms of Johnson's philosophy, the intellectual light was the means by which men obtained knowledge of two kinds of spiritual objects. First, it was what enabled men to have notions, to be conscious of their own minds and other minds. Secondly, it was the way men knew the archetypes.[70]

Strictly speaking, the intellectual light was not a separate human faculty over which men had control. Johnson emphasized that "our minds are as passive to this intellectual light as they are to sensible light." It was a power that depended entirely on "the universal presence and action of the deity, or a

68. The texts Johnson read and cited most often were: Ralph Cudworth, *The True Intellectual System of the Universe* (London, 1678); John Norris, *An Essay Towards the Theory of the Ideal of Intelligible World* (London, 1722); François de la Fénelon, *A Demonstration of the Existence and Attributes of God* (London, 1724). Professor Murray Murphey has pointed out stylistic and lingual similarities between Johnson and Fénelon, whom Johnson referred to as the Archbishop of Cambray. Johnson does not include any of Malebranche's works in his reading list, although he does cite him in *Elementa Philosophica*. He might have picked up Malebranche through Norris, who closely followed the French philosopher. See also John Muirhead, *The Platonic Tradition in Anglo-Saxon Philosophy* (London, 1931), chaps. 1–4. See Cragg, *From Puritanism to the Age of Reason*, for Cambridge Platonism. For Johnson's view, see Johnson to Berkeley, Jr., 10 December 1756, *Career*, 2 : 337–39. For the influences of Platonism on Berkeley, see Hicks, *Berkeley*, pp. 220–38, and Wild, *George Berkeley*, pp. 311–19.

69. *Career*, 2 : 379.

70. Ibid., pp. 379–80.

perceptual communication with the great father of lights, or rather his eternal word and spirit." In this sense the intellectual light was God's way of granting his creatures intuitive knowledge of eternal truth by bridging the gap that separated the sensible from the spiritual world. Like the infusion of grace, it depended wholly on God. The divine agent became the central figure in Johnson's philosophy, not only because he was the cause of every idea that men perceived, but also because he was directly responsible for providing men with a glimpse into the archetypes. Since the intellectual light was the result of a divine act, however, it only explained man's knowledge of the supernatural in supernatural terms. Johnson admitted that he could only describe the intellectual light by means of a metaphor: it was like the light of the sun. This preserved the mystery of the divine and satisfied Johnson's theological requirements, but it also left him with the same philosophical question that the intellectual light was supposed to answer.

In 1746 Johnson had published *A System of Morality*, in which he attempted to set out his views on ethics.[71] The final section of his *Elementa Philosophica* consisted simply of a revised version of this earlier piece, tacked on to his discussion of Berkeleyan metaphysics and epistemology. Since Johnson made little effort to connect the earlier and later works, his comments on ethics did not emerge naturally out of the metaphysical propositions that preceded them. The two sections were definitely the work of a man with the same philosophical perspective, but Johnson's discussion of ethics lacked the rigor and precision that characterized his analysis of ideas. At their worst, his comments on ethics were a string of disjointed homilies that compromised serious moral problems by positing solutions at such a general level that they meant nothing. At its best, Johnson's ethics fused his philosophical and religious beliefs to sanction the traditional dictates of Christian morality.

In the search for the good, Johnson discovered that God had so arranged the universe that seemingly disparate values coin-

71. The original treatise is in the Johnson MSS. The revised version is in *Career*, 2 : 442–515.

cided. On the one hand, since God was "a most kind and benevolent Being," he undoubtedly created men "with a design that they might be, in some good degree, happy." Happiness, Johnson reasoned, was clearly the end for which man was made. On the other hand, the Bible showed that "God made all things for his own glory." This apparent discrepancy between human happiness and divine glory did not bother Johnson, because he believed that the greatest happiness accrued to those persons who honored God. If their reward was not provided in this world, as it sometimes was not, then God would provide it in the next. Therefore, "the glory of God, and our happiness . . . come in effect to one and the same thing." [72]

Similarly, those persons concerned with the distinction between acting truthfully and acting ethically need not worry, because the model for both kinds of action was the same: namely, the archetypes. Truth and goodness were "only the same thing under diverse conditions," for each had a common source in the mind of God.[73] Finally, if truth and goodness were identical, then the intellectual light, which provided intuitive truth, also provided knowledge of what was good. Men did not have a separate moral sense, as Hutcheson and Shaftsbury had suggested, but God did give them sudden exposures to the moral order, which produced "a quick and almost intuitive sense of right and wrong." [74]

By tracing ethical values back to God and making man's awareness of the good dependent on divine intervention in the form of the intellectual light, Johnson moored his system of ethics in the same mysterious harbor as his metaphysics—the mind of God. In this sense his ethics, like his metaphysics, buttressed traditional religion and countered the secular morality of the deists in much the same way as the religio-philosophical works of Englishmen like William Law and Joseph Butler. On the other hand, by blurring the distinction between religion and philosophy Johnson unwittingly paved the way for secular moralists of the future. After all, *Elementa Philosophica* enjoined

72. Ibid., pp. 449–51.
73. Ibid., pp. 390–91, 448.
74. Ibid., pp. 450–51.

men to act morally in imitation of the archetypal standards. Johnson did not hold out threats of eternal punishment as a means of enforcing his system of ethics. Men were advised to be virtuous, not because hell awaited the non-virtuous, but because the life of virtue was in accord with the archetypes. This was a philosophical sanction for moral behavior that such deists as Franklin and Jefferson could accept, once they had jettisoned the notion that God was the source of the archetypes.

Although Franklin did not know what to do with the printed but unsold copies of *Elementa Philosophica*, Johnson was hopeful that the public might, by a dramatic turnabout, buy up the first edition, and demand a second. He therefore sent Franklin an extensive list of errata, to be annexed to future editions. The public demand never materialized, and Johnson was forced to face the fact that, as a philosopher, he was a popular failure.

Historians of philosophy have tended to agree with Johnson's contemporaries.[75] *Elementa Philosophica* is not brilliant or sophisticated. It is riddled with imprecision and inconsistency, a derivative work that often mimics Berkeley, a good example of the intellectual disarray of American colonial philosophy. And yet it is a significant historical document precisely because of its deficiencies. For *Elementa Philosophica* is the work of a mind attempting to serve several masters and incapable of synthesizing their various directives into a coherent whole. Johnson's analysis of the sensible world was rigorous, avoided theological mysticism, satisfied the highest empirical standards, and indicated his ability to assimilate the refined epistemological doctrines of the emerging British empiricists. His analysis of spirits and archetypes abandoned philosophical rigor in favor of religious mystery, conserved selected features of the old Puritan metaphysic, borrowed from the Cambridge Platonists—all to guarantee the primacy of God. The fundamental division in *Elementa Philosophica*, the division that made logical consistency impossible, was the division between the critical philosopher and the devout believer. Johnson was both.

75. See above, n. 2.

9

The King's College Controversy

Benjamin Franklin never worried about the inconsistencies of Johnson's metaphysics. His problem with *Elementa Philosophica* was more fundamental; it lost his publishing house money. But he had loftier considerations on his mind than money. Franklin wanted Johnson to come down to Pennsylvania to head the new college that was just getting under way in Philadelphia. Whether or not *Elementa Philosophica* made a profit, its publication evidenced Franklin's admiration for Johnson's scholarship and provided the opportunity for the wily Franklin to maintain contact with a likely candidate for the college presidency. Franklin told Johnson what he wanted to hear: that his "name for learning would give it [the college] a reputation," that his son, William, could be appointed a tutor, that the trustees were willing to pay his expenses if he would visit Philadelphia, that he was the trustees' first choice and, finally, that the job carried a handsome annual salary of £100 sterling.[1]

Johnson's refusal might have been mistaken for a cautious acceptance. It was customary for a prospective college president to belittle his qualifications, to exhibit the proper disdain for the turbulence of college life, to plead old age and ill health, and then acknowledge the wisdom of the officials who insisted that he was the only man for the job. After offering the familiar reasons for his rejection of Franklin's offer, Johnson discovered that Franklin still expected him to move his family and belongings to Philadelphia any day. Finally, after *Elementa Philosophica*

1. Franklin to Johnson, 9 August 1750; Franklin to Johnson, 13 September 1750, *Career*, 1 : 140–43.

was safely in press, Johnson made it clear that he meant what he said. He did not want the job.[2]

The chief reasons he gave for remaining in Stratford were not fabrications. In October of 1752 he celebrated his fifty-sixth birthday. His commitment to reading and study had prohibited regular exercise, so he had entered middle age badly overweight. A leg injury suffered in 1747 had not healed properly and gave him recurrent trouble throughout the rest of his life, especially when the weather was damp. His handwriting, once a model of neatness and legibility, began to degenerate around 1750 at the same time that he complained of cramps in his right arm. Within two years his letters were barely decipherable and he was sometimes forced to postpone replies to correspondents for weeks at a time. His legs periodically broke out in sores, "little pustles daily rising, breaking and rising." The sedate environment of Stratford put a minimum of strain on these minor ailments. If he accepted the presidency of the Academy at Philadelphia, he would not only be expected to be more active, he would also be more exposed to the dangers of smallpox, the disease which had killed many of Johnson's Anglican friends and disciples and would soon kill the newly named president of the College of New Jersey, Jonathan Edwards. All in all, Philadelphia did not seem the place for an aging and somewhat fragile philosopher.[3]

Nevertheless, the debilities of middle age did not lessen Johnson's involvement in colonial education. In 1753 he argued with Thomas Clap, president of Yale, over the treatment of Anglican students at his alma mater. Clap, who saw himself as a defender of the Puritan principles on which Yale was founded, had a reputation for a kind of zeal that verged on dogmatism.[4] In 1745 he

2. Johnson to Franklin, January 1752, ibid., pp. 155–56.

3. This paragraph is based on many different kinds of evidence, some of it indirect. The painting of Johnson in the Columbiana Room of the Columbia University Library shows him to be fat. Chandler referred to him as "considerably corpulent" in *Career*, 1 : 54. The deterioration of the handwriting can be seen by comparing manuscripts from the late 1740s with documents written five years later. For a discussion of his leg problem, see S. Johnson to W. S. Johnson, 24 November 1769, *Career*, 1 : 463.

4. Louis L. Tucker, *Puritan Protagonist: President Thomas Clap of Yale College* (Chapel Hill, 1962), offers the most recent and fullest secondary account of Clap's life.

had obtained a new college charter that increased his presidential power at the expense of that of the trustees of the Yale Corporation. He had then launched a campaign to consolidate his control and strengthen Yale's image as a pillar of Puritan orthodoxy. Unfortunately for Clap, Yale's trustees and students were divided over the question of what orthodoxy had come to mean. In the midst of a protracted squabble between Old and New Light factions, in which Clap managed to alienate both sides, students were ordered to attend church services in the college hall, where Clap could supervise religious instruction. Ebenezer Punderson requested that his two Anglican sons be excused from this new requirement and allowed to attend Sunday worship in the recently constructed Anglican church, but Clap would have none of it. All students, said Clap, must "attend worship in one place." Anglican parents were free to send their sons to Yale, but once admitted, all students were obliged to uphold the doctrines of Puritan orthodoxy as Clap interpreted them.[5]

Johnson responded with an indignant and outspoken defense of religious toleration. Admitting that Yale's Corporation had the right to enact laws that regulated college life, he wondered "whether there ought of right to be any such law in your college [that] . . . forbids the liberty we contend for?" [6] He argued that any law which infringed a student's religious principles was null and void, because it violated a superior English law, the Act of Toleration. And then, in the most explicit terms in which he ever phrased the problem, Johnson articulated his conception of the moral underpinning of liberal legislation:

> If, indeed, with *Hobbs*, [*sic*] etc., you thought power to do anything would give a right to it, then your argument from possession is just; but I trust that it is not your tenet. The question then is, first, *Whether it be right in itself for any society, however voluntary or independent to require as a condition of enjoying the privileges of it (and especially so great a privilege as that of public education), that any person*

5. Thomas Clap, *The Religious Constitution of Colleges* . . . (New London, 1754), pp. 4, 15; also Clap to Johnson, 30 January 1754, *Career*, 1 : 174–76.
6. Johnson to Clap, 5 February 1754, *Career*, 1 : 177.

that is free of that society, or born in it, should be obliged to act contrary to his conscience, or, to what he is really persuaded is his duty in matters of religion, supposing that his religious principles be not in their nature subversive of the state? [7]

Clap was astonished that Johnson chose to base his defense of Anglican rights on the principle of liberty of conscience. In so doing, Clap wrote, "you have undertaken to state the case . . . upon a foundation very different" from other Anglican critics.[8] Once again, Johnson had borrowed from the liberal heritage of English Puritanism to defend the minority rights of colonial Anglicans.

The clash with Clap was another episode in Johnson's fight to further the cause of the Anglican churches in Connecticut. But it was also an indication of Johnson's increasing involvement in college affairs. He kept the pressure on Yale, threatening an exposure of the college's somewhat tenuous legality.[9] And when the Anglican students were slow to take advantage of the right to attend their own services, a right that Clap grudgingly conceded in 1754, Johnson exploded: "What! Are they so mean and abject that having been so long under restraint, they now are come even to hug their chains, and when the prisons are set open, are they of so low and base a spirit as not to embrace or even accept of liberty?" [10]

By the spring of 1754 Johnson's concern for the religious freedom of Anglican students at Yale had to compete with his growing interest in a projected college in New York City. As early as 1749, long before Franklin's offer of the Philadelphia job, Johnson had confided to Bishop Berkeley that he had his eyes on the "College of New York." [11] And in 1752 an anonymous contributor to the *New York Mercury* had recommended Johnson as

7. Johnson to Clap, 19 February 1754, ibid., pp. 181–82.
8. Clap to Johnson, 30 January 1754, ibid., p. 175.
9. Louis L. Tucker, "The Church of England and Religious Liberty at Pre-Revolutionary Yale," *William and Mary Quarterly*, 3rd ser., 17 (1960): 314–28, emphasizes Johnson's threats as the determining factor in the liberalization of Clap's policies.
10. S. Johnson to W. S. Johnson, June 1754, *Career*, 1 : 191.
11. Johnson to Berkeley, 10 September 1750, ibid., pp. 135–36.

first president of the proposed college.[12] In 1746 and 1748 the New York legislature had authorized public lotteries "for Advancement of Learning" and in 1751 had vested the resulting £3,443 in a board of temporary trustees empowered to lend the money at interest and receive proposals for the site of a college. Johnson's Anglican friends in New York City had kept him posted on all these developments.[13]

These developments were also bandied about in the press. William Livingston wanted New York to have a "publick seminary of Learning" in order that the colony's cultural and intellectual life might match her commercial growth.[14] Another pamphleteer surmised that a college would keep young men off the streets and discourage "the practices of breaking windows and wresting off knockers." [15] But it was William Smith who offered the most far-reaching proposals and gave form to the different points of view that were soon to divide the people of New York.

Smith, like Johnson, was an Anglican and a somewhat eclectic but serious scholar. (He was soon to accept the job that Johnson had rejected and become provost of the Philadelphia Academy.)[16] He assumed that future colonial colleges would be public rather than private, for he felt that there were not enough interested and wealthy colonists to support private academic institutions. Although the funds raised by the lotteries were under the control

12. *New York Mercury,* 6 November 1752.

13. *The Colonial Laws of New York,* 5 vols. (Albany, 1894), 3 : 609–16, 675–85, 842–44. See also John B. Langstaff, "Anglican Origins of Columbia University," *Historical Magazine of the Protestant Episcopal Church* 9 (1940): 257–66. The best history of Columbia is by John Howard Van Amringe, et al., *A History of Columbia University* (New York, 1904).

14. William Livingston, *Some Serious Thoughts on the Design of Erecting a College in New York* (New York, 1749), p. 2. Available only at Columbia University Library.

15. Hippocrates Mithridate, *Some Serious Thoughts on the Design of Erecting a College in the Province of New York* (New York, 1749), p. 13.

16. Albert F. Gegenheimer, *William Smith, Educator and Churchman, 1727–1803* (Philadelphia, 1943). I am sad to report that there were four men with the name William Smith active in the King's College controversy. They will be identified as follows: William Smith, the Scottish Anglican and future provost of the Philadelphia Academy; William Smith, Sr., father of the author of the *History of New York;* William Smith, Jr., author of the *History of New York* and member of the New York triumvirate; William Peartree Smith, Yale 1742, also a member of the triumvirate.

of the Assembly, Smith insisted that the New York college could be chartered only by the king through his representative, the governor, to whom the trustees would be answerable. Such a college would serve the entire community by offering a broad curriculum in literature, mathematics, and the sciences and would prepare students for a variety of professions in addition to the ministry. He was particularly critical of colleges like Clap's Yale, which had a totally religious vision of their function and a narrow sectarian base.[17]

And yet, immediately after he had denounced sectarianism, Smith articulated a decidedly Anglican set of policies. The college in New York must reflect the fact that the Anglican Church was established in New York. It must have an Anglican president, and here Smith specifically suggested Johnson, and it must use some form of the Anglican liturgy as the basis for public prayers.[18] Somehow, the college was to be nonsectarian and Anglican at the same time. It was to be supported financially by all the public, but it was to serve one portion of the public more fully than the rest. It was to have a broad, secular curriculum, but a partisan religious atmosphere.

Smith's inconsistent proposals not only foreshadowed some of the future points of contention in the controversy over King's College (later Columbia University), they also reflected the confused state of colonial education. The Great Awakening had fostered the development of numerous sects no longer satisfied with the orthodox Puritan churches. Known as the New Lights in New England and the New Side in the middle colonies, these sects began to demand separate educational facilities for their future ministers and followers. The New Side Presbyterians founded the College of New Jersey at Princeton (1746). Evangelical Baptists established Brown (1764). The followers of Theodore Frelinghuysen in the Dutch Reformed Church set up Queens (1766) later renamed Rutgers. And Dartmouth (1769) grew out of

17. William Smith, *Some Thoughts on Education* . . . (New York, 1752), and *A General Idea of the College of Mirania* (New York, 1753).
18. William Smith, *Mirania*, pp. 84–86; See also Smith's comments in the *New York Mercury*, 6 November 1752, and the *New York Gazette or Weekly Post-Boy*, 6 November 1752.

an Indian missionary school under the control of New Light Congregationalists. Ironically, the Awakening, which based its appeal on an emotional experience of conversion and minimized the importance of education (as opposed to conversion) in the ministry, produced a revitalized concern for colonial education and a new crop of colleges.[19] While the initial thrust of these new colleges was sectarian, none of the founders went as far toward sectarianism as Clap did at Yale. Ultimately, the schismatic tendencies of the Awakening produced sectarian antagonisms so profound that colleges were eventually forced to follow a policy of toleration in order to avoid doctrinal disputes that threatened their stability. Moreover, sectarianism was forced to compete with a growing secularization, evident in the broadening of curricula to include more science and a modification of theology, as well as the dramatic increase in the number of college graduates who went into professions other than the ministry.[20]

King's College (1754) was founded in the midst of this clash between sectarianism and secularization. In addition, despite William Smith's confidence that the governor alone had the power to sanction a college, New York had a long history of conflict over the question of where the governor's prerogative ended and the Assembly's power began.[21]

There were, then, a number of fundamental questions about the direction of colonial education that were being debated at the time when King's was getting underway: what was the purpose of a college? who should control it? to what extent were religion and learning related? King's College showed every sign of be-

19. Gaustad, *The Great Awakening in New England*, chap. 7; Hofstadter and Metzger, *The Development of Academic Freedom in the United States* (New York, 1955), pp. 114–34; Rudolph, *The American College and University: A History* (New York, 1962), pp. 13–16.
20. Louis F. Snow, *The College Curriculum in the United States* (n.p., 1907), pp. 59–60; Hornberger, *Scientific Thought in the American Colleges*, pp. 23–28. Bailey B. Burritt traces graduate professions in *Professional Distribution of College and University Graduates* (Washington, 1912), pp. 74–75.
21. Leonard Labaree, *Royal Government in America* (New York, 1958), pp. 176, 287–88; also William Smith, Jr., *History of the Late Province of New York, from Its Discovery to 1762* (New York, 1829–30), p. 171.

coming embroiled in an extended controversy over these issues. For a man like Johnson, who had an aversion to discord, the New York situation must not have appeared totally inviting. Moreover, all the reasons Johnson had given for snubbing the trustees at Philadelphia were equally applicable to King's. Nevertheless, Johnson saw certain unique and promising features in the New York scene, features which drew him closer and closer to an outright acceptance of the college presidency.

One thing he saw was a cosmopolitan city. Then, as now, New York City was a place about which an observer could say anything without qualification, and every observation had some truth. One traveler reported that the city was an assemblage of "different nations, different languages and different religions" and that "it is almost impossible to give them any precise or determinate character." [22] Originally founded as part of a Dutch colony, New York City had been transformed into a commercial and cultural stronghold of the British empire. The several newspapers reported the arrivals of ships loaded with cargoes of black slaves or English manufactured goods. English styles were imported too. A contemporary historian of the colony remarked that "In the city of New York . . . we follow the London fashion, though by the time we adopt them, they become disused in England." [23] Vestiges of the Dutch origin remained, however, and by the middle of the eighteenth century there was still enough Dutch spoken to cause problems for sheriffs in search of jurors. The ethnic pluralism of the city was further enhanced by the presence of a large black slave population, which was regarded with some fear by the white citizenry because of serious slave uprisings that had occurred in the city in 1712 and 1741. A survey in 1749 reported the ratio of whites to blacks at five to one. [24]

The area of the city was confined to the present borough of Manhattan, and the contemporary historian William Smith, Jr.,

22. Andrew Burnaby, *Travels Through the Middle Settlements of North America in the Years 1759 and 1760* (New York, 1904), p. 117.

23. William Smith, Jr., *History of New York*, p. 270.

24. Ibid., p. 265; E. B. O'Callaghan, *The Documentary History of the State of New York*, 9 vols. (Albany, 1849–51), 1 : 695.

estimated that the city was "a mile in length and not above half that in width." One of the most impressive of the approximately 2500 buildings was Trinity Church, the chief place of worship for the Anglicans, who comprised 10 to 20 percent of the colony's population but were concentrated in the city. Trinity was 148 feet long and 72 feet wide; it had a towering steeple 175 feet in height. On some Sundays over 2000 people crowded into the pews. The church was "ornamented beyond any other place of public worship," with an organ, huge pillars topped with angels' wings, and the coats-of-arms of its benefactors hung on the walls. A monument to the considerable wealth of the Anglican residents of the city, it dwarfed the Presbyterian and Dutch Reformed churches, the two dominant sects in terms of numbers, as well as the single Jewish synagogue.[25]

Of the twenty-seven representatives in the colonial Assembly, six came from the city, where the colonial government held its regular sessions. The political history of the colony, like that of the city, was a morass of conflicting economic interests, family rivalries, religious tensions, and ethnic divisions. On the one hand there was a long tradition of friction between the royally appointed governor and the popularly elected members of the Assembly; the Assembly had successfully resisted demands to provide a permanent revenue for the governor's salary and used its control of money bills to subvert the instructions of each new royal appointee. On the other hand there was an equally strong tradition of party rivalry within the Assembly that usually took the form of two political factions organized around powerful and wealthy men or families that contended vigorously for popular support.[26]

25. William Smith, Jr., *History of New York*, pp. 252–53; Milton M. Klein, "The Cultural Tyros of Colonial New York," *South Atlantic Quarterly* 64 (1967): 218–32.

26. The best and most recent account of New York politics is by Stanley Katz, *Newcastle's New York: Anglo-American Politics, 1732–1753* (Cambridge, Mass., 1968). Carl Becker's classic, *The History of Political Parties in the Province of New York, 1760–1776* (Madison, 1909) is still useful. Two articles by Milton M. Klein, "Democracy and Politics in Colonial New York," *New York History* 40 (1959): 221–46, and "Politics and Personalities in Colonial New York," *New York History* 47 (1966): 13–16, are excellent summaries of current historical opinion.

In sum, the city where King's College was to be located was a
melange of cultural and ethnic patterns, a jumble of lingual differences, religious sects, family feuds, and political wars. New
York had always been as diverse as Connecticut was becoming. If
one was looking for the polar opposite of Stratford and the "land
of steady habits," the city and colony of New York were it.

Another thing that Johnson noticed when he surveyed the
New York scene was the impressive assemblage of Anglican talent
that was pushing for the college's establishment and encouraging
him to take on the presidency. Johnson had never met William
Smith, but he knew his reputation as a brilliant Scotsman from
the University of Aberdeen who was eager to throw his talent
into the battle for colonial Anglicanism. Samuel Seabury, Jr.,
another young Anglican hope who was assisting Smith in writing
weekly articles in the *New York Mercury,* was the son of one of
Johnson's earliest converts.[27] Samuel Auchmuty was one of the
most prominent Anglican clergy in the city and an outspoken
supporter of Johnson's candidacy.[28] The pastor of Trinity Church,
Henry Barclay, was a Yale graduate and an old friend of Johnson's; he sent a steady stream of letters to Stratford informing him
of the trustees' plans.[29] Finally, Benjamin Nicoll, Johnson's stepson, was a prominent New York lawyer and active Anglican layman who also happened to be a trustee of the lottery funds for the
proposed college.[30]

There is reason to believe that Johnson's negotiations with
Franklin over the Philadelphia job were a ploy, not only to assure
publication of *Elementa Philosophica,* but also to enhance his
appeal to the King's College governors. Cadwallader Colden,
though skeptical about Johnson's metaphysics, began to champion
his prowess as an educator soon after the New York legislature
approved the lottery bill in 1746. Johnson encouraged Colden's

27. E. E. Beardsley, *Life and Correspondence of the Right Reverend Samuel
Seabury, D.D.* (Cambridge, Mass., 1881), 8–9.

28. William Smith to Johnson, 23 July 1753, *Career,* 4 : 4–5, describes
Auchmuty.

29. Johnson to Frances Astry, 30 October 1752, *Career,* 1 : 160–61, gives
Barclay's background; Barclay to Johnson, December [1753], *Career,* 4 : 5–6.

30. Correspondence between Johnson and Nicoll, whom Johnson referred to
as "Benny," is scattered throughout *Career,* vols. 1 and 4.

1. Samuel Johnson, painted in the 1730s by John Smibert, an artist who had accompanied Bishop Berkeley to America. The original hangs in the Trustees' Room, Columbia University.

2. "Southeast View of the City of New York," ca. 1763. Drawn on the spot by Captain Thomas Howdell of the Royal Artillery. Engraved by P. Chanot. This so-called "palm tree print" shows the college building, completed in 1760, and Trinity Church just beyond.

3. "View of Columbia College in the City of New York," taken from an engraving by Sidney L. Smith. The engraving depicts the first college building at King's College, constructed in 1760.

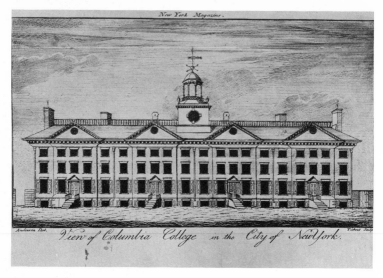

4. Sketch by E. P. Chrystie which depicts Samuel Johnson and his eight students as they probably appeared on the morning of the first class at King's College on July 17, 1754. It also shows Trinity Church and the vestry house where classes were held.

5. Johnson teaching his first class at King's College as recreated by Howard Pyle. The sketch first appeared in *Harper's Magazine*, October 1884.

6. Samuel Johnson. The artist and the date are unknown, but the painting was probably done about the time Johnson assumed the presidency of King's College. It now hangs in the King's College Room, Columbia University.

efforts, saying he was "glad that you are at length resolved to have
a college in your Government . . . I heartily wish success to it, I
shall willingly correspond with you in any thing in my little
power that may tend to promote it." At this same time some of
the leading families in New York, including the DeLanceys, the
Stuyvesants, and the Van Cortlandts, began to send their children
to Stratford for precollege training under Johnson. They had
heard of his intellectual prowess from Colden; they knew Charity
Johnson to be descended from one of the finest New York families.
Now, in 1753, this fine man with whom their sons were studying
was about to be snatched away by a rival college in Pennsylvania
before King's College could make him an offer. The King's
trustees were urged to speed up their deliberations on presidential candidates. Word reached Johnson in January of 1754:
"At a meeting of the said trustees the 22nd of November last, they
unanimously made choice of you for the chief master or head of
our seminary and agreed to offer you the sum of 250 pounds this
currency." [31] A few days earlier he had received a letter from the
vestry of Trinity Church, offering him the job of assistant minister
as a supplement to the college presidency, with an additional
annual salary of £150.[32] He waited two weeks, then wrote an
equivocal but revealing response, again dredging up the problems
posed by his age and health. Deleted from the final draft of the
letter was the following sentence: "And I would humbly suggest
considering the great expense of house rent, whether it would
not be advisable to put up a house for the President with as
much dispatch as may be?" [33] Although the trustees did not know
it, Johnson was eager to take the job.

By January of 1754 developments in New York had caused
Johnson to regard the King's College job as a unique opportunity
to advance the cause of Anglicanism. First, there was the governor. A new royal appointee, Sir Danvers Osborn, had arrived
in the autumn of 1753. Osborn was an Anglican who also carried
a new set of instructions that condemned the Assembly for "their

31. William Livingston and Trustees to Johnson, 7 January 1754, *Career*,
4 : 7.
32. Extract from the Minutes of the Vestry of Trinity Church, New York,
20 December 1753, *Career*, 1 : 172–73.
33. Johnson to Livingston and Trustees, 17 January 1754, *Career*, 4 : 8–9.

neglect of, and the contempt they have shown to, our Royal
Commission" and called for the immediate approval of a permanent gubernatorial revenue that would be "indefinite and
without limitation." (Horace Walpole had described the instructions as "better calculated for the latitude of Mexico and for a
Spanish tribunal than for a free rich British settlement.") Although Osborn was so confounded by the perplexities of New
York politics that he committed suicide a few days after his
arrival, James DeLancey, the lieutenant governor, was a local
Anglican leader who let it be known that he intended to carry out
Osborn's instructions and reassert the governor's authority over
the Assembly. Henry Barclay took note of DeLancey's Anglicanism
and surmised that the governor's power and Anglican influence
would rise together. Unlike Connecticut, where the governor was
traditionally hostile to episcopacy, in New York the Anglicans
could count on his support.[34]

Second, the Anglican churches in the New York area enjoyed
preferential treatment. Under the terms of the Ministry Act of
1693 the Anglican pastors in four surrounding counties were supported by public taxes. The law stipulated that tax money would
be used to support "a good sufficient Protestant minister," but
royal governors had established the policy of excluding non-
Anglicans.[35] As a result, Trinity Church paid its minister out of
public taxes while members of the Presbyterian and Dutch
churches were forced to support their clergy by private collections. In fact, the New York Presbyterians were in exactly the
same position as the Anglicans in Connecticut. It must have
seemed like an act of divine retribution to Johnson, who had
complained of the Connecticut tax laws for thirty years, when he
realized that the salary he would receive from Trinity Church
would come, in part, from Presbyterian pockets.

34. The best primary account of the Osborn-DeLancey affair is in the
New York Mercury, 22 October and 5, 12 November 1753.
35. Hugh Hastings, ed., *Ecclesiastical Records of the State of New York*, 7
vols. (Albany, 1901–16), 5 : 3220; R. T. Henshaw, "The New Ministry Act of
1693," *Historical Magazine of the Protestant Episcopal Church* 2 (1933): 199–
204. See also *Colonial Records of New York*, 1 : 328–31, and Milton M. Klein,
"Church, State and Education: Testing the Issue in Colonial New York,"
New York History 45 (1964): 291–303.

Third, the most likely site for the proposed college had been contributed by the Anglicans. On March 5, 1752, the vestry of Trinity Church had offered the trustees part of King's Farm, a thirty-two acre plot they had received from the crown in 1705.[36] Although the vestrymen made the offer without stipulation, they eventually conceded that the gift was "a means of obtaining some Priviledges to the Church." [37] In the course of the debate it would become clear that the King's Farm gift was contingent on a guarantee that the college president always be an Anglican and the college prayers be taken from the Anglican liturgy.

And finally, the temporary board of trustees appointed in 1751 to administer the lottery funds and decide on the King's Farm site was dominated by Anglicans. Of the ten lottery trustees, seven were Anglicans. William Livingston was the lone Presbyterian member. The remaining positions were filled by two members of the Dutch Reformed church.[38] This in a colony which, like Connecticut, had an Anglican population that comprised only a fraction of the whole.

The imbalance of the board was, however, an accurate reflection of a mounting Anglican desire to get a college of their own. Harvard and Yale had always been Puritan strongholds. The success of the New Side Presbyterians in establishing the college of New Jersey only heightened Anglican eagerness for their own school. Until 1753 Johnson had criticized the sectarian policies of the Puritan colleges, especially Yale. The thrust of his arguments had been for liberalization of the existent Puritan institutions rather than the establishment of a separate Anglican college. But by the summer of 1753 he was referring to King's as "a Seminary of the Church" and "our college" and plotting with Barclay to get a college charter that assured Anglican domination. Although he continued to insist that any "Episcopal College" must grant "a free and generous toleration of other denomina-

36. E. B. O'Callaghan, ed., *Documents Relative to the Colonial History of the State of New York,* 15 vols. (Albany, 1853–87), 4 : 327, 335, 393, 434, 463, 527.
37. Vestry of Trinity Church to Secretary, 3 November 1755, S.P.G. MSS, B, 315; Morgan Dix, *A History of the Parish of Trinity Church in the City of New York,* 4 vols. (New York, 1898), 1 : 141–45.
38. *The Colonial Laws of New York,* 3 : 842–44.

tions," he wanted to be president of a college in which the Anglicans made the rules.[39] New York presented the Anglicans with an opportunity to manipulate the political machinery in a way that was impossible in Connecticut. He was not going to make the mistake of repeating Clap's intolerant policies, but neither was he going to throw away the advantages accumulated by zealous Anglican advocates in New York.

These advantages had not only been won, they had been given intellectual reinforcement during the summer and fall of 1753. William Smith was apparently the moving force in a campaign to justify Anglican control of King's in the pages of the *New York Mercury*, which was owned by a prominent Anglican, Hugh Gaine. Johnson, along with Barclay, Seabury, and Thomas Wetmore, was asked to draft a few essays.[40] Whether or not he contributed to the weekly series is uncertain. (Most of the essays were signed X Y Z.) These articles in the *Mercury* presented a clear picture of Anglican goals in New York and, incidentally, provided the most articulate statement of Anglican ideas about government and education that had yet appeared in the colonies.

The authors set out to discredit several notions about social order. They were particularly opposed to any political program based on the doctrine of natural rights. All arguments that depended on a Lockean conception of a state of nature were products of a "modern Imaginus," [41] or were "effluviums . . . too senseless to need curious and strict examination." [42] Quoting David Hume as their primary political authority, the Anglican writers insisted that men had always lived in a social state. The state of nature was a piece of fiction. There never existed a "natural man" who surrendered certain freedoms in return for security against encroachments by other men. Yet the Anglicans agreed that there had always been a social division between governors and governed that was based on the manner in which God distributed human talent. Scripture showed that "kings

39. Johnson to Archbishop of Canterbury, 25 June 1753, *Career*, 4 : 3.
40. William Smith to Johnson [May 1753?], *Career*, 1 : 169.
41. *New York Mercury*, 27 August 1753.
42. Ibid., 10 September 1753.

reign and Princes decree Justice." And Scripture also contradicted the belief in the equality of "natural man" because such a belief, the Anglicans claimed, "will wholly destroy the Doctrine Of Original Sin." [43] Furthermore, the Anglicans suspected that those "Whimsical Noodles" who preached "the Notions of the Origin of Power in the People" were only striving to accumulate power for "their own wicked designs" and were probably in league with the deistic and atheistic followers of Tindal.[44]

Secondly, the Anglicans were opposed to all attempts to separate the religious and civil functions of rulers. They posed the problem in the form of a question: "The main point is to consider, whether the Interest of Societies is so connected with Religion, as to Justify the Guardians of the Public in making use of their Power for promoting and encouraging true Religion?" [45] And they answered their own question in the affirmative. There was no compact between rulers and ruled, they said, but there was a compact between God and man which the civil magistrates were obliged to maintain. This compact required men to establish godly societies. Anglicans who argued "the Absurdity of the Civil Magistrates not interfering in Matters of Religion" were concerned with preserving the *Religious Harmony of Society*." In order to buttress their positions with historic evidence, the Anglicans quoted from an address by William of Orange to the effect that a ruler had both an obligation and a duty to concern himself with the godliness of the community.[46]

Third, the Anglican writers disparaged the idea that civil rulers should assume an impartial attitude toward different religious sects. They challenged anyone to show "when *the perfect, the precious, never-to-be surrender'd Equality* . . . had a real Existence in *Britain,* or in any other place but his own romantic Brain." [47] If the governor of New York attempted to treat all sects impartially, he would reproduce "the Confusions of Babel" and create "Disputes and Jealousies which would far more en-

43. Ibid., 17 and 24 September 1753.
44. Ibid., 24 September 1753.
45. Ibid., 17 September 1753.
46. Ibid., 27 August, 9 July, 10 September 1753.
47. Ibid., 23 July 1753.

gage the Attention of our College, than the Promotion of true Literature." [48] It was clear to the Anglicans that a balancing of sects was impossible, that "a preference then, must of necessity be given to some one denomination among us." Moreover, only if the state threw its weight behind one group could "the full social advantages arising from Religion" be realized. Only an established church could prevent the "dreadful convulsions" that resulted from a conflict of sects. Opposition to the established church was to be expected, but it would soon die out. In the end the established church would be accepted, for "no new sects will spring out of it, as no change is permitted in it; and the Majority of the People will adhere to it, especially if it is a qualification for Civil Offices." [49]

There was no doubt, wrote the Anglicans, that the established church of New York was episcopacy. Legal precedent was not as straightforward as they wanted it, but an act of Parliament during the reign of Queen Anne established Anglicanism in England and "the territories thereunto belonging"; and "territories" obviously meant all royal colonies.[50] If a skeptic challenged this interpretation, as many New Yorkers did, the Anglicans reverted to pragmatic grounds. They asked, "What denomination has an equal title to this preference with the Established church? . . . In a Word, what Church is there that has given so great Instances of Moderation in Power, as she?" [51] Surely not the Presbyterians or other Puritan sects. Here the Anglicans drew upon their bitter experience in New England to score their point.

> Look around you, on their manifest abuse of Power in the neighboring Provinces and you'll soon be convinced how unfit they are to be trusted even with equal Share of the Government of our College; for if they are once suffered to put in a finger, they'll soon thrust in their whole Hand.[52]

Johnson had once opposed Connecticut Presbyterianism on the grounds that no established church was justifiable. Now that law

48. Ibid., 30 April 1753.
49. Ibid., 18 June, 23 and 30 July 1753.
50. Ibid., 30 July 1753.
51. Ibid., 30 April 1753.
52. Ibid., 30 April 1753.

and circumstance were on the side of episcopacy, his Anglican friends modified the argument. It was not that all religious establishments were bad. It was just that some establishments were better than others.

One could take issue with this version of things yet admit that the Anglican spokesmen had done a commendable job of articulating the assumptions that underlay their position in New York. They had attacked illusory visions of a state of nature, equality, and nonsectarianism. They had taken their stand on a realistic estimate of what was possible in society, on the kind of wisdom that "let the Measures of Obedience run in the old Channels." [53] They envisioned an orderly tranquil society as the ideal and were willing to sacrifice the rights of dissenting groups to achieve their goals. And challenging the Anglican ideas must have seemed futile to non-Anglicans, since these ideas only justified an irrefutable fact—the college and the government of the colony were in their hands.

Not quite. In the way of Anglican hegemony stood a twenty-nine-year-old New Yorker by the name of William Livingston. He was the youngest son of Philip Livingston, second lord and patriarch of Livingston Manor. After spending his college years at Yale, William prepared for a career in the law, but when he publicly attacked the vanity of his employer's wife, he was fired. It was a typical display of Livingston's contentious character, the kind of impropriety that a man like Johnson abhorred. Despite this early setback, the Livingston name was too prominent and his talent as a jurist too great to ruin his legal career. But his real love was not the law anyway; it was writing. He had a gaunt, hawkish appearance that caused him to be self-conscious about the unattractive figure he cut in the courtroom. He compensated for his public shyness by writing out his opinions whenever possible. And he could write. His most famous literary creation, *Philosophic Solitude, or The Choice of A Rural Life,* was a long imitation of Dryden and Pope that appears tiresome and trite to a modern reader, but went through thirteen editions in the

53. Ibid., 15 October 1753.

eighteenth century. More durable are his political writings, especially a weekly series of essays entitled *The Independent Reflector*.[54]

James Parker printed the first issue of the *Reflector* on 30 November 1752. Three of Livingston's friends—William Smith, Jr., John Morin Scott, and William Peartree Smith—collaborated with him in the venture, in the same spirit they had joined with him to found a "Society for the Promotion of Useful Knowledge" in the city in 1748. They believed the intellectual life of the colony needed improvement. (Here they sound like Johnson and his college friends who gathered around the Dummer books in 1715.) And they perceived the Anglican control of the proposed college as a threat to the cultural growth of young colonists as well as a violation of their Whig principles. The *Reflector* was, then, a joint effort.[55] But it was Livingston's mind and energy that guided the project, his understanding of political theory that made the magazine so powerful, his synthesis of English and American ideas that was so befuddling to Johnson and the Anglicans. In fact, Livingston's arguments were so far-reaching, so ahead of their time, that one historian has judged them to be "more advanced than anything heard in influential political circles in England at any time in the eighteenth century, or, in fact, in the nineteenth century too." [56] And these, were the arguments that the Anglicans had to combat.

Livingston accepted the description of the origin of government that Locke had set down in his *Second Treatise on Government*. Prior to the establishment of any political order, men were free to act as they pleased. Whether or not there was a historical period in which men had enjoyed complete freedom of action

54. Theodore Sedgwick, Jr., *A Memoir of the Life of William Livingston* (New York, 1833), for the full-length biography of Livingston; see also Dorothy Dillon, *The New York Triumvirate: A Study of the Legal and Political Careers of William Livingston, John Morin Scott, and William Smith, Jr.* (New York, 1949); and Milton M. Klein, ed., *The Independent Reflector . . . by William Livingston and Others* (Cambridge, Mass., 1963), 1–50.

55. Klein, *Independent Reflector*, pp. 13–18; Dillon, *The New York Triumvirate*, pp. 48–100; Dexter, *Yale Biographies*, 2 : 55–60, 85–89.

56. Bernard Bailyn, *The Origins of American Politics* (New York, 1968), p. 114.

was irrelevant. The crucial point for Livingston was that there were certain rights that men possessed by virtue of being men. Government, then, was simply "an Erection or Elevation of one or more Men above the Rest, dependent upon the free Exertion of the Will of the Latter, for the Good of the Whole." [57] Civil magistrates received their power from their constituents, not from God.[58] That power enabled magistrates to act in the "Pursuit of the Welfare of the Community, and in compelling the Practice of Justice, and prohibiting the Contrary." [59] But magistrates possessed no arbitrary power. They were obliged to observe the terms of the original compact made with their constituents. Magistrates who violated this compact "act with unauthorized Power . . . Hence they are to be considered as in a State of Nature, to have broken the original compact, abdicated their thrones, and introduced a Necessity of repelling Force by Force." [60] Such a magistrate was "a private Trespasser, which every Man . . . may lawfully repel." [61]

The upshot of this line of reasoning was revolutionary for colonial leaders twenty-four years later. For Livingston, Lockean theory had a more immediate lesson; namely, "that a People should be careful of yielding too much of their original Power, even to the most just Ruler, and always retain the Privilege of degrading him." [62] One power that the people should always reserve for themselves was the power to tax; another was the power or "indisputable Right to direct the Education of their youthful Members." [63] In both cases, Livingston argued, the proper representatives of community opinion were the members of the Assembly. Since they were more susceptible to public pressure, Assemblymen were more inclined to shape the college according to the wishes of the community.

57. Klein, *Independent Reflector* (39), p. 331. In this note and those that follow, the number in parentheses refers to the original number of the *Reflector* published by Parker and the second number refers to the page in the Klein edition.
58. Ibid. (33), pp. 285–291.
59. Ibid. (39), p. 332.
60. Ibid. (4), p. 77.
61. Ibid. (39), p. 332.
62. Ibid. (33), p. 289.
63. Ibid. (2), p. 62; (20), p. 193.

Moreover, the college was supported by funds raised in a public lottery. The act approving the lottery had been passed by the Assembly and the resulting monies "ought to be considered as the voluntary Gift of the People, to be applied to such uses as they, by their Representatives, shall think expedient." It followed that "if the Colony must bear the Expense of the College, surely the legislature will claim the Superintendency of it." [64]

Livingston's vision of natural rights and the power of the Assembly was not original. It came straight out of Locke, had been expressed earlier and in similar terms by John Wise and Jonathan Mayhew, and was only a distillation of the arguments that several colonial legislatures, including New York's, had been using to oppose royal governors for many years.[65] But the precision of Livingston's prose clarified certain points of disagreement that most colonial legislatures preferred to leave ambiguous. And Livingston stated the case in completely secular terms, thereby dispensing with the notion that Wise and Mayhew found most compelling—that magistrates should be turned out when they ceased to obey God's will. Finally, Livingston's abstract reasoning had practical implication in a specific case—King's College. Here was a public controversy in which these ideas could be tested in action.

Crucial to the test was the way Livingston applied his Lockean tools to pry apart the church-state relationship that the Anglicans had fused together. There was a limit, Livingston believed, to what a magistrate could do.

Nothing therefore, but what is injurious to the Society, or some particular Member of it, can be the proper Object of civil Government; because nothing else falls within the design of forming the Society. . . . But the religious opinions and speculations of the Subject, cannot be prejudicial to the Society . . .

64. Ibid. (18), p. 182; (20), p. 193.
65. John Wise, *A Vindication of the Government of New England Churches* (Boston, 1717); Jonathan Mayhew, *A Discourse Concerning Unlimited Submission and Non-Resistance to the Higher Powers* (Boston, 1750). For a good statement of legislative power in New York, see DeLancey to Board of Trade, 18 March 1755, *New York Colonial Documents*, 6 : 940–41.

Matters of Religion relate to another World and have nothing to do with Interests of the State.[66]

Starting from the Lockean notion of a social compact, Livingston felt that logic carried an impartial student of society to the conclusion that civil and religious concerns were totally divorced from one another.[67]

The disagreement between Livingston and the Anglicans on this matter was not merely a disagreement over Locke. At issue was one's understanding of religion and how it operated within society. For Livingston religion was essentially an "inward Persuasion of the Mind." It was a private and personal experience not subject to the control of civil rulers, because their power could only be exercised in public ways, in matters that were susceptible to "outward Force." [68] Religion was too fragile and delicate to be maintained by coercion. It was an intimate relationship between God and man that left no room for politicians.

Livingston's conception of the religious experience came out of the Puritan tradition that condemned intermediaries between the human and the divine; he gave expression to a resurgence of an old Puritan suspicion not only of magisterial interference in church affairs but also to a strong anticlericalism. It was best, wrote Livingston, if we all "read Scriptures with our own Eyes, and practice the Meaning without being Hoodwink'd by Jugglers and other Visionaries." [69] He recalled a fundamental principle of the Cambridge Platform, "that Religion existed long before the Clergy, and that the Clergy may exist without Religion." [70] His anticlerical comments were a reinvigoration of a strain of Puritan thought that was enjoying a revival throughout the colonies, partly in reaction to the extremism of the New Light clergy, partly because of a growing secularism among the population at large. But Livingston's observation that "a black Petticoat, like Charity, often *covers a Multitude of Sins*" was in-

66. Klein, *Independent Reflector* (36), p. 307.
67. Ibid. (36), p. 308.
68. Ibid. (37), p. 315.
69. Ibid. (31), p. 276.
70. Ibid. (34), p. 295.

terpreted by the Anglicans as a direct slap at the episcopal ministry.[71]

More importantly, however, his suspicion of any public tampering, be it civil or clerical, with an individual's religious beliefs enabled Livingston to advocate a completely secular brand of education. He proposed a college in which students enjoyed "an unrestrained access to all Books in the Library," in which "all public disputations on Divinity be forbidden."[72] Like the magistrate and the minister, the professor had no right to intrude upon the religious opinions of students. Livingston even suggested that there be no divinity courses offered in the college and no formal prayers.[73] A public education was intended "to render our Youth better Members of Society . . . , to make them more extensively serviceable to the Common-Wealth."[74] Neither the Anglicans nor any other sect had a right to suppose that an infusion of their peculiar dogmas made a man a better citizen.

Livingston's final attack on the conception of an Anglican-controlled college was the most devastating. It was not borrowed from Locke or from the religious traditions of New England. Rather, it was an imported but greatly modified version of radical English thought. The political theorists of the Whig opposition had compiled a body of attitudes and ideas that had begun to filter into the colonies in the 1730s.[75] Two English writers, John Trenchard and Thomas Gordon, were most frequently quoted in the colonies as representatives of this radical point of view. Livingston had not only read Trenchard and Gordon, he had consciously modeled his *Independent Reflector* after their chief publications, *The Independent Whig* (1720) and *Cato's Letters*

71. Ibid. (34), p. 292. The Anglicans published two pamphlets in response to Livingston's charges: the anonymous *A Scheme for the Revival of Christianity* (New York, 1753), and a reprint of a 1723 pamphlet by Francis Squire, *An Answer to . . . the Independent Whig* (New York, 1753).

72. Klein, *Independent Reflector* (31), p. 203.

73. Ibid. (31), p. 202.

74. Ibid. (37), p. 172.

75. Caroline Robbins, *The Eighteenth Century Commonwealthmen* (Cambridge, Mass., 1959), pp. 115–25 discusses the English context of opposition thought. The impact of these ideas on American thought is the subject of two books by Bernard Bailyn: *The Ideological Origins of the American Revolution* (Cambridge, Mass., 1967), and *The Origins of American Politics.*

(1723). The New York Anglicans tried to belittle Livingston's essays as carbon copies of extremist English journalism, chiding

> He rose dread Foe to Priests and Fetters,
> Deep skill'd in Church and Civil Matters;
> For he had read all Cato's Letters.[76]

But Livingston's words were more than just an echo of English opposition thought. They were an affirmation of the possibility of a college governed not by one religious faction, but by all the people of New York.

He began with the problem posed by the Anglicans—how could a scheme for a stable, nonsectarian college be devised? The Anglicans were sure it could not. Livingston was equally sure that a sectarian college would be a disaster. He worried that if "any particular sect be invested with the supreme rule in that seminary, what can hinder their indoctrinating its youth in the controlled principles of their own party?" [77] Instead of "Reason and Argument," students would be infused with "the Doctrines of Party, enforced by the Authority of the Professor's Chair." [78] He was critical of any sect that aspired to control a public institution, arguing that "Whatever denomination shall monopolize its government will easily jockey all the rest of the province. Adieu then to peace and liberty!" [79] But he was aware that the Anglicans constituted the greatest threat. They already controlled a majority of the trustees, although they were "utterly devoid of every qualification to recommend them for such a trust, save only their notorious, inflexible bigotry." [80]

It was absurd to suppose, as the Anglicans seemed to do, that one sect would be more generous than another. For this reason, Livingston did not recommend a Presbyterian-controlled college. He admitted that Yale and the College of New Jersey "savor too much of party; and as far as they are culpable in this particular,

---

76. *New York Mercury*, 23 July 1753.
77. "Extract from the Preface to the Independent Reflector," 19 January 1754, *Career*, 4 : 160–61.
78. Klein, *Independent Reflector* (17), p. 180.
79. "Extract from the Preface," *Career*, 4 : 166.
80. Ibid., p. 162.

they fall under the lash of any animadversions." [81] It was also absurd to believe that the governor or the crown could stand above sectarian interests and mediate disputes. The governor was part of the persistent and inevitable clash of interest groups that constituted the political life of any state. He himself was a faction.[82]

Livingston had no faith in any system of government that ultimately rested on trust, on the granting of prerogatives or arbitrary powers in the hope that the recipient would rule impartially. "Power of all kinds is intoxicating," he observed, "but boundless Power, is insupportable by the giddy and arrogant Mind of MAN." [83] History showed that "most absolute Monarchs have acted more like imperial Wolves, or rather Beasts in human Shape, than rational and intelligent Beings." [84] To invest the governor of New York with control of the college was to invite injustice.

The only way to govern a public college was to ensure that all points of view represented in the colony were also represented in the governing body. The result would not be anarchy, as the Anglicans implied, because "the Jealousy of all Parties combating each other, would inevitably produce a perfect Freedom for each particular Party." [85] It followed that the college, if governed by the Assembly, would belong not to one sect but to all. It would be nonsectarian.[86]

At a time when the fundamental assumptions of a culture are in a state of flux, a public controversy over some local problem often evolves into an argument about philosophy. This is what happened in New York in 1753. Time would show that Livingston's ideas were the most enduring, that his mixture of Lockean and radical Whig thought foreshadowed the ideology

81. Ibid., p. 167.
82. Klein, *Independent Reflector* (19), pp. 184–89. Bailyn regards this as Livingston's most insightful and important comment on the political process. See Bailyn, *The Origins of American Politics*, p. 129.
83. Klein, *Independent Reflector* (4), p. 76.
84. Ibid. (4) p. 77. See also (12), pp. 143–48.
85. Ibid. (20), p. 195.
86. Ibid. (20), p. 196.

of the American Revolution as well as the republicanism of James Madison and the Federalists. His vision of the ideal society sacrificed a portion of the order and tranquility that Anglicans held so dear in order to guarantee the rights of all interest groups. But contemporaries who did not have the advantage of hindsight could not be sure whether *The Independent Reflector* was the wave of the future or a historical footnote to Anglican hegemony in New York.

Even Johnson was not sure. At the center of the storm over the college, he remained quiet. His son William Samuel advised silence, warning that it would be "highly prejudicial" if the future college president was known as "the head of a party, or promoting any particular scheme." [87] Johnson certainly hated Livingston and believed it was his intention "to make it [the college] a sort of free-thinking latitudinarian seminary." [88] And whether or not he spoke out in the debate, Johnson was the official leader of the Anglican party. He believed that the Anglicans were not unreasonable in their insistence that the office of president be reserved for an Anglican and that the college prayers come from the Anglican liturgy, because "the Church have given 1000 pounds worth of land [the King's Farm] on that condition." [89] But Livingston had raised an issue that troubled Johnson's conscience. Was it not inconsistent to oppose the Presbyterian domination of the Connecticut government and Yale College and then advocate a similar control by the Anglicans in New York? [90] Henry Barclay assured him that such thoughts were irrelevant; Johnson had committed himself; the entire Anglican cause would collapse if he did not take the job. "In a word," wrote Barclay, "it seems you have put your hand to the plow, and I know not how you can look back." [91]

Meanwhile, the Anglicans were going forward with their plans, fearful of the influence of the *Reflector* on public opinion, but determined to get their way. Livingston hoped that his essays had

87. W. S. Johnson to S. Johnson, 13 June 1754, *Career*, 4 : 17–18.
88. Johnson to Archbishop of Canterbury, 25 June 1753, ibid., p. 4.
89. S. Johnson to W. S. Johnson, 27 May 1754, ibid., p. 11.
90. W. S. Johnson to S. Johnson, 3 May 1754, ibid., p 9.
91. Barclay to Johnson, 4 November 1754, ibid., p. 25.

upset the Anglicans and told his friends he had "repaid their [Anglicans] anger by laughing at their resentment." [92]

But Livingston knew that the odds were against him. Despite the great and unexpected demand for Livingston's pamphlets that forced James Parker to reprint back issues, the Anglicans had swamped his office with letters demanding an end to the *Reflector*. DeLancey had threatened Parker's newspaper with the loss of public business if he continued to publish Livingston's essays.[93] By November of 1753 *The Independent Reflector* had ceased to exist—Livingston said it had been "tyrannically suppressed." The arbitrary power that Livingston had argued against had been used to crush his criticism.[94]

By the spring of 1754 it appeared that the *Reflector* would have to wait for history to resurrect its arguments and recognize their brilliance. The magazine was dead, and the Anglicans had drafted a college charter that guaranteed their control. When Johnson came down to New York in April to confer with Barclay, he was told the charter was sure to be approved. He smelled further difficulty and wrote home, "I expect trouble if I stay, but where can I go to be free from that?" [95] He stayed on. In June he was conducting admissions exams for prospective students in the yet uncharted college.[96] He said he would wait for the approval of the charter before he officially accepted the presidency, but, for all practical purposes, he was in the fight.

92. Livingston to Whittlesey, 22 August 1754, ibid., p. 23.
93. *Occasional Reverberator*, 7 September 1753.
94. The only other newspaper available to Livingston, the *New York Post,* had ceased to exist earlier in 1753. Livingston eventually gained access to a one-page section of the *New York Mercury* and began a new series entitled "The Watch-Tower" with the help of William Smith, Jr.
95. S. Johnson to W. S. Johnson, 27 May 1754, *Career*, 4 : 12.
96. Advertisement from *New York Gazette or Weekly Post-Boy*, 3 June 1754.

President of King's

The standards for admission to King's College that Johnson set down in the *New York Gazette* were conventional. If a young man could demonstrate his proficiency in Latin and Greek and could "write a good legible hand," if he knew the rudiments of arithmetic "as far as Division and Reduction" and paid the tuition, he was in. Although the opening class was scheduled to meet "in the new *School-House* adjoining to *Trinity Church* in *New York*," Johnson went out of his way to assure the community that the school's proximity to Anglican headquarters was not symptomatic of his desire to establish a college that catered only to Anglicans. He announced that he had "no intention to impose on the Scholars, the peculiar Tenets of any particular sect of Christians; but to Inculcate upon their tender Minds, the great Principles of Christianity and Morality, in which true Christians of each Denomination are generally agreed." He portrayed himself as a man who stood above the clash of factions, a president who, in terms of his own philosophy, embodied archetypal values that transcended worldly concerns.[1]

In keeping with this public stance, Johnson promised his son that he would steer clear of the "bristle and racket" and "not put pen to paper in any of these controversies . . . I will write nothing pro or con." [2] In private, however, he denounced the "reflectorial spirit" that he felt was responsible for the turmoil, and

1. *New York Gazette or Weekly Post-Boy,* 3 June 1754.
2. W. S. Johnson to S. Johnson, 6 December 1754; and S. Johnson to W. S. Johnson, 8 December 1754, *Career,* 4 : 31–34.

refused to admit to his Anglican friends or himself that the Puritan fear of Anglican domination had any justification.[3] At the same time that he publicly announced his commitment to nonsectarian goals, he wrote boastfully to the Bishop of London about the newly drafted college charter which stipulated that "the service of the Church is to be always used in the college, and the president to be always of the Church of England."[4]

Johnson, like William Smith in the *Mirania* pamphlet, seemed to think that the college could be Anglican and nonsectarian at the same time. In Johnson's mind the ultimate test of the religious atmosphere established at the college was the treatment accorded to non-Anglican students. On this issue the charter was clear. The trustees were forbidden "to exclude any Person of any religious Denomination whatever, from equal liberty and Advantage of Education, or from any [of] the Degrees, Liberties, Privileges, Benefits or Immunities . . . on Account of his particular Tenets to Matters of Religion."[5]

Although Johnson was insensitive to the inconsistencies of the proposed charter, William Livingston was not. The constant reference in the charter to "the Church of *England* as by Law established," as well as the insistence on an Anglican president and liturgy, confirmed Livingston's worst fears.[6] He registered the only dissenting vote when the lottery trustees approved the charter; then he listed twenty reasons why he regarded the charter as "an artifice to purchase the rights and liberties of the people."[7]

3. Criticism of the Livingston faction is sprinkled throughout Johnson's correspondence during the summer and fall of 1754. See especially S. Johnson to W. S. Johnson and W. Johnson, 10 June 1754, ibid., p. 16.

4. Johnson to Bishop of London, 6 July 1754, ibid., p. 20.

5. *The Charter of the College of New York in America* (New York, 1754), p. 10. The charter had been drafted during the spring of 1754 by John Chambers and Benjamin Nicoll. It was modeled on the New Jersey College charter of 1748, which itself followed the outline of the Yale charter of 1745. Specifically Anglican references were added to guarantee an Anglican president and liturgy. Johnson was consulted about the wording, and he made a visit to New Jersey in May with Nicoll to look over the college there. Beverley McAnear, "American Imprints Concerning King's College," *The Papers of the Bibliographical Society of America* 44 (1950): 318. See also W. S. Johnson to S. Johnson, 21 June 1754, *Career*, 1 : 189.

6. The charter is reprinted in *Career*, 4 : 219–22.

7. "Extract from the Journal of the General Assembly of New York" [16 May 1754], ibid., pp. 177–90.

As long as Livingston's criticism was unleashed within committee, where the Anglicans held the upper hand, no harm was done. And as long as Hugh Gaine and James Parker kept their presses closed to him, he had no ready-made public vehicle for his views.[8] Throughout the summer of 1754, while Johnson interviewed applicants for the college and then began regular sessions with his younger son, Billy, as tutor, the Anglican grip on the college remained firm. It was Johnson's hope to make the college prosper and let academic success squash whatever political or religious criticism the Livingston forces were able to muster.

The dream ended in October. The Assembly began to debate the merits of the college charter and all the old wounds were reopened.[9] Livingston successfully encouraged his friends in the Assembly to create enough public pressure to force Hugh Gaine to open his *New York Mercury* to the Presbyterians. A weekly column called the "Watch-Tower" afforded Livingston and his colleagues the opportunity to carry the issues to the people.[10] Meanwhile Robert Livingston, William's older brother, introduced a bill in the Assembly for the establishment of a "free college" under the control of the Assembly "with a Presbyterian president." [11] Johnson continued to meet his classes and pray that the Assembly would approve his election as president. He had hoped that the Livingston forces would dissipate their energies by bickering among themselves; now it appeared that "however so much they are otherwise at variance among themselves, yet they unite with their utmost force against us." He confessed disillusionment to his son; "It seems we must be in a state of war." [12]

The "Watch-Tower" articles kept the war in the open. Liv-

8. Not that Livingston and his colleagues remained silent. He published 150 copies of his dissenting opinion of the charter in May 1754 and began a new series of pamphlets entitled *The Plebeian* under the pseudonym "Noah Meanwell" in August. The latter pamphlet series died quickly, however, and only one issue is extant. McAnear, "American Imprints," p. 320.

9. *Journal of the Votes and Proceedings of the General Assembly . . . 1743 . . . 1765* (New York, 1766), 2 : 396. Hereafter cited as *Assembly Journal.*

10. The column first appeared on 25 November 1754.

11. *Assembly Journal*, 2 : 404.

12. Johnson to Secker, 25 October 1754, *Career*, 2 : 334–35; S. Johnson to W. S. Johnson, 8 December 1754, *Career*, 4 : 33.

ingston's first column summarized the events leading up to the submission of the Anglican charter and announced his intent to assure that "the Whole Province is upon the Watch, respecting the Transactions of the Legislature." He described the debate over King's College as "the most important Affair that ever fell under the considerations of any American Legislature." [13] Throughout Livingston's weekly comments ran the same refrain that he had voiced in the *Reflector*: the projected college belonged to the people, had been financed by the people, and should be governed by popular representatives in the Assembly; the Anglicans were a minority faction; if they regained control of the college, the remainder of the community had "nothing to look for, but a gradual succession of Incroachments, 'till the scene closes in a final and perpetual Oppression." [14]

Livingston proclaimed his dependence upon and appeal to popular opinion. He published the petitions from the freeholders of five counties that demanded Assembly approval of the "free college" bill. He appeared at the door of the Assembly with "sundry Petitions from a great Number of the Freemen and Freeholders of several of the cities and counties in this Colony," all denouncing the King's College charter. He publicized the inability of the trustees to sell tickets for a new lottery for the college, portraying the failure as "a Demonstration that the popular Voice is opposed to that Dirty Purpose." And he condemned Anglican attempts to force a vote on the college bill before all the members of the Assembly were seated. By July of 1755 Livingston had developed such a following that David Jones, the speaker of the Assembly, had to take out an advertisement in the *New York Gazette* testifying that he had not voted for the Anglican-backed charter.[15]

The Anglicans, on the other hand, were contemptuous of appeals to the public. Replies to the "Watch-Tower" by Auchmuty, Wetmore, and William Smith warned the members of the Assem-

13. *New York Mercury*, 25 November 1725.
14. The quotation is from ibid., 24 March 1755.
15. Petition of the Freemen of New York, against . . . the College established by Charter [1755], College Papers, Columbia University; *Assembly Journal*, 2 : 468; *New York Mercury*, 15 September and 23 June 1755; *New York Gazette or Weekly Post-Boy*, 28 July 1755.

bly not to allow themselves "to be biased by a few forced Petitions, from distant Counties, signed by ignorant People, that know not what they are about." [16] "The Common Run of the Species," they wrote, "Seldom examine things with Attention. They take all upon Truth; and follow their Leaders with an implicit Faith." [17]

No matter what the Anglicans thought of Livingston's tactics, they were no match for his pen. He constructed dialogues in which "a Churchman" became so frustrated that he blurted out his conspiratorial schemes to "a Dissenter." [18] He described a nightmare in which he saw the front page of a New York newspaper in 1775, after Anglican domination of the colony was complete.[19] He contrasted the school over which Johnson was presiding—"our little obscure Embryo, which consists, I am informed, only of about half a Dozen Lads"—with Harvard and Yale.[20] He searched in vain for clear legal precedent for Anglican supremacy in the colonies, concluding that "If we wade into the Statutes, no Man can tell what the law is." [21]

The Anglicans simply restated their earlier position in the form of a plea:

> The Members of the Church of England, never did, nor do, wish to monopolize the intended College to themselves. They only desire that since they have given the largest Donations, and have such a Relation to the Establishment of the Nation (which surely demands some Degree of Respect) and Since they are very numerous, and the most wealthy in this and many other of the Provinces—that the President, for ever shall be a Member of said Church, and that the Liturgy of the Church of *England*, or a Collection from it, shall be used in their daily prayers. Is this Request any Way unreasonable? [22]

16. *New York Mercury*, 2 December 1754.
17. Ibid., 3 March 1755.
18. Ibid., 2 and 16 December 1754.
19. Ibid., 3 February 1755.
20. Ibid., 10 February 1755.
21. Ibid., 17 February 1755.
22. Ibid., 2 December 1755. See also the Anglican position repeated in *John Englishman In Defence of the English Constitution* (New York, 1755), and *John Englishman's True Notion of Sister Churches* (New York, 1755).

Livingston said it was, not because the conditions in the college would be unbearable, but because the Anglicans would possess the arbitrary power to change those conditions as they wished.[23] A few readers, refusing to believe that the Anglican position had been presented fairly, wrote into the *Mercury* accusing Livingston of composing the Anglican articles himself. Livingston denied the charge and, incredibly, the Anglicans confirmed that they had written their own defense.[24]

While the ideological and rhetorical fight continued in the press, the crucial political struggle was going on in the legislature. Apparently the Anglicans had expected some opposition from the Assembly but felt that the DeLancey faction would beat down opponents to the charter and provide enough votes to guarantee its passage. Although Johnson thought the debates of May 1754 had been "pretty warm," his decision to begin classes reflected Anglican confidence in the outcome. In June he wrote his son William that "everybody are more and more persuaded there will be no doubt of the Assembly." Throughout the months that followed, Johnson persisted in his opinion that "the Majority will next Session be for us." [25]

But other Anglicans who were more realistic about Livingston's effect on public opinion and less sanguine about Anglican voting power in the Assembly revised their political strategy. They decided to sidestep the Assembly and request direct approval of the charter from the governor. Benjamin Nicoll articulated the new Anglican view that the incorporation of the trustees named in the proposed charter did not require an act approved by "the governor, council and general assembly," but only "a charter from the crown." [26] Clearly, the Anglicans wanted Assembly approval

23. *New York Mercury*, 6 January 1755.

24. Ibid., 23 December 1754.

25. S. Johnson to W. S. Johnson, 6 May 1754; S. Johnson to W. Johnson, 17 June 1754, *Career*, 1 : 184–87; S. Johnson to W. S. and W. Johnson, 2 December 1754; Johnson to Secretary, 3 December 1754, *Career*, 4 : 26–30.

26. Benjamin Nicoll, *A Brief Vindication of the Proceedings of the Trustees Relating to the College* . . . (New York, 1754) as reprinted in *Career*, 4 : 191–207. The quotation is from 197. Johnson had argued with Thomas Clap about the legality of the Yale charter, insisting that mere Assembly approval was insufficient because "a corporation cannot make a corporation without his Majesty's Act." See *Career*, 1 : 178. Nicoll's pamphlet was preceded by

of the charter, for such approval would have blunted Livingston's accusation that the college lacked popular sanction. But once Assembly approval appeared unlikely, they were willing to disregard the popular representatives and make use of the governor's prerogative powers, which, they claimed, included the power to make corporations. On October 31, the Council approved the King's College charter. Two days later DeLancey incorporated the trustees named in the same charter.[27]

Livingston responded immediately. He did not challenge DeLancey's power to incorporate the trustees. But he did charge that the lottery trustees were not empowered to draw up a college charter; they were empowered to administer the lottery monies and choose a location for the school: that was all. According to Livingston's view, a charter could only be drafted by the Assembly or by a committee charged with that task by the Assembly.[28]

A majority of the Assembly not only agreed with Livingston, they also possessed the leverage to make their opinion felt. For, although King's College was now officially chartered and the Assembly was incapable of having it rescinded, the Assembly retained control over the lottery funds needed to begin construction, purchase books, and pay the faculty. On 6 November 1754, the Assembly recorded its will in terms that would be repeated often in years to come: "this House will not consent to any Disposition of the Monies raised by Way of Lottery . . . in any other Manner whatever, than by Act or Acts of the Legislature of this Colony." [29]

The Anglicans found themselves standing with the governor in another of the constitutional disputes over control of the purse, disputes that the legislature had a long history of winning. Even those representatives who did not oppose the King's College

yet another pamphlet by William Livingston entitled *The Querist* . . . (New York, 1754), listing 48 allegations against the proposed charter.

27. See Draft of Petition to the Assembly for a Charter [1754], for confirmation of initial Anglican intent to seek Assembly approval for the charter. The charter DeLancey signed was a revised version of the charter first drafted the previous spring. The various drafts are arranged chronologically in College Papers, Columbia University Library. In all drafts, the safeguards for Anglican control remained substantially unchanged.

28. *Assembly Journal,* 2 : 397–99, 413–14.

29. Ibid., p. 404.

charter aligned themselves against the Anglicans in order to oppose the governor's control over locally collected monies. During
the next year the Assembly employed parliamentary delaying
tactics learned in past confrontations with the royal prerogative.
The result was predictable; King's College remained penniless.[30]
Johnson continued to hope for a miracle. Anglican political
strategists, including Nicoll and Auchmuty, began to woo members of the Dutch Reformed church to their side in an effort to
shift the balance in the Assembly. In 1755 the college trustees approved an "Additional Charter," establishing a professorship of
divinity and stipulating that a Dutch Reformed minister would
hold the chair "from Time to Time." [31] The attempt to buy off
the Dutch was quashed almost immediately, when Theodore
Frelinghuysen, the leading Dutch divine in the colonies, joined
the Presbyterians.[32] Under the pseudonym "Marin Ben Jesse,"
Frelinghuysen attacked the Arminianism of the Anglicans and
characterized their role in the college as an "astonishing Imposition of the incroaching Party." He called the *Independent Reflector* "the happiest Phenomenon of the Age" and advised the
Dutch to ignore Anglican pledges of friendship. After he had
finished, the Dutch were more firmly enlisted with the Livingston
forces than before.[33]

The Anglican predicament became even more difficult in
March of 1755, when French and Indian forces began to threaten
the city with occupation. Now that the war was on the doorstep,

30. Ibid., pp. 468–520.

31. *An Additional Charter Granted to the Governors of the College of
New York* (New York, 1755). See also Petition of the Governors . . . for an
Additional Charter [draft], 30 May 1755, College Papers, Columbia University.
Joannes Ritzema, a Dutch minister and one of the trustees, suggested the
appeal to the Dutch churches at the first meeting of the trustees. See *Early
Minutes of the Trustees, 1755–1770* (New York, 1932), 7 May 1755.

32. Frelinghuysen was a pastor of the Dutch Church in Albany who was
active in the movement to establish the autonomy of the American wing of his
Church and free it from the control of the governing classis or assembly in
Amsterdam. He regarded an Anglican college as a threat to his plan for a
separate Dutch college in New York. Hastings, ed., *Ecclesiastical Records of
New York*, 5 : 3495–3500, 3546–64. For evidence of his authorship of the
anti-Anglican pamphlets, see McAnear, "American Imprints," pp. 327–28.

33. Marin Ben Jesse, *A Remonstrance* (New York, 1755), and *A Remark on
the Disputes and Contentions in This Province* (New York, 1755), pp. 5–7.

the legislature postponed discussion of all nonmilitary matters, including the college.[34] With people fleeing the city each day, Johnson felt that he must demonstrate his willingness to keep the school open in spite of war and recalcitrant legislators. His wife had remained in Stratford, which indicated his awareness of the tenuous nature of his job. In March he instructed her to move into the city and set up a permanent household. William Samuel reported that his mother was worried, that "Mammy . . . thinks it odd she should be hastening there when those who are there are endeavoring to get away." [35]

In the midst of the chaos Johnson admitted that the chances for funding were slim, since "nothing can now be thought of but war." The college, he confessed, "cut a poor figure," and he was "melancholy that my aims and endeavors meet with so much embarrassment." But instead of blaming his troubles on war or Livingston, he traced the failure "to the want of resolution in our principal persons, and especially to the want of vigor and activity in the gentlemen [trustees] at the helm." [36] Johnson also blamed "our steersman" [DeLancey] for his inability to alter the stance of the Assembly.[37]

The affair dragged on for almost two more years. DeLancey's political reputation barely survived the ordeal; the Livingstons emerged as the most formidable party in the colony.[38] A new governor, Sir Charles Hardy, arrived in 1755 and gave the college £500, enough to keep it alive, but not enough to make it flourish.[39] In December of 1756 Hardy effected a political compromise. Half the lottery money went to King's College; the other half went toward the construction of a new jail and a detention house for sailors from disease-ridden ships.[40] By then William Smith, Jr.,

34. *Assembly Journal*, 2 : 459; O'Callaghan, ed., *N.Y. Col. Doc.*, 6 : 99.
35. W. S. Johnson to S. Johnson, 20 March 1755, *Career*, 1 : 214.
36. S. Johnson to W. S. Johnson, 20 January 1755 and February 1755, ibid., pp. 209–211.
37. S. Johnson to W. S. Johnson, 31 March 1755, ibid., pp. 216–17.
38. William Smith, Jr., *History of New York*, 2 : 238–39; Klein, *Independent Reflector*, pp. 44–45.
39. Johnson to Bishop of London, 27 October 1755, *Career*, 4 : 36–37.
40. Johnson to Secretary, 27 October 1755, *Career*, 1 : 227; O'Callaghan, ed., *N.Y. Col. Doc.*, 7 : 217; *Colonial Laws of New York*, 4 : 160–67; *Assembly Journal*, 2 : 512–13, 520.

said that the college was in such sad shape that the money had
been divided "between the two pest houses." [41] Livingston was
unhappy that the college survived at all, but gained a modicum
of satisfaction from the knowledge that he had raised the specter
of Anglican educators warping the tender minds of young New
Yorkers, a specter that continued to haunt the college long after
the controversy was officially ended.

Curiously, none of Livingston's attacks was ever aimed directly
at Johnson. As an Anglican president he set a precedent that
Livingston had warned against. There was also the implication
that Johnson was one of the culprits disseminating Anglican
propaganda inside the classroom. But Livingston, who showed no
reluctance to vilify an opponent's character when it furthered his
cause, never specifically mentioned Johnson. In fact, Livingston
had voted for Johnson's appointment as president and had even
drafted the letter offering him the job. In all likelihood Livingston recognized that Johnson's impeccable academic credentials,
his intellectual stature, and his image as a moderate Anglican
who tried to get along with Puritan neighbors gave him a
reputation that was difficult to tarnish.

While the fight between the trustees and the Assembly kept
sectarian passions alive, Johnson was establishing an educational
program that seemed designed to discourage sectarianism and to
encourage a broader vision of colonial education than anyone
could expect from an Anglican partisan. In an advertisement in
the *New York Gazette* he promised that King's College would
train students "in the best manner expressive of our common
Christianity." Then he spelled out his educational goals. He
proposed

> to instruct and perfect the youth in the learned languages,
> and in the arts of reasoning exactly, of writing correctly, and
> speaking eloquently; and in the arts of numbering and meas-
> uring, of surveying and navigation, of geography and history,
> of husbandry, commerce and government, and in the knowl-
> edge of all nature in the various kinds of meteors, stones,

41. William Smith, Jr., *History of New York*, 2 : 238.

mines, and minerals, plants and animals, and of everything useful for the comfort, the convenience and elegance of life, in the chief manufactures relating to any of these things; and, finally, to lead them from the study of nature to knowledge of themselves, and of the God of nature, and their duty to him, themselves, and one another, and everything that can contribute to their true happiness, both here and hereafter.[42]

The most arresting feature of this proposal was its breadth. As one historian of colonial America has observed, "Had Johnson himself offered a specific course for each of these fields, he would have been presiding, *mutatis mutandis,* over the equivalent of a twentieth-century university." [43] The encyclopedic scope of Johnson's own mind undoubtedly encouraged him to offer a college program that covered everything from inanimate matter to God. More specifically, Johnson's familiarity with Franklin's plans for the Academy in Philadelphia and with William Smith's projected curriculum there made him aware of the current drive toward practical educational goals (i.e. surveying, geography, government). If King's College was to serve the needs of a cosmopolitan community, it would have to prepare men for professional life as well as teach the classics. Moreover, Johnson apparently felt that King's had an obligation to serve all sectors of New York society, not just the sons of prominent Anglican and Dutch families. Edward Antill, a former New York merchant who had retired to his New Jersey estate, was optimistic about Johnson's plans for the college. "We shall then in a little time see a tast [sic] for learning rearing its head," he wrote, "[and] it is the Wisdom of a State to make the Children of the Poor . . . Servicable [sic] to the Community" as well as "the Children of the Rich." [44] Even a skeptical observer of the King's College scene, and Livingston certainly qualified as a skeptic, must have been heartened by the educational blueprint the Anglican president had outlined. There was no mention of ministerial training of any sort. The emphasis

---

42. The *New York Gazette or Weekly Post-Boy,* 3 June 1754.
43. Richard Gummere in *The American Colonial Mind and the Classical Tradition* (Cambridge, Mass., 1963), p. 65.
44. Antill to Johnson, 14 December 1758, College Papers, Columbia University.

was on intellectual preparation for service to the community, an emphasis that agreed completely with Livingston's cherished goal of public education, even though the public was denied legal control over the college.

In 1755 it was becoming clear that neither the Anglican trustees nor the Livingston factions of the Assembly had practical control over the college: Samuel Johnson did. He and his younger son Billy constituted the entire faculty. He led the students in the morning and evening prayers, taught five classes a day, and, most important of all, drafted the rules that would govern King's College throughout his tenure.[45]

He insisted on a four-year residency requirement for a bachelor's degree, thereby eliminating speculation that King's, like the College of New Jersey, would grant advanced placement to some students. He also stipulated that the senior exams, conducted six weeks before commencement, be rigorous tests of what the undergraduates had learned and not just the pro forma exercises conducted at most other colonial colleges. Although Johnson required that students complete three years of postgraduate study before they could receive an M.A., he established no residency requirement; King's, like Harvard and Yale, soon fell into the practice of granting an M.A. to any former student who showed up at commencement three years after his graduation and paid the necessary fee.

The college affairs that Johnson did not regulate were as revealing as the matters he did. While each student was obliged to attend some form of Sunday worship, he was free to pick the church and denomination he preferred. While students were required to remain in their rooms except for classes, college prayers, meals, and scheduled recreation, they were not required to speak to each other in Latin outside of Latin class. And while Johnson encouraged close contact between students and faculty, he did not follow the established colonial pattern of assigning tutors to

45. Johnson to Archbishop of Canterbury, 10 April 1762, *Career*, 1 : 318; also *New York Mercury*, 26 June 1756, and the *New York Gazette or Weekly Post-Boy*, 30 August 1756. Johnson continued to serve as an advocate for Anglican missionaries in Connecticut, even while he resided in New York. See S.P.G. MSS, B, 2 : 75–85.

particular classes. He prohibited a tutor from taking charge of
an entering class and carrying it through the four-year curriculum.
Johnson preferred that tutors teach subjects rather than students.

The college rules followed the tradition of the New England
colleges by setting high moral standards for the students. They
were warned against "houses of ill Fame," prevented from "laughing or jostling one another" during class, required to uncover
their heads in the presence of the president, and reminded of "the
duties of a serious Christian." An elaborate table of fines was
established for different forms of misbehavior. When an entering
student read the section of the college rules dealing with discipline, he was supposed to conclude that president Johnson ran a
tight ship.[46]

It soon became evident that Johnson did not see himself as a
ship captain or a head seminarian, but as a father. Although he
gave regular lectures on the value of piety and "Christian
morality," he found that his fondness for the students often
militated against strict enforcement of the college laws. He himself admitted that he exhibited "too much tenderness and leniency
in discipline." [47] At the end of his tenure, for example, the
trustees were forced to reiterate that "no women on any pretence
(Except a Cook) be allowed to reside within the college for the
future, and those that are now there be removed as soon as conveniently may be." [48] Even in his lectures to the students he
conveyed an attitude of benevolent paternalism in which the
capacity to forgive ranked higher than the desire to chastise. He
told one class of seniors that they were still "under [his] immediate care" but would soon be "going forth into a treacherous
and vexatious world, to act your part in this uncertain course of
life; assure yourselves that I [will] part with you with inexpressible
tenderness, and great concern for your best good and shall always
be solicitous to hear well of you." [49] One of the reasons he was
so eager to have the trustees approve the funds for a new build-

46. The college rules are in *Early Minutes of the Trustees*, 3 June 1755.
47. *Career*, 4 : 95.
48. *Early Minutes of the Trustees*, 1 March 1763.
49. *Career*, 4 : 278.

ing in which students could live, eat, and study was his conviction that King's College was a large family. Parents of entering freshmen apparently appreciated Johnson's paternal vision. One mother wrote a friend that "Mr. Johnson is to teach him [her son] &, I was in the hope he would have lodg'd with him also." [50] In 1755 Edward Antill asked Johnson to watch over his son and, if possible, "to take him into Your House." [51]

In sum, by the time the political controversy over the proceeds from the lottery was resolved, Johnson had assumed control of the day-by-day operation of the college; had established academic standards that were modeled on selected features of the programs of Harvard, Yale, the College of New Jersey, and the Academy at Philadelphia; had declared himself opposed to any narrow or sectarian conception of education; and, most importantly, had infused the college atmosphere with his personal brand of moderation and tolerance. Far from being an urban "pest-house," in 1756 King's College looked as if it was ready to grow into a vital member of a thriving colonial metropolis.

Already, however, the college was beset with internal problems that would plague Johnson throughout his presidency. Moreover, they were problems whose solution transcended both his presidential powers and his personal talents.

One of the first problems Johnson noticed was the reluctance of Presbyterians, who constituted the bulk of the colonial populace, to send their children to King's. In 1756 he wrote Billy that he had "admitted a considerable dissenting pupil, and another principal dissenter with good humor assures me he will enter his son next May." [52] But it soon became clear that, in spite of Johnson's assurances that the college welcomed all pupils, only Anglican and prominent Dutch Reformed parents were sending their sons to King's. The most recent study of the student body at

50. Mrs. Peter DeLancey to Mrs. Cadwallader Colden, 7 June 1756, The Letters and Papers of Cadwallader Colden . . . 1711–1775, Collections of the New York Historical Society (1917–35), 68 : 155.

51. Antill to Johnson, 29 October 1755, College Papers, Columbia University.

52. S. Johnson to W. Johnson, 8 November 1756, Career, 1 : 268.

King's College during the pre-Revolutionary period shows that about 60 percent of the students were Anglicans and almost all the others were Dutch Reformed. Furthermore, over 75 percent of the students came from prominent families who lived within a thirty-mile radius of the campus. From the very beginning, King's College was "the preserve of the prosperous middle and upper-middle classes of the New York City area's Anglican-Dutch community." Since about 80 percent of the colony's population lived outside the city, and the majority of them were Presbyterians, King's College was drawing only a fraction of its potential supporters.[53]

Johnson blamed the recruiting problem on the sectarian stigma that the *Independent Reflector* had affixed to King's College. And surely many Presbyterians declined to support the school because it was run by Anglicans. Another source of disenchantment, which Johnson did not mention, was the high cost of a King's College education. Tuition, room, and board at King's totaled £33 a year, considerably more than any of the other colonial colleges. Additional expenses attendant upon life in the city, where prices were inflated, usually doubled this figure and raised the total cost for four years at King's to approximately £240. Only the wealthier families could afford to spend this much money on education. Most Presbyterian parents preferred to send their children to Princeton or Yale which, though farther away, were both cheaper and religiously safer. Thrifty Anglican families could and did save money by sending their children to study under William Smith in Philadelphia.[54]

Whether the cause was sectarian suspicion or economy, the result was the same—King's College had the smallest student body of all the colonial colleges. Over half of the students who matric-

53. David C. Humphrey, "King's College in the City of New York, 1754–1776" (Ph.D. diss. Northwestern University, 1968), pp. 246–54, 642–61. Humphrey's dissertation is a mine of information about the early years of King's, one that I discovered only after I had repeated much of his research. His analysis of the student body, however, is based on a wide range of documents that I have not examined.

54. Beverley McAnear, "The Selection of an Alma Mater by Pre-Revolutionary Students," *Pennsylvania Magazine of History and Biography*, 73 (1949): 432–35; also Humphrey, "King's College," 373–76.

ulated dropped out before graduation. Johnson's records show
that some went "into the army," others "to merchandizing," and
still others "to nothing." A significant number transferred to other
schools, most "to Philadelphia College." Only thirty boys received a B.A. during Johnson's tenure. This was about half the
number graduated from the College at Philadelphia and one-
fifth the number who received undergraduate diplomas from
Princeton, even though both of these schools, like King's, were
just under way.[55]

A second problem that emerged in the early years of King's and
exacerbated a host of other difficulties was the unequal division
of power between the trustees and the president. The charter
vested ultimate power to determine college policy in the trustees.
They could select the president, make the college laws, hire and
fire the faculty, and even "direct and appoint what books shall
be publicly read in the college." The president was entrusted
with the "immediate care of the education and government of the
students," but he was only allowed one vote as an ex officio member of the board of trustees. In effect, he had responsibility for
all college affairs, but almost no power.[56]

Since Johnson had been involved in the drafting of the charter,
it is hard to understand why he consented to terms that so restricted presidential authority. The King's charter was modeled
on the New Jersey College charter of 1748, and New Jersey had
followed the trail blazed by Clap in the Yale charter of 1745, in
which the president was granted special prerogatives that made
him the most important member of the governing board. But
the King's charter did not divide power between the president
and trustees, like Yale and Princeton, nor did it, like Harvard
and the English universities, grant the faculty a voice in decisions.
The King's trustees had complete control of the college; the president, officially at least, had less power than any college president
in the colonies. Since the King's charter was drafted during the
height of the controversy with Livingston and the Assembly, it
is possible that the diminished role of the president was intended

55. Bailey Burritt, *Professional Distribution of College and University
Graduates*, pp. 84–88. *Career*, 4 : 244–49 for a list of graduates.
56. *Career*, 4 : 220–221.

as a safeguard against eventual capture of the office by the Presbyterians. Whatever may have been the motives of the trustees, Johnson made no initial fuss about his lack of official power.[57]

But then why should he complain, when the trustees seemed so willing to surrender to him the right to make the college laws, devise the curriculum, hire his son, and, in general, run the show? The board of governors was an unwieldly body, consisting of forty-four members; over half the board were ex officio members unlikely to take their duties seriously. The president was the only member in daily contact with college affairs. All the early evidence indicated that the trustees would accede to his superior knowledge of the college and sanction his proposals. Barclay assured Johnson that the trustees who would bother to attend meetings were all "good friends" who had selected him for the presidency precisely because they trusted his judgment. No matter what the charter said, Johnson was in charge.[58]

He remained in charge for about three years, from 1754 to 1757. During that time the trustees met infrequently and, when they did meet, a small group of "4 or 5 friends" saw to it that Johnson's requests were speedily approved.[59] Johnson wanted a qualified replacement for Billy, who was leaving his tutorial post to be ordained in England. In 1755 the trustees got Leonard Cutting, an Anglican graduate of Cambridge with excellent recommendations, to take over Billy's Latin and Greek classes.[60] When Johnson insisted that King's needed a man trained in natural philosophy added to the faculty, the trustees began a search that brought to King's Daniel Treadwell, a former student of Harvard's renowned John Winthrop. In 1757 Treadwell became

57. Franklin B. Dexter, *A Sketch of the History of Yale University* (New York, 1887), pp. 29–32, for the Yale charter of 1745. S. Johnson to W. S. Johnson, June 1754, *Career*, 1 : 190–91, for the influence of the College of New Jersey. Humphrey, "King's College," 74–85. Also see n. 5.

58. Barclay to Johnson, 4 November 1754, *Career*, 4 : 25.

59. Proposed to the Gov^{rs}, 16 January 1759, College Papers, Columbia University. Humphrey, "King's College," pp. 70–74.

60. For Cutting's credentials see Seabury to Johnson, 2 November, 1755, College Papers, Columbia University.

professor of mathematics and natural philosophy.[61] When Johnson told the trustees that King's could not become a first-rate
college until it had a permanent residence hall, the trustees approved the funds. The cornerstone was laid in 1757.[62]

Ironically, in the same year that the college building began to
go up, Johnson's hopes for King's College began to go down.
Until 1757 he had been optimistic. Although the lack of students
had disappointed him, he was confident that news of the increased competence of the faculty and of his fair but firm leadership would allay public apprehension. After 1757 his most positive statements about King's were apologies. He confessed that
King's was "in its first rudiments and very imperfect" or "in a
very suffering condition." He was not sure when the college would
"lift up her head and flourish." By the time he retired, he admitted that his successor's first chore would be to bring the
college "out of the clouds." [63]

This turnabout was not caused by any increased pressure from
Livingston or the Presbyterians. It was the result of a serious
division within the ranks of the Anglicans. Just as his missionary
activities in Connecticut had been victimized by the hostility of
foreign-born missionaries and the apathy of the S.P.G. officials,
Johnson's plans for King's College were spoiled by the intran-
sigence of the Anglican-dominated board of trustees.

Trouble actually began in 1756, when a smallpox epidemic hit
the city. Johnson had obtained an agreement with the trustees
that allowed him to leave the college whenever the dreaded smallpox endangered his family; he retired to Westchester in November as the epidemic became severe. The trustess appointed a committee "to Visit and Overlook the College during the absence of
the President, Doctor Johnson." But the epidemic lingered on for
over a year, leaving the Committee of Visitation in charge of the
college until Johnson returned in December of 1757.[64]

61. *Early Minutes of the Trustees,* 8 November 1757.
62. Ibid., 13 May 1755.
63. Johnson to East Apthorp, 5 March 1760, *Career,* 4 : 64; Johnson to
Secker, 20 November 1760, ibid., p. 74; Johnson to Daniel Horsmanden, 11
March 1763, ibid., p. 97.
64. Johnson to Secretary, 31 December 1757, ibid., pp. 42–43; *Early Minutes
of the Trustees,* 16 December 1756.

As soon as he returned, it became apparent that the trustees were no longer willing to surrender the control they had exercised during his absence. Johnson undoubtedly assumed that he had the same hold on policy decisions as before his departure, for he routinely recommended the establishment of a grammar school to prepare potential King's students in Latin and Greek. He contrasted King's with the Academy at Philadelphia, which had an elaborate preparatory school system that supplied students for the college. Until New York developed secondary schools on a par with those in Massachusetts, Connecticut, and Pennsylvania, he claimed, King's College would be "obliged to admit them [students] very raw." But the trustees refused to act on Johnson's recommendation. Rather than oppose Johnson directly, they simply made sure that there was not a quorum at their meetings. Johnson suggested that the charter be amended so that "less than fifteen might make a board," but even his former allies, the "4 or 5 friends" that had pushed his recommendations through in the past, would not support his suggestion. "The stupidity of the governors," Johnson wrote his son, "is such that it looks as if they would let their college come to nothing in spite of all that I can do to save it." [65]

The split that appeared in 1757 over the establishment of a grammar school was the first sign of what was perhaps an inevitable breach between Johnson and the trustees. Although the charter gave official control of King's to the trustees, Johnson thought that they were out of touch with the immediate problems of the school and ought to delegate authority to his office. The trustees were mostly lawyers and merchants, businessmen of New York City whom Johnson regarded as "utter strangers to Learning and Colleges." Even though the majority of the trustees were Anglicans, they did not share Johnson's love for the intellectual life or his knowledge of colonial education. From their perspective Johnson must have seemed an insistent old character, always demanding money for new faculty, new buildings, and now a new grammar school. Worse still, he had deserted the college for over a year, but maintained the illusion that he was in charge.

65. Johnson to East Apthorp, June 1760; Johnson to Governors of King's College, 2 November 1762, *Career*, 4 : 69, 85.

Whatever the basis for the sudden break between Johnson and the trustees, events did not allow tempers to cool. The smallpox struck the city again in October of 1759, forcing Johnson to retire to Stratford and leave his superiors in charge of the college once more. He returned in May of 1760, only to find that Daniel Treadwell had died of consumption during his absence and that the school was in a state of near collapse. He admitted to William Samuel that "my absence, together with the long sickness and death of my best tutor has been a great damage, five or six having left the college." Johnson even confessed to Edward Antill that Livingston's former assessment of King's was now almost accurate; the college had "fallen much into disrepute" and affairs were "dragging on very heavily." Only six students entered King's in 1760. The ever small student body now threatened to disappear altogether.[66]

The trustees agreed with Johnson's morose description of the state of the college. They could also count heads and conclude that word of the school's desperate condition had scared potential students away. But the trustees saw these developments as a direct result of Johnson's absences. When he had accepted the presidency he had cautioned them about his advanced age and poor health. Yet who could have guessed that he would be away from the college for so long? Even after he returned in May, he refused to venture outside his room to teach, because he had heard that the "smallpox is much about." Instead of organizing an effort to restore the college to its former promise, he was running up and down the stairs in his study in order to exercise his bad legs. By 1760 a number of the trustees had decided that the first step toward reviving King's College was the removal of Samuel Johnson.

Firing Johnson was not going to be easy. The trustees were empowered to replace any college official, but they did not want to advertise the rupture within Anglican ranks and provide Livingston with additional ammunition. Moreover, by 1760 John-

66. *Career*, 1 : 36–38; Johnson to Secker, 20 October 1759, Cooper to Secker, 23 June 1763, *Career*, 4 : 51, 99; Johnson to Antill, 16 January 1759, College Papers, Columbia University.

son had suffered a series of losses in his family that left him depressed and lonely. It was not an appropriate time for the trustees to tell him he was fired. They had hopes that the aging president would avert embarrassment by stepping down voluntarily. Meanwhile the college languished.

11

Morality and Education

By 1760 Johnson could have used his experiences at King's College as evidence for his metaphysical contention that reality was a pale imitation of archetypal ideals. At King's reality had taken the form of smallpox epidemics, widespread Anglophobia, and a watchdog board of trustees, all of which seemed about to reduce Johnson's hopes for the college to the level of wishful thinking. In fact in 1760 the trustees initiated a search for a successor to Johnson, obviously thinking the old man would soon realize that he was not the one to extricate the college from its current predicament.

But Johnson did not want to leave. He knew about the quest for his successor; it only increased his hatred for the trustees. He knew that the college was an administrator's nightmare; disputes about the uncompleted building, the need for a grammar school, and the president's powers were all unresolved. Yet Johnson did not think that a litany of administrative problems was an accurate measure of the college's stature. What counted most in the end, he believed, was not what happened in the trustee meetings but what happened in the classroom and in the minds of the students. In those areas he honestly felt that he had been able to implant some of his academic ideals, and that those ideals had proven themselves capable of surviving the administrative crises the trustees called reality. The trustees seemed to think the business of a college was business. Johnson thought it was learning and claimed quite openly to know more about learning than anyone else at King's College.

Most of Johnson's ideas about education were borrowed from John Locke, then refashioned so that they fitted neatly into Johnson's theological and metaphysical categories. He first read Locke's *Some Thoughts Concerning Education* in 1729, read it again in 1747, then reviewed it a third time in 1753, just before accepting the job at King's.[1] What most arrested Johnson's attention was Locke's contention that human nature was susceptible to a variety of environmental influences that might be monitored by a skilled teacher so as to encourage the development of desirable characteristics. It was an insight founded on the epistemology of Locke's *Essay*, but wholly compatible with the empirical side of Berkeley's *Principles of Human Knowledge* and Johnson's *Elementa Philosophica*. It was an elevating insight for a prospective college president, since it endowed education with awesome powers and responsibilities. In fact, as the Lockean doctrine developed in the colonies into an acceptable truism if not a self-evident truth, it suggested that the keeper of the schools, as much as the keeper of the churches, possessed the keys to the Kingdom of God.[2]

Johnson saw fit to spell out his own version of the Lockean message in a section of *Elementa Philosophica* devoted to epistemology. It followed from his previous analysis of human perception that each person "is a limited dependent being, that he is every moment affected by various impressions and sensations that do not all depend upon his power . . . in all of which he is merely passive." [3] Both Locke and Berkeley directed attention toward the malleability of human nature and the decisive impact that environmental influences had in the shaping of character. Even infants who were incapable of speech were undergoing significant personality changes, and Johnson hypothesized that "those little creatures, from the beginning, do consider, reflect and think a prodigious deal more than we are commonly apt to imagine." [4] As a result Johnson surmised that "it is mightily in-

1. *Career*, 1 : 509, 522.
2. James L. Axtell, ed., *The Educational Writings of John Locke* (Cambridge, 1968), passim.
3. *Career*, 2 : 375.
4. Ibid., pp. 423–424.

cumbent on those to whose care they [children] are by providence committed, whether parents, nurses, guardians, masters or tutors, to consider them, with great candor." [5] Once men recognized the extreme plasticity of human nature, they possessed the insight that opened a new vista for colonial education. By controlling the intellectual environment within which a person advanced toward maturity, a teacher in effect controlled the way the mature man would think. Those entrusted with the power to educate could even alter the next generation's conception of right and wrong "by steadily affecting them with applause or blame, pleasure or pain, joy or grief, according as they affect or do the one or the other." [6] Here was an insight that informed and inflamed both sides in the fight for control of King's College.[7]

It was also an insight loaded with heretical potential. Fifty years after the King's College controversy, it still inflamed the Reverend Samuel Miller. In his *A Brief Retrospect of the Eighteenth Century,* Miller was critical of those colonial intellectuals who had preached the doctrine that education

> has a kind of intellectual and moral omnipotence; that to its different forms are to be ascribed the chief, if not all the differences observable in the genius, talents and dispositions of men: and that by improving its principles and plan, human nature may, and finally will, reach a state of absolute perfection in this world, or at least go on to a state of unlimited improvement. In short, in the estimation of those who adopt this doctrine, man is the child of circumstances.[8]

From his perspective Miller saw quite correctly that those advocating the omnipotence of education were Arminians who had translated their theological views into a more secular language.

5. Ibid., p. 426.
6. Ibid., p. 425.
7. See an excellent article by J. A. Passmore, "The Malleability of Man in Eighteenth Century Thought," in Earl Wasserman, ed., *Aspects of the Eighteenth Century* (Baltimore, 1965), pp. 21–46, for an insightful analysis of Lockean psychology and its impact on educational theory.
8. Samuel Miller, *A Brief Retrospect of the Eighteenth Century,* 2 vols. (New York, 1803), 2 : 295. See also Lawrence A. Cremin, *American Education: The Colonial Experience, 1607–1683* (New York, 1970), pp. 561–63.

Those who insisted that human nature was completely malleable denied that man was born with an innate moral character. They rejected the doctrine of original sin. They took from God and gave to men the control over human development. They tended to adopt a utilitarian approach to morality that equated civil behavior with godliness, thereby encouraging hypocrisy. New Englanders had debated these issues for generations. The old dispute over grace and free will had given way to a dispute over nature and nurture, but the point at issue remained unchanged: how can men be remade?

Small wonder then that the educational ideals that Johnson brought to King's College were well thought out, for they not only followed naturally from his carefully formulated philosophical principles, but they had also been refined in the long battle over his Arminian theology.

Just as he refused to subscribe to the Arminian view of original sin, Johnson rejected the Lockean view of human nature. The students at King's College he regarded as extremely impressionable young men. The tutors and other architects of the curriculum, he thought, had enormous influence over them. But Johnson always retained the Puritan conviction that human nature was essentially evil. Man was not completely malleable. Those in charge of a young man's education were not making impressions on a blank tablet. If human nature was allowed to develop on its own, Johnson felt sure that it would be "carried down the stream of a senseless, untoward, impetuous humor, and have not resolution to muster up force of mind and thought sufficient to stem the current." If removed from all forms of influence, Johnson believed that men would always allow "appetite, passion, interest, anything to bear sway" until they became "a miserable species of animal . . . called human kind!" [9] The only thing that might deter a man from damnation was God's grace. And the only thing that might free a man from his baser instincts was a Christian education.

Johnson thought that education, like conversion, was a long and difficult process. In *Elementa Philosophica* he outlined the

9. *Career*, 2 : 525.

various stages through which a person must advance in order to
overcome his depraved tendencies. From infancy children should
"be taught and inured to the practice of self-denial, and the
moderation and restraint of their appetites and passions." [10]
They should begin to learn reading and writing "from their
first capacity for it." By the time they are twelve or fourteen,
children should be "well versed in the construction of speech,
both Latin and French, as well as English; and in two or three
more [years] of Greek and Hebrew." At some time during childhood each person should be "initiated in the study of nature, by
being led into the easiest and most delightful things in natural
history, and a general survey of the mighty works of God, both in
heaven [astronomy] and earth [physics]." Johnson also prescribed
early doses of logic, metaphysics, mathematics, and theology,
subjects which a young man should explore more fully in college.[11]

At some point during the pre-college years Johnson believed
that each person who underwent this rigorous intellectual program would gain control over the passionate side of his nature and
relegate his instincts "to a ready submission to the dictates of reason and conscience." In fact, Johnson claimed that "the great
concern of culture, and right education, is to awaken . . . attention to this inward intuitive sense of true and false, good and
bad, right and wrong." [12] In his sermons he had described the
way in which each person was presented with grace and given
the opportunity to become a "New Creature" capable of loving
God and neighbor. In his educational writings Johnson preached
the same kind of message: through education men developed the
capacity to act rationally and morally.[13]

Underlying the similarity between Johnson's views of conversion and of education was his conviction that religion and
learning were different means to the same end, namely, a life of
Christian virtue. By this he did not mean a life of "merely ex-

10. Ibid., p. 427.
11. Ibid., pp. 428–41.
12. Ibid., p. 425.
13. See above chap. 7, for a discussion of Johnson's view of religious conversion.

ternal morality." Like his Puritan ancestors, he was unwilling to
settle for appearances because he believed that God would judge
men according to their deepest convictions. Just as a man who
performed a variety of good works was not necessarily a saint, a
man who demonstrated remarkable proficiency in languages,
logic, and natural philosophy was not necessarily wise. A truly
educated man was one who used his finely tuned intellectual tools
in accordance with God's will. Education could raise a man to
the level at which he was capable of activating what Johnson
called "this inward intuitive sense" or "the intellectual light," but
it could not guarantee that the man would have the final insight. Johnson believed that true virtue was unteachable. Like
Ralph Cudworth, he thought that educators "cannot teach it
[virtue] to us like a mechanical art or trade." [14]

Johnson, then, though an ardent believer in the power of education and an adherent of the Lockean doctrine of man's sus-
ceptibility to environmental influences, did not carry Lockean
doctrines to the extremes that Samuel Miller warned against. He
harnessed his educational theory to traditional religious goals and
he recognized that education was bounded by the same conflicting forces that operate within each personality. Still, the main
impression he generated in his writings on education was opti-
mism. Education could not do it all, he seemed to say, but it
offered a deliberate and systematic way to develop man's inherent potential, a way to organize experience so that people
would be more receptive to divine messages. Unlike Hobbes, he
believed that men were more than just finite bundles of self-in-
terest. Unlike the utilitarians, he believed that education should
aspire to a higher goal than the cultivation of civil behavior.
Like Plato and a host of other idealists in western philosophy, he
believed that there were absolute standards that all men who
came out of the cave of ignorance should strive to emulate. Most
optimistically of all, he thought he knew how to organize a
curriculum that put his educational theories into practice.

Johnson lifted a maxim from Berkeley and put it on the title
page of the third edition of *Elementa Philosophica*. It was also

14. Quoted in Passmore, "The Malleability of Man," p. 30.

a kind of summation of his academic goals and a guiding principle in his organization of the curriculum. It read, in part, "He, who hath not much meditated on God, the human mind, and the Summum Bonum, may possibly make a thriving Earth-worm, but will undoubtedly make a sorry Patriot and a sorry Statesman." [15]

When Johnson selected the subjects to be offered at King's and the authors to be read in the classes, his first concern was always their moral impact on the students. In terms of his own educational philosophy, he seemed to ask if the work under consideration helped to subdue the passions and nourish the rational faculties. Did it provide models for virtuous action? Did it clarify the way that God preached to man through nature? Did it show how to become a better Christian?

Although these were moral concerns that reflected a rejection of knowledge for its own sake (real knowledge, Johnson thought, must have a moral purpose), it soon became evident that Johnson did not mean to rule out the study of subjects that were primarily secular in orientation. In fact, the only traditional discipline that Johnson dropped from the King's College curriculum was theology. There were no Saturday lectures from either Anglican or Puritan theological sources, primarily because Johnson realized that the Presbyterians would charge that he used his academic position to propagate Arminian doctrines. Rather than rotate the theology lectureship among the various ministerial leaders of the city, a possibility he considered for a time, Johnson decided to eliminate all formal instruction in theology. Otherwise, the subjects offered at King's were identical to the subjects Johnson had studied when he was a student at Yale—languages, logic, natural philosophy, mathematics, and metaphysics. What made the King's curriculum different was not the subjects offered, but the content of the subjects and the moralistic vision of the man who determined that content.[16]

15. *Career*, 2 : 345.

16. Johnson to East Apthorp, 1 December 1759, *Career*, 4 : 56–57, contains the fullest account of the curriculum that I could find. From this letter and scattered references I have compiled a list of the courses and the books read in each course. There was no college library during Johnson's presidency. Students purchased books privately through a local bookseller. See Account

A first-year student at King's had a course load almost entirely devoted to Latin and Greek. Johnson openly admitted that entering students were inadequately prepared in the classical languages and required additional grammar instruction before they could begin to study the classics as literature. "Our first year is chiefly grammatical," he wrote to East Apthorp, and he never allowed the trustees (who had delayed the funding of a new grammar school) to forget it.[17] Johnson recognized that grammar was a tedious business both for students and teachers, but he also thought that it inculcated disciplined mental habits. It was a kind of academic training that prepared the rational faculties for more challenging subjects. It was so basic and so important in Johnson's view that, at one time or another, every faculty member was required to teach it. Johnson taught it as long as he was president. Billy, Leonard Cutting, and Daniel Treadwell each took at least one class through the various conjugations, moods, tenses, and cases.

But learning languages at King's did not mean just learning grammar. Once a class proved itself proficient in grammar and capable of translating simple works like Caesar's *Commentaries,* it moved on to the study of the Latin and Greek classics. Johnson knew that Cicero and Homer were pagans, but he also thought that they had insights into the human condition that were perfectly compatible with the principles of Christian morality. The main reason for requiring students to read Latin and Greek, he suggested, was "to make them intelligent and serious Christians . . . giving them a plan of Christianity with its evidences, and inculcating it upon their hearts." [18]

For example, one of the texts used at King's was Cicero's *De Officiis,* a book that promised to examine "the practical principles of conduct to which all of life's experiences may be con-

---

of Garrat Noel, 4 September 1761, in College Papers, Columbia University. After I had completed this chapter I was directed to the dissertation by David C. Humphrey, "King's College," which contains a full-blown account of the King's curriculum. While I disagree with Humphrey on certain points, revisions of this chapter benefitted from material that he caused me to re-examine.

17. Johnson to Apthorp, 1 December 1759, *Career,* 4 : 56.
18. Ibid., p. 243.

formed." [19] It was a handbook of political honesty and personal
rectitude that Cicero addressed to his son in the hope of impressing on him the distinction between moral rightness (*honestas*)
and usefulness (*utilitas*). Although *De Officiis* at times degenerated
into a compilation of witty epigrams and anecdotes, Cicero's concern for personal virtue and a commonwealth of justice paralleled
Johnson's concern for Christian morality. In addition, Cicero
wrote *De Officiis* in 44 B.C., immediately after the assassination of
Caesar, when the stability of the Roman republic was being undermined by political divisiveness and social degeneracy. It was
also a time when a variety of doctrines and philosophical schools
(i.e. Stoicism, Epicureanism, the Academics, the Peripatetics) were
in conflict with one another for intellectual supremacy. Cicero
called attention to the clash of philosophies and argued for a
skeptical and eclectic outlook that would blend selected features
of the different schools into a balanced world-view capable of
giving direction to men during a confusing period of history.[20]
Whether or not Johnson analogized Rome to the British empire
or recognized the similarity between Cicero's philosophical dilemma and his own, it seems safe to say that he did not select *De
Officiis* as a Latin text for its stylistic achievements alone.

Johnson required sophomores to read a Latin treatise by
Samuel Pufendorf, entitled *De Officio*. Pufendorf was a Saxon
jurist and political philosopher who gained fame as an advocate
of natural law and reason over biblical revelation and faith.[21]
While Johnson did not agree with the emphasis Pufendorf gave to
rational as opposed to biblical evidence, he felt that Pufendorf's
exposition of the respective duties of rulers and citizens contained
a great many moral insights. In *Elementa Philosophica* Johnson
himself had distinguished among a man's duties to God, to himself, and to other men, a set of distinctions lifted straight from
Pufendorf.[22] Johnson also agreed with Pufendorf that "no animal
is fiercer or more untameable than man," especially man removed

19. Hubert M. Poteat, trans., *Marcus Tullius Cicero . . . On Duties*
(Chicago, 1950), p. 468.
20. Ibid., pp. 3–5.
21. I have used the James B. Scott translation of Pufendorf's *De Officio
Hominis et Civis Juxta Legem Naturalem* (New York, 1927).
22. Ibid., pp. 22–42.

from the socializing influences of the community.[23] Pufendorf
re-enforced Johnson's conviction that the inherent potential of
human nature could be developed only within structured communities, where "citizens' minds [can] be imbued with them
[right teachings] from boyhood." Pufendorf even rated a ruler's
power over education on a par with his power over the legislature
and the courts.[24]

Throughout Pufendorf's book there ran the persistent theme
that rulers and ruled were bound together in an interlocking network of mutual responsibility which, when it operated effectively,
made the state "a composite moral person." [25] Although his vision
of the origin of society followed Hobbes more closely than Locke
(and therefore Pufendorf did not sanction the right of revolution), he did insist that a ruler was bound by the same moral laws
as the governed. And in the end he granted that "the welfare
of the people is the supreme law." [26] Here then was a work that
suggested that man was depraved but educable; that laws were
not just arbitrary restraints but also moral precepts; that rulers
as well as ruled must observe these laws—a work that constantly
reminded men to recognize the responsibilities attendant upon
the observation, "Thou art not alone in the world." It seems
probable that the Latin classes Johnson taught on Pufendorf
were as much classes in moral philosophy as grammar.

Sophomores also read Latin selections from Scripture gathered
together in a convenient edition by Jean Heuzet, who described
his book as "an Assemblage of several Strokes of Morality and
History, many of which may serve as Rules and Models for the
Conditions of Life." [27] Initially Johnson probably regarded the
scriptural translations as a way to balance Pufendorf's emphasis
on a rational moral system. But in 1757 Johnson announced a
sudden shift in his intellectual outlook, a shift that had profound implications for the curriculum and the role of Scripture
at King's.

23. Ibid., p. 104.
24. Ibid., pp. 110–12.
25. Ibid., p. 108.
26. Ibid., pp. 117–21.
27. Jean Heuzet, *Selectae E Profana Scriptoribus Historiae* . . . (London,
1758), pp. vi–vii.

The immediate cause of his metamorphosis was a book by John Hutchinson entitled *Moses' Principia*. From Johnson's perspective Hutchinson suggested an approach to learning that opened up new insights at the same time it showed the folly of many respected philosophies. "I have been now more thoroughly canvassing [Hutchinson] in regard to the philosophical as well as the theological part," he wrote "and to my unspeakable satisfaction am much convinced it is, in both, entirely satisfactory."[28]

Hutchinson was, in fact, a kind of linguist and amateur philosopher who was recognized as a charlatan by his contemporaries as well as succeeding generations of scholars.[29] His appeal was partly due to the simplicity of his message—namely, that all knowledge was contained in the original Hebrew version of the Old Testament. Hutchinson claimed that God had revealed himself to the prophets and they had written down his revelations in Hebrew. But at the Tower of Babel God had punished man for his vanity by burdening him with a multiplicity of languages that prevented him from understanding the Hebrew truths. As time passed and the number of languages grew, the translations of the Old Testament became more barbarous and misrepresentative. Now, in the eighteenth century, Hutchinson claimed to have uncovered some previously unnoticed grammatical principles of ancient Hebrew, which allowed him to unlock the long-lost meaning of the Old Testament. In *Moses' Principia* Hutchinson not only announced his discovery, but condemned scientists like Newton who persisted in searching for truth in nature. According to Hutchinson, if scholars would stop exploring the natural world and devote themselves to the analysis of languages, they would discover the ways in which men had perverted divine truths. They should give special attention to Hebrew, the primal language, and apply what they learned to the Old Testament.

Johnson's belief in Hutchinson was much like Berkeley's belief in tar water—a sad, misguided phase of a generally distinguished career. He had read *Moses' Principia* before coming to King's, but had the good sense to reject most of Hutchinson's arguments. But he was fascinated with Hutchinson's contention

28. S. Johnson to W. S. Johnson, 30 January 1757, *Career*, 1 : 270.
29. John Hutchinson, *Moses' Principia* (London, 1724), passim.

that the source of human ignorance was a matter of grammatical imprecision, faulty translations of God's revealed words. In *Elementa Philosophica* he had written

> He [God] hath condescended to accommodate himself to the low capacities of the general rate of mankind, by using various types and emblems, and a most beautiful and instructive language taken from what is familiar among us, wherewith to represent and shadow forth his perfections and dispensations, which are vastly above our comprehension.[30]

Here he was using the word "language" in a broad sense to mean the entire natural world as well as the Bible. Nevertheless, he had seen fit to footnote Hutchinson and insert a paragraph on the "original symbols and instructions" contained in the Old Testament. In the London edition of *Elementa Philosophica*, William Smith, whom Johnson had authorized to handle the publication in England, excised the references to Hutchinson and thereby prevented Johnson from embarrassing himself before English readers.[31] Johnson, however, was outraged at Smith's unsolicited editorial assistance. He thought his restrained commentary on Hutchinson's curious theory was perfectly justifiable.[32]

Between 1757 and 1760 Johnson's opinion of Hutchinson grew less and less restrained. When East Apthorp tried to steer him away from Hutchinson, Johnson asserted that Hutchinson had proved that "our first parents and the ancient patriarchs and earliest nations" embodied all the moral truths of Christianity.[33] The Archbishop of Canterbury informed Johnson that one of the candidates for a position at King's had been rejected because he was "deeply tinctured with Mr. Hutchinson's notions in philosophy and Hebrew, both of which I take to be groundless." [34] At this very time Johnson was trying to coax the sophomores at

30. *Career*, 2 : 434–35.
31. Ibid., pp. 346–51, for Smith's introduction to the London edition.
32. Johnson to Secker, 25 October 1754, ibid., p. 333, for Johnson's comment that he was "not a little surprised" at Smith's free-handed editing, "there being scarce a page in which he had not made some alterations, many of which I think are by no means any advantage to it but much the contrary."
33. Johnson to Apthorp, 22 December 1760 [?], ibid., p. 342.
34. Secker to Johnson, 4 November 1760, *Career*, 4 : 71.

King's to concentrate on Hebrew grammar in an effort to recover
the lost meaning of the Old Testament. Johnson was gravitating
more and more toward the view that the Bible, properly translated, was the sole source of truth:

> I have heretofore been long wandering after the wisdom of this
> world, and eagerly pursued the philosophy so much in vogue
> [the New Learning], but of late after the example of some
> others [Hutchinson] . . . I have been almost entirely devoted
> to the study of the Holy Scriptures, and especially the pure and
> noble original.[35]

It was highly ironic that the man who had once denounced the
antiquated curriculum of Yale and called for the study of Newton,
Locke, and other modern philosophers should become an advocate
of biblical literalism when he gained control of the King's College
curriculum. But Johnson looked back at his fascination for the
New Learning with regret and scorned those former intellectual
idols who "had led me for many years into the reasoning humor
now so fashionable." [36] In the past he had been able to combine
a respect for Scripture with an appreciation of modern scholarship, a strong faith with a commitment to the development of
human reason, a religious temperament with a concern for scientific discoveries. Exposure to Hutchinson's work apparently
convinced him that religion and modern scholarship were fundamentally antithetical.

Yet a single book can seldom produce such a dramatic turnabout by itself. Johnson had always been wary of thinkers like
Collins and Tindal who extend human reason beyond its limited
boundaries. In his theology he was careful to distinguish between
his moderately Arminian doctrines and the exhalted claims of the
deists. And in his philosophical writings he insisted that the
human pursuit of truth was never destined to bridge the gap
between types and archetypes or resolve the deepest mysteries of
life. Hutchinson's enjoinder to trust only in the word of God as
revealed in Scripture played on a mind that had shown itself mis-
trustful of the growing tendency to ignore the crippling dis-

35. Johnson to Mrs. Anne Watts, 24 February 1757, ibid., 1 : 273.
36. Johnson to Horne, n.d., ibid., 2 : 340.

abilities that impeded man's understanding. Finally, at the very time when he was rereading Hutchinson, Johnson was reminded that God did not always subscribe to rational laws. In the spring of 1756 his grandson (William Samuel's boy) died unexpectedly. In June of the same year Billy, who was in England to receive Anglican orders, was struck down by the smallpox and died. In 1758, soon after Johnson and his family had fled New York to avoid the smallpox, his wife Charity contracted the disease; she too died. In June of 1759 Johnson's daughter-in-law, who had agreed to keep house for him at the college, came down with a fever that proved to be fatal. Then in 1760 both Benjamin Nicoll (his stepson) and tutor Daniel Treadwell also passed away quite suddenly. The string of deaths gave Johnson a series of emotional jolts that shook his belief in a God of reason. Those who convinced themselves that the theories of Locke and Newton allowed man to understand the mental and physical principles underlying human existence were deluding themselves, for they ignored the instant and arbitrary way that God might scramble all rational principles. The Hebraic scheme of *Moses' Principia* required no commitment to reason, only a simple faith in the word of God as revealed to the prophets. For an old man who had seen his plans for King's College victimized by the irrationality of the trustees and who now saw his relatives and friends snatched away, the Bible had an enormous appeal; Hutchinson's strange theory was merely an intellectual device that allowed an aged and disconsolate scholar to find comfort in biblical dogmas.[37]

In one sense Johnson's denunciation of the New Learning and his retreat to the shallow theory of John Hutchinson had an impact on King's College: they were symptomatic of Johnson's increasing despondency during the difficult years from 1757 to 1760. It was during this period that the trustees became disenchanted with the president and began the search for his successor. From a historical perspective it is clear that Johnson's move toward the Hebraic version of the Bible was an intellectual retreat that signaled his demise as a critical thinker. His most significant intellectual achievements had been the product of his efforts to

37. For accounts of these deaths see Johnson's correspondence in ibid., 1 : 38–39, 257, 259–63, 277, 280–81, 333–35.

reconcile the religious insights of New England Puritanism with the scientific and philosophical discoveries of the eighteenth century. By rejecting the New Learning and embracing Scripture Johnson effectively eliminated the tension between these two intellectual traditions, but he gained peace of mind at the cost of intellectual vitality. The trustees did not know this (they never mentioned Johnson's biblicism), but they did know that the man in charge of King's College in 1760 was not the man they had hired in 1754.

In another sense the shift in Johnson's intellectual positions had little if any effect on the college. He made no effort to impose the doctrines of *Moses' Principia* on unwilling students. He may have supplemented his own Latin classes with the observation that the study of grammar and philology was a useful way to prepare oneself for an understanding of the Bible. And he did make an effort to popularize Hebrew at King's, an effort that proved futile. He admitted to Edward Antill that he was unable to "prevail on above three or four while I had the care of the college at New York to give any attention to it [Hebrew]." [38] Students continued to translate from Caesar, Cicero, Pufendorf, and Homer as well as the Bible. All the traditional academic subjects remained in the curriculum. In fact, Johnson continued to preside over a college in which students were steeped in the same New Learning that the president had disavowed. Although Johnson had retrogressed to a crude biblicism, the King's College curriculum embodied the enlightened notions he had defended at the height of his intellectual powers.

For example, despite Johnson's increased sense of the weakness of human reason, he continued to insist that students read logic late in their sophomore and early in their junior years. The book used was *The Elements of Logic* by William Duncan, a Lockean text that denounced the a priori categories of Ramist logic in favor of an empirical approach that emphasized the ordering of information received through the senses.[39] Students learned that their "capacity for reflection" depended less on the mastery of prescribed rules than on the ability to distinguish

38. Johnson to Antill [1759], College Papers, Columbia University.
39. William Duncan, *The Elements of Logic* (Philadelphia, 1792).

between reliable and unreliable evidence. Duncan, like Johnson in *Elementa Philosophica*, suggested there were limits to man's rational development and gave a special role to intuition (what Johnson called the intellectual light) as a guide to truths that lay beyond the realm of reason. Here Duncan, again like Johnson, implied that the ultimate goal of the logical mind was to recognize the moral imperatives that governed all intelligent men. Perhaps because of Duncan's hostility toward systems of logic that encouraged verbal trickery at the expense of empirical arguments, King's did not require students to engage in formal disputations. As of 1759, Johnson reported, "We have not as yet had any syllogistic disputations." [40] *The Principles of Logic* was probably the best logic text available in the colonies at the time and served as the standard work at William Smith's Academy as well as at King's.[41]

Third-year students at King's spent most of their time studying mathematics and natural philosophy. These were subjects that had increased in importance as the eighteenth century progressed and colonial scholars grew more aware of the benefits to be gained by applying their rational faculties to a study of the natural world. In Philadelphia William Smith devoted fully one-third of his school's curriculum to the mastery of algebra, trigonometry, fluxions (integral calculus), astronomy, and Newtonian physics.[42] At Princeton president Aaron Burr, also recognizing the scientific upsurge, required his juniors to spend a full year with Newton, and brought in guest lecturers to demonstrate the principles of electricity.[43] Harvard not only had John Winthrop, Hollis Professor of Natural Philosophy, and after Benjamin Franklin the most renowned colonial scientist of the day, but also boasted an elaborate assemblage of instruments with which to demonstrate physical principles and conduct ex-

40. Johnson to East Apthorp, 1 December 1759, *Career*, 4 : 57.
41. Smith's curriculum, complete with required texts and suggested reading, is reprinted in Cremin, *American Education*, pp. 382–83.
42. Ibid., pp. 378–84; also Edward P. Cheyney, *History of the University of Pennsylvania, 1740–1940* (Philadelphia, 1940), pp. 82–107.
43. T. J. Wertenbaker, *Princeton, 1746–1896* (Princeton, 1946), pp. 90–93; also Francis L. Broderick, "Pulpit, Physics, and Politics: The Curriculum of the College of New Jersey, 1746–1794," *William and Mary Quarterly*, 3rd ser. 6 (1949): 51–57.

periments. Finally, at Yale, the chief advocate of natural philosophy was none other than Thomas Clap, who managed to
combine his religious zeal with a personal commitment to the
Baconian method and Newtonian mechanics. As always, Clap
insisted that the Yale students share his commitment.[44]

Johnson did not require the King's students to share his commitment to Hutchinson's antiscientific bias. For years he had
accepted Clap's comfortable view that an appreciation of the
Newtonian universe led inexorably to an admiration of God's
handiwork. Between 1757 and 1760 he had decided that *Moses'
Principia* was more trustworthy than Newton's, not because
Newtonian mechanics was scientifically in error, but because a
rational analysis of nature had shown a tendency to produce
skeptical deists rather than God-fearing Christians. What Johnson perceived more clearly than college presidents like Smith,
Burr, or Clap was that the long-range impact of the scientific
method was disastrous for religion. The scientific approach to
nature was not wrong in itself, but it had demonstrated a tendency to woo men away from the mysteries of a supernatural God
and to create the expectation that the universe was comprehensible to mortal men. And yet, despite his profound fear of
the scientific method, Johnson did more than anyone else at
King's to assure the students of a first-rate education in mathematics and natural philosophy.

It was Johnson who demanded that the trustees conduct a
search for a man qualified to teach these subjects. By 1757, just
as the oldest class at King's entered its junior year, the trustees
came up with Daniel Treadwell, a Harvard graduate recommended by Winthrop as possessing "uncommon proficiency in
mathematical learning." [45] Everyone who met Treadwell seems
to have been impressed with his competence. John Adams, who
happened to ride in the coach with him on the way to New
York, saw fit to comment favorably on Treadwell in his diary.[46]

44. John E. Van De Wetering, "God, Science, and the Puritan Dilemma,"
New England Quarterly 38 (1965): 494–507; Tucker, *Puritan Protagonist*, pp.
100–21.
45. John Winthrop to Samuel Auchmuty, 19 April 1757, College Papers,
Columbia University.
46. Quoted in *Harvard Graduates*, 13 : 795–98.

A correspondent for the *New York Mercury* also reported that "Mr. Treadwell, in a clear and concise manner demonstrated the Revolution of the Earth around the Sun, both from astronomical observations, and the Theory of Gravity." [47] Johnson was sufficiently impressed with the young man's ability to request that he became the college's first professor of mathematics and natural philosophy. Treadwell became the only professor at King's in November of 1757. It was also Johnson who obtained for Treadwell's classes the expensive scientific apparatus needed to demonstrate the principles of natural philosophy.

When Treadwell died of consumption in 1759, Johnson again took the lead in the search for an adequate replacement. Upon his return to the college in 1760 the trustees agreed to hire a temporary instructor named Samuel Giles and begin a search for a permanent professor.[48] It was Johnson who wrote to English friends, complaining that "we extremely want a tutor to teach mathematics and experimental philosophy." [49] By December of 1760 Johnson's letters had turned up Robert Harpur, a graduate of the University of Glasgow, who began teaching at King's the next month. Although Harpur was a Presbyterian, Johnson felt his scholarly qualifications were more important than his religious preference. "This [hiring of Harpur] seems a very particular providence," Johnson wrote to William Samuel, "for we were suffering extremely and the scholars are so pleased." [50]

It is difficult to know how sophisticated the King's College course in mathematics and natural philosophy was. The basic mathematical text was Edmund Stone's edition of *Euclid's Elements,* but whether Treadwell or Harpur supplemented Euclid with lectures on trigonometry and calculus is unknown. In natural philosophy the students read John Rowning's *A Compendious System of Natural Philosophy,* a clear presentation of the Newtonian explanation of mechanics, hydrostatics, optics, and other natural phenomena.[51] Judged on the basis of the books

47. *New York Mercury,* 26 June 1758.
48. *Early Minutes of the Trustees,* 25 March 1761.
49. Johnson to Secker, 20 November 1760, *Career,* 4 : 74.
50. S. Johnson to W. S. Johnson, 12 October 1761, ibid., 1 : 314.
51. I perused the London edition of 1772.

assigned, which again were the same as those used at the Philadelphia Academy, the King's College offerings in science appear
quite advanced. And certainly Treadwell and Harpur had training that qualified them to offer excellent instruction. In general, however, the sciences taught at King's during Johnson's
tenure probably did not meet the highest standards. For that
matter most of the genuinely original scientific research in the
colonies was going on outside the colleges. And the schools that
developed a reputation for their offerings in natural philosophy
tended to be places where a single man like Winthrop (Harvard) or William Small (William and Mary) remained for a
long time. The faculty at King's was too unstable to permit
a tradition of scientific excellence to develop while Johnson was
president. The class that reached its junior year after Treadwell had died and before Harpur was hired probably learned
very little natural philosophy at all. Yet, despite the inadequacies,
it seems clear that Johnson did all that was humanly possible
to establish the sciences at King's. The professorship in mathematics and natural philosophy was a permanent fixture that his
successors could use to advance scientific study in years to come.
And the early years, thanks largely to Johnson's efforts, provided
the beginnings of a scientific tradition that no one need be
ashamed of.[52]

In his final year at King's a student found himself in the
classroom with the college president, studying from a book his
teacher had written, entitled *Elementa Philosophica*. If there was
any field in which King's led all the other colonial colleges, it

52. Hindle, *Pursuit of Science*, pp. 80–101; also Hornberger, *Scientific
Thought*. The place of science in the King's curriculum is one of those
tantalizing historical problems that derives its vitality from the fact that
the small amount of existent evidence can be used to support several conflicting interpretations. Hornberger, for example, regards Johnson's conversion to biblicism as evidence that the sciences at King's had no prominence.
In *American Education* Cremin uses Johnson's curricular proposal of 1754
as evidence that the sciences were as important at King's as at the College
of Philadelphia. In my view Cremin is closer to the truth, but, as I have tried
to suggest, the problem is complex, involving Johnson's personality, the
discrepancy between curricular goals and actual offerings, and faculty stability.
See Cremin, *American Education*, pp. 405–407; also Humphrey, "King's College," pp. 447–67.

was in what Johnson and other scholars had come to call moral
philosophy. It was a subject, for example, in which William
Smith publicly announced Johnson's supremacy and also used
Johnson's book as the standard text.[53] (Smith supplemented
Elementa Philosophica with his personal lectures on moral philosophy, which in 1758 he delivered from the city jail, where he
was serving a three-month term for libel.) The moral philosophy
course at King's was supposed to be the capstone of a young
man's education; in this and many other ways it was reminiscent
of the senior year course in metaphysics offered to Yale students
at the beginning of the eighteenth century. Johnson, in fact,
regarded moral philosophy as the modern version of the old
idea of technologia, a kind of summary or synthesis of all that
an educated man should know. Gone was the dated metaphysical
scheme of William Ames; it was replaced by the Berkeleyan
philosophy as explicated in Johnson's *Elementa Philosophica*.
Gone was the elaborate web of distinctions of Ramus or John
Alsted; in its place Johnson had put the empirical epistemology
of Berkeley as well as the nonempirical philosophy of Cambridge
Platonists like Richard Cudworth and John Norris. Gone was
the scholastic vision of the physical world; despite the dangerously seductive nature of Newtonian doctrines, they were far
superior to the antiquated physics of the Aristotelians, especially
if discussions of Newton were laced with comments from John
Hutchinson.

But in a fundamental way moral philosophy was the intellectual heir of technologia. Both were broadly based subject areas
meant to encompass every conceivable relationship between
God and man, to include all subjects now referred to as the social sciences. In addition to serving as the ultimate in interdisciplinary learning, both moral philosophy and technologia
had the same educational goal. The Puritan theologian William Ames would have said that only after men had prepared
their souls to receive God could grace come and genuine morality
be possible. The mid-eighteenth-century moralist like Johnson

53. *Career*, 2 : 346–47 for Smith's praise; Cremin, *American Education*, pp.
382–83 for the use of the text in Philadelphia.

translated this into the view that men are capable of real knowledge only after they have prepared their minds through the study of the meaning of virtue. Both moral philosophy and technologia were expressions of one of the oldest traditions in western thought, a tradition that Johnson could find in either the Old Testament or Plato: namely, that knowledge and virtue are interdependent, and the search for truth is simultaneously a search for morality.

The beauty of the course in moral philosophy lay in the fact that it encouraged respect for religion without giving preference to one particular sect. Like latitudinarianism, moral philosophy was able to appeal to a broad spectrum of religious men precisely because it was an amorphous discipline that gathered a variety of doctrinal perspectives under a single canopy. One of the most recent and perceptive commentators on the history of moral philosophy in America has characterized it as "the semi-secular way station between the great era of theological dominance and the present when objective science presses so hard on all other modes of experience." [54] In this sense moral philosophy represented not only an attempt to preserve the moral insights of religion against the inroads of science, but also to show God-fearing men of many doctrinal persuasions what they had in common.

Despite its many metaphysical flaws (often because of them), *Elementa Philosophica* was an excellent vehicle for teaching moral philosophy. There were several sections of the work that Johnson probably played down to the King's seniors. References to the rationality and benevolence of God and the inherent logic of nature made less sense to him in 1760 than they had in 1754. And the scattered references to John Hutchinson undoubtedly received extra attention. But Johnson did not need

54. The quotation is from Norman Fiering, "President Samuel Johnson and the Circle of Knowledge," *William and Mary Quarterly*, 3 ser. 28 (1971): 233. Fiering's article, along with his lengthier account of Johnson in "Moral Philosophy in America, 1650–1750, and Its British Context" (Ph.D. diss., Columbia University, 1969), pp. 253–376 have made me more aware of the significance of moral philosophy as an intellectual bridge between Puritanism and the Enlightenment.

to tamper with the basic philosophical scheme of *Elementa Philosophica* in order to drive home the moral lessons he wanted to impart. According to his Berkeleyan framework every human perception was the direct result of some divine action and therefore had a moral meaning. Since all principles of knowledge originated with God, they served simultaneously as guides to truth and virtue.[55]

The central message of the moral philosophy course was that all intelligent men should strive to lead their lives in accordance with these eternal moral principles. Students were encouraged to begin the quest for virtue, not in expectation of any rewards or punishments beyond the grave, but because a virtuous life produced three positive consequences: it gave happiness and self-satisfaction to the individual, it contributed to God's glory, and it promoted the well-being of one's neighbor.[56] Johnson tried to show the seniors how the four-year experience at King's was intended to produce men capable of both moral and intellectual leadership. The study of languages not only disciplined the mind, but also exposed the future leaders of New York to the moral wisdom of the classics. Those few who studied Hebrew grammar were better able to interpret the divine messages contained in Scripture. In logic the students had learned how to employ reason as an instrument to discover moral principles. In mathematics and natural philosophy they had observed how God had imbedded moral signposts in nature as nonscriptural guides that, properly taught, reinforced the lessons of the Bible. Now in moral philosophy class they were inspecting the entire intellectual landscape, observing how the different parts of curriculum, like the different departments of learning, came together in the service of virtue.

In September of 1759, soon after Charity died and at a time when the smallpox epidemic was at its height, Johnson drafted a letter which he requested be read to the trustees "at their next meeting After my Decease or Dismission." Apparently

55. See above, chap. 8.
56. *Career*, 2 : 497–501.

Johnson thought he was either about to die or be fired, and he wanted to fire a parting shot at the trustees. He reviewed the troubled history of King's College, noting the various administrative problems that had plagued the fledgling school, noting also that he shared in the failure to make King's the great institution he hoped it would become in the future. But he wanted the trustees to know that he was not ashamed of the college or his role in its development. The students at King's, he wrote, had received a rigorous grounding in several disciplines; most importantly, they had begun to learn the meaning of virtue. In a "dangerous and vexatious age" they had been taught to take pride in the enduring values of the Christian religion, values that transcended the sectarian disputes of the day. Johnson asked the trustees to assure him that King's would follow the course that he had set. He advised that the next president "should always be not only a serious Christian, but a clergyman, a divine as well as a philosopher." [57]

Although it was a self-serving judgment, it was based on an honest and fairly accurate appraisal. Students of colonial education have tended to notice the sectarian controversy over the founding of King's College, to take the criticism of the Livingston faction at face value or to accept the trustees' complaints about administrative chaos as an indication of academic failure. In fact, the curriculum established at King's when Johnson was president implemented almost all the educational goals that Johnson had announced to the public in 1754. There were no courses in practical subjects like navigation and surveying, as Johnson had promised there would be. But in the more traditional academic areas King's offered a program that most resembled the much-praised program of William Smith's Academy of Philadelphia. The year-long course in moral philosophy, which was to become a fixture in American higher education for the next century, had allowed Johnson to offer religious instruction that dampened sectarian differences at the same time that it recognized the legitimacy of scientific learning. It would not be until after the American Revolution that King's College, renamed

57. Ibid., 4 : 115–16.

Columbia, would take full advantage of its location and its urbane clientele to become a major center of learning. But, as Johnson told the trustees, the initial years were "a respectable beginning."

Johnson's personal choice as the man to carry King's into the future was East Apthorp, a prominent Anglican minister of the Boston area. But after an exchange of letters Johnson realized that Apthorp did not want the job. There was the lame excuse that "his voice is not strong enough for our churches," but the underlying reason was that Apthorp "is unwilling to leave Cambridge." [58] Meanwhile the trustees had perceived Johnson's letter of 1759 as an indication of his imminent and voluntary retirement. They had begun a search of their own for a successor and had come up with a young Englishman named Myles Cooper. The Archbishop of Canterbury had not recommended Cooper in the strongest terms; other candidates were better qualified, he suggested, but Cooper was an educated gentleman who had received little of his father's estate and was therefore most available.[59] At first Johnson disapproved. He warned that Cooper, "being so young," would not be able to cope with the trustees, "most of whom care for little else but their gain and pleasures." [60] But after Cooper arrived in New York Johnson changed his mind.

In 1761 Johnson apparently began to emerge from the gloom produced by the death of his relatives and friends. In June of that year he married Sarah Beach, who was the mother of William Samuel's wife. The new wife helped buoy his spirits and give him the companionship that had been lacking since Charity's death. He threw himself into another battle with the trustees, this time over the management of a funding drive that he accused the trustees of mishandling. King's had planned to enlist the financial support of English benefactors, but had allowed the Academy at Philadelphia to steal the idea. "And

58. Apthorp to Johnson, 11 February 1760, ibid., p. 58; Johnson to Archbishop of Canterbury, 15 February 1760, ibid., pp. 59–60.
59. Secker to Johnson, 4 November 1760, ibid., pp. 71–73; *Early Minutes of the Trustees*, 5 January 1762.
60. *Career*, 1 : 40–42.

now here comes Dr. Smith of Philadelphia going home to beg for
their college," Johnson wrote, "so we have lost an opportunity
for that . . . such our stupid doings." [61] It was a rejuvenated
Johnson that welcomed Cooper to King's College and put him
up in his new household. Although Cooper was younger than
Johnson would have preferred, he was also eager to learn. And
Johnson was now in the mood to stay on as president for a few
more years in order to make sure that his successor learned the
right lessons.

The trustees would have none of it. They wanted Johnson
to retire immediately. At their meeting in January of 1762 the
trustees refused to vote approval of the much-needed grammar
school until Cooper was installed as president. They also em-
barrassed Johnson by refusing to make Cooper vice president
of the college, as Johnson had requested, haggling over Cooper's
salary, and finally appointing him as a "Fellow of King's College" and professor of moral philosophy.[62]

By the fall of 1762 the dispute between Johnson and the
trustees had grown more acute and poor Cooper was finding it
difficult to remain neutral. The new issue was Johnson's pen-
sion, how large it should be and when he would receive it. William Samuel thought that the situation again demonstrated "the
ingratitude and barbarity of the Governors." In November, however, barbarity again took the form of smallpox, this time striking
down Johnson's new wife. "The thing I feared is upon me,"
wrote Johnson when he learned of Sarah's death. William Samuel
observed that his father again looked like a "Poor Gent"
hounded by the fates and the trustees. He could not go on. In
February of 1763 Johnson hired a sleigh to carry him through
a snow storm and back to Stratford. He wished Cooper well and
expressed the hope that "he will never meet with such severe tests
of patience as I have had." He had no way of knowing that

61. S. Johnson to W. S. Johnson, 1 February 1762, *Career*, 4 : 77–78. See
Beverley McAnear, "The Raising of Funds by the Colonial College," *Missis-
sippi Valley Historical Review* 38 (1952): 591–612, for the full story of the
competition for funds between the Academy at Philadelphia and King's.
62. *Early Minutes of the Trustees*, 5 January 1762.

Cooper would also be driven from the presidency of King's College, not by the smallpox or the trustees, but by a mob and a revolution.[63]

63. W. S. Johnson to Daniel Horsmanden, 18 November 1762, *Career*, 4 : 86–87; "A True and Just State of the Case Between the Reverend Dr. Johnson and the Governors of King's College in New York," 31 [?] January 1763, ibid., pp. 93–96.

12

Religion and Politics

Stratford was peace and quiet, a comfortable apartment that his son provided, a chance to mingle with old parishioners, a way-station for Anglican friends on the road from Boston to New York, an opportunity to rethink his life, and a box seat for the coming of the American Revolution. During his tenure at King's College Johnson's pastorate at Stratford had been occupied by Edward Winslow, but when Johnson learned that the people of Braintree, Massachusetts, wanted the promising young Winslow (and when he learned that his own tour at King's was almost over), he advised the Society to send Winslow to Braintree, "for the better support of his very large and growing family." With Winslow gone, Johnson assumed the duties and salary of his old parish job.[1]

During these years parish chores kept Johnson busy and prevented him from regarding himself as a decrepit drain on his son's pocketbook or a permanent intruder at his daughter-in-law's dinner table. Missionary duties also maintained his contact with the Society, particularly with Thomas Secker, the recently appointed Archbishop of Canterbury. Secker had a strong interest in the colonial church and regarded Johnson as the grand old man of New England Anglicanism. His frequent letters to Stratford not only confirmed Johnson's secret belief in his own importance, they also allowed the aging missionary to believe that he might yet salvage something for the episcopal

1. *Career,* 1 : 42.

cause in the colonies. Secker's letters, filled with probing questions about colonial episcopacy, received lengthy answers.[2]

The most striking feature of Johnson's correspondence with Secker during these years was the attention given to the political reform of the colonial governments. Johnson had advocated an overhaul of the Connecticut charter government as early as 1732, but he usually refrained from making specific suggestions about political matters because he felt neither qualified nor disposed to discuss imperial politics.[3] Now, in the 1760s, his letters were filled with political advice. As he looked back over his life, he recalled how Connecticut's taxation of Anglicans, the ability of local officials to implement laws as they saw fit, the power of the New York Assembly to block the funding of King's College, the political pressure available to anti-Anglican popular movements—how all these experiences revealed the extent to which royal officials and agents of episcopacy were at the mercy of entrenched local leaders who were hostile to the church. He concluded that the political balance of power in the colonies required readjustment if Anglicanism was ever to flourish.

This conclusion appeared to blend nicely with current imperial policy. Two months after he returned to Stratford, Johnson received word from Secker that "our ministry will be concerting schemes this summer, against the next session of Parliament, for the Settlement of his Majesty's American dominions."[4] The accession of George III and his ministry, coupled with the cessation of war with the French, provided the occasion for imperial reorganization. Johnson sensed that it was an opportune time to offer the new leaders at Whitehall the benefits of his long experience in the colonies. "I conclude schemes are now concerting for the Settlement of America," Johnson wrote Secker, "and I strongly hope the interests of religion will not be forgotten."[5]

While his most frequent plea was for American bishops, John-

2. Sykes, *From Sheldon to Secker;* also Bridenbaugh, *Mitre and Sceptre,* pp. 30–31, 268–69.
3. See above, chap. 6.
4. Secker to Johnson, 10 December 1761, 30 March 1763, *Career,* 3: 260–69.
5. Johnson to Secker, 10 August 1763, ibid., p. 273.

son advised his superiors that the religious reformation of the colonies must be accompanied by political reform.[6] What was most in need of change, he suggested, was the popular form of the colonial governments. In Connecticut the Anglican cause was hamstrung by the wicked union of "rigid enthusiastical notions and practices in religion and republican mobbish principles and practices in politics." Governments cast in this republican form only promoted "confusion and 'high notions of liberty'"; the latter led inevitably to "intrigue and faction" that made the orderly operation of public affairs impossible. The charter governments were particularly chaotic, because they allowed "vastly too numerous and unequal a representation" in their legislature. In all the northern colonies, wrote Johnson, "rulers [are] afraid to do what is best and right for fear of disobliging them [the people]." Invariably, anti-Anglican proposals were concealed behind the political confusion that accompanied "popular governments." Since the Anglican colonists constituted a minority, any colonial government that accurately reflected popular opinion could be expected to oppose pro-Anglican proposals. Both the efficiency of the empire and the survival of episcopacy demanded greater administrative uniformity and a reordering of political power.[7]

6. For hints of this linkage, see Johnson to Secretary, 14 April 1751, and Johnson to Secker, 1 March 1759, *Career*, 1 : 145–48, 282–87.

7. Johnson to Archbishop of Canterbury, 12 July 1760, ibid., p. 295. Perhaps it is worth noting that Johnson's analysis of the relationship between religious enthusiasm and republicanism is analogous to but not the same as Alan Heimert's more recent interpretation of colonial religion and politics. Heimert sees a connection between the New Light ministers who supported the Great Awakening and the colonial Whigs who supported the Revolution. Johnson did not go so far as to claim that the men who defended religious revivals were also the same men who opposed the royal prerogative. One reason Johnson did not argue in terms of specific personalities was that he knew that men like Charles Chauncy and Jonathan Mayhew were able to mix their hostility to religious enthusiasm with republicanism. Heimert's attempt to identify two antithetical traditions in colonial society forces him either to count Chauncy and Mayhew as exceptions or to distort their positions so that they fit his categories. In Johnson's view there is a certain affinity between the ideas underlying religious enthusiasm and the ideas underlying a popular conception of government, but individual ministers and politicians were capable of shifting their allegiances as they moved from religion to politics. In general, then, Johnson's analysis suggests that Heimert's

The first thing the politicians at Whitehall should do, advised Johnson, was to demolish "these pernicious charter governments, reducing them all to one form, in immediate dependence on the King." Every colony should have a royal governor with clear prerogative powers over the legislature. There should also be a "principle of union" among all the colonies. This could be accomplished by the creation of a new office filled by a "Lord Lieutenant or Vice Roi" who would "preside over all colonies from New York and serve for three years." Each colony would send two representatives to New York, one from the Council and one from the Assembly. Together these representatives would advise the Lord Lieutenant "and consult whatever may contribute to the union, stability, and good of the whole. . . . Here the common affairs of war, trade, etc., might be considered and the confirming or negativing laws passed in each government and the result to be confirmed or negatived by the King." The only objection to such a scheme that Johnson could imagine was "an apprehension in the course of time of an affectation of independency from the Mother Country." [8]

Johnson regarded such an objection as an ironic misunderstanding of the colonies. The existence of a single colonial government would not cause the colonists to think of America as an independent country. It would serve as a vehicle for imperial control, not for colonial self-rule. As it was, some colonial governments (like Connecticut) already enjoyed virtual independence. Johnson tried to convince Secker that such colonies were already moving away from the church and the crown. "Did our benefactors know the real state of things in New England," he wrote in 1763, "they would allow that missionaries are as much needed here as in other parts of America." [9] English officials who ad-

---

thesis has merit, but that colonial leaders did not always think or act in accord with Heimert's ideological pattern. See Heimert, *Religion and the American Mind,* pp. 1–24.

8. "Questions Relating to the Union and Government of the Plantations," appended to letter from Johnson to Archbishop of Canterbury, 13 July 1760, *Career,* 3 : 297–301. Similar ideas are expressed in Some Considerations concerning the better Government and Settlement of the Church of England in the Plantations till Bishops can be sent abroad [1760], Johnson MSS, Hawks Papers, Archives of the Episcopal Church, Austin, Texas.

9. Johnson to Secker, 20 December 1763, *Career,* 3 : 279.

vised that Whitehall do nothing did not understand the extent
to which both religion and politics had already deteriorated in
the colonies. To do nothing was to allow these subversive tendencies to grow. The Anglicans in America needed the legal assistance of royal officials equipped with new powers; royal officials needed Anglican colonial allies. Johnson warned Secker
that colonial Puritans "are really no more friends to monarchy
than episcopacy; and against people of both these sorts episcopacy is really necessary towards the better securing our dependence, as well as many other good political changes." [10] Samuel
Auchmuty was even more of an alarmist: "It is my opinion . . .
that his Majesty has very few subjects whose loyalty he can depend upon on the Continent, *besides the Members of the Church
of England*. The rest are down right republicans." [11]

Secker explained that the ministry was hesitant to make any
drastic alteration in the ecclesiastical or political framework of
the colonies for fear that it might provoke a revolution. Johnson
continued to warn that the erosion of royal authority had already
reached dangerous proportions; and throughout his analysis ran
the persistent theme that the re-establishment of royal control
over the colonies was inextricably linked with the strengthening
of Anglicanism.

Johnson was neither a politician nor a prophet, but his experiences in New England and New York had given him a sense of
the colonial situation that the policy-makers in England lacked.
Benjamin Franklin did not share Johnson's religious views or his
political persuasion, but he too was a perceptive critic of the
current relationship between England and the colonies. Franklin
also believed that the imperial political machinery was in dire
need of a major overhaul and that a perpetuation of the existent governmental system would produce only mutual distrust
and resentment. Franklin, like Johnson, advised English officials
to make fundamental changes in the structure of the empire
in order to "strengthen the whole, and greatly lessen the danger
of future separations." Similarly, Thomas Pownall and Francis
Bernard were seasoned colonial observers who were attuned to

10. Johnson to Secker, 20 September 1764, ibid., 1 : 345–46.
11. Auchmuty to Johnson, 7 October 1765, Johnson MSS, Hawks Papers.

the need for a redefinition of English authority in the colonies. Both Pownall and Bernard agreed that disputes between local representatives and English officials would continue to grow more serious until leaders in the mother country established guidelines that clarified the relationship between English law and colonial practice. All these men—Johnson, Franklin, Pownall, and Bernard—as well as a host of others, had come to the conclusion that the imperial management of the colonies required reform. Johnson's advice to Secker, then, was merely one voice in an entire chorus that echoed across the Atlantic in the early 1760s.[12]

What made Johnson's voice distinctive was his vision of the relationship between political and religious reform. Johnson did not regard the strengthening of colonial episcopacy as a means by which to establish the political supremacy of the crown; he saw the strengthening of royal power as a means by which to establish the Anglican religion and halt what he perceived as a spiritual degeneration of the colonists. Whether political or religious reform was the ultimate goal of the English officials did not seem important at first, since they appeared to go hand in hand. In a short time appearances proved to be deceptive.

In 1763 two colonial critics of Anglicanism published pamphlets that, at first glance, appeared to be a repetition of earlier ecclesiastical controversies. Noah Welles, the Presbyterian minister at Stratford, reiterated the legitimacy of Presbyterian ordination in terms reminiscent of Jonathan Dickinson. He questioned the motive for the Anglican missionary crusade in New England, claiming the Anglicans had "no liberty, no right, to forsake the communion of these [non-Anglican] Churches, under the want of ministerial authority in them." [13] At about the same time the fiery Puritan minister from Boston, Jonathan Mayhew, resurrected some of Noah Hobart's old ideas and lambasted the Anglican expenditure of money and energy on New England.

12. Edmund S. and Helen M. Morgan, *The Stamp Act Crisis: Prologue to Revolution* (Chapel Hill, 1953), chap. 1.
13. Noah Welles, *The Divine Right of Presbyterian Ordination Asserted* . . . (New York, 1763), p. 78.

The £35,000 spent by the Anglicans in New England should have been used to minister to Indians on the frontier, Mayhew argued, rather than on missions in Massachusetts and Connecticut where the majority of the population were devout Protestants. The symbol of Anglican decadence and misplaced priorities was the home of East Apthorp in Cambridge, "the *Palace* of one of the humble successors of the apostles." [14]

There was a great deal of old hat in the pamphlets of Welles and Mayhew, but there was also something new, something that reflected the more politicized atmosphere of 1763. It was the suspicion that "the grand design of episcopizing . . . all New England" might have had a political motive. Perhaps the Anglican crusade in New England was not an ignorant misapplication of resources, but a subtle conspiracy designed to undermine colonial liberties in the heartland of liberty-loving Puritans. Perhaps the Anglican missionaries were the advance unit of a royal assault team.[15] It was not a thought new to New England Puritans, but it was a thought enjoying wider acceptance than ever before. Mayhew was the most explicit spokesman for this heightened sense of Anglican political motives; it was to Mayhew that Secker addressed his anonymous *Answer,* a moderate defense of Anglican policies intended to assure colonists of the devout intentions of American missionaries.[16] Mayhew responded immediately, making his suspicions even more explicit. He granted that Anglican clergy were careful and cautious men, but added, "People are not usually deprived of their liberties all at once, but gradually, by one encroachment after another, as it is found they are disposed to bear them." In Mayhew's opinion the Anglican effort to get American bishops was part of a devious scheme to smuggle political functionaries into the colonies by clothing them in religious robes.[17]

14. Jonathan Mayhew, *Observations on the Charter and Conduct of the Society for the Propagation of the Gospel in Foreign Parts* . . . (Boston, 1763), p. 56.

15. Charles Akers, *Called unto Liberty,* chap. 6; Bernard Bailyn, ed., *Pamphlets of the American Revolution* (Cambridge, Mass., 1965), 1 : 204ff.

16. *An Answer to Dr. Mayhew's Observations* . . . (Boston, 1764). See also [Henry Caner], *A Candid Examination of Dr. Mayhew's Observations* . . . (Boston, 1763).

17. Mayhew, *Remarks on an Anonymous Tract* . . . (Boston, 1764), p. 62.

Apthorp admitted that Mayhew was too much for any one Anglican to handle. As "an unequal antagonist who disclaims the contest," Apthorp suggested that the Anglicans tone down their activities in New England. "As far as I can judge," he wrote, "the worthy part of the dissenters will make advances to us with a better grace, the less they are solicited." A year later Apthorp acted on his own judgment and returned to England.[18]

The debate had also made a deep impression on Secker, who confided to Johnson that Mayhew's accusations, while not completely accurate, had an impact on the ministry "and therefore it may be best, not absolutely to justify, but to excuse ourselves in that respect."[19] What Secker meant soon became clear. The church was going to redirect its missionary activity away from New England in order to avoid antagonizing the Puritan colonists concentrated there. As Secker explained to Johnson, "there are so great numbers in other parts destitute of all instruction . . . , I mean the new and frontier settlements, that I think we cannot avoid preferring the latter."[20] The recent uproar created by Mayhew had verified Secker's belief that "the Dissenters in America are closely connected with those in England, and both with such as, under color of being friends to liberty, are many of them enemies to all ecclesiastical establishments." Since the influence wielded by this combination of English and American Puritans threatened "the present weak state of the ministry," Secker informed Johnson that the politicians at Whitehall would not "meddle with what will certainly raise opposition."[21] As a result, the redirection of imperial policy, far from strengthening Anglican power in the colonies, called for a reduction of missionary activity in New England and an indefinite postponement of the question of bishops.[22]

18. Apthorp to Johnson, 26 March 1763, *Career*, 3 : 268.
19. Secker to Johnson, 28 September 1763, ibid., p. 277.
20. Secker to Johnson, 30 March 1763, ibid., p. 269.
21. Secker had warned of the political influence of the Puritans as early as 1758. The quotation is from Secker to Johnson, 27 September 1758, ibid., p. 259.
22. The final decision to avoid antagonizing New Englanders was announced to Johnson in Secker to Johnson, 30 March 1763, ibid., pp. 269–70. Johnson's reaction is in a letter to the Secretary, 14 September 1764, S.P.G. MSS, B, 23 : 187.

The turmoil that followed the passage of the Stamp Act in 1765 merely confirmed the contradictory opinions of Johnson and Secker about the need for a strengthened episcopacy. Johnson undoubtedly approved of the section of the act that mentioned ecclesiastical courts, thereby implying the imminent arrival of bishops. Ironically, he disapproved of the stamp tax itself, which he felt was unwarranted.[23] Whether or not the tax was warranted, Johnson pointed to "the principles and practices of those factious people that falsely call themselves Sons of Liberty" as proof of his contention that colonial society was on the verge of revolution. He claimed the "present unhappy Condition of things" demanded a zealous Anglican commitment.[24] Auchmuty concurred that these were "bad times" and that "some heavy Judgment is ready to come upon our Nation" unless the church was strengthened.[25]

Secker, however, perceived the colonial uproar as a death blow to Anglican hopes. "It is very probable," he wrote, "that a bishop or bishops would have been quietly received in America before the Stamp Act was passed here. But it is certain, that we could get no permission here to send one now." [26] Johnson did not bother to point out that Secker had been pessimistic about bishops and New England missions before the passage of the Stamp Act. Instead, he wrote that the Anglican clergy in the colonies were "much grieved that the Society declines making

23. Edmund S. Morgan, *Prologue to Revolution: Sources and Documents on the Stamp Act Crisis, 1764–1766* (Chapel Hill, 1959), p. 36, for the act itself. For a typical Anglophile reaction to the crisis, see Auchmuty to Johnson, 2 September 1765, Johnson MSS, Hawks Papers. T. B. Chandler had an intriguing reaction to the act in Chandler to Johnson, 5 September 1766, *Career*, 1 : 367: "What reasons can there be for consulting the Parliament? How in the name of goodness does it concern them whether such a bishop as we have requested be sent us any more than whether an astronomer or a poet should come over to America; for he is to receive no powers nor perquisites [*sic*] from them . . . all that we desire is that they will not oppose us, and we will promise never to molest them." Apparently Chandler did not think Parliament had any authority over the proposed colonial bishops and resented the Stamp Act for its implication of parliamentary power.

24. Johnson to Secker, 10 October 1766, Johnson MSS, Hawks Papers.

25. Auchmuty to Johnson, 2 September 1765, ibid.

26. Secker to Johnson, 31 July 1766, *Career*, 3 : 286.

any more Missions in New England." [27] By the time the smoke surrounding the Stamp Act crisis had cleared, Johnson had concluded that the political and religious well-being of the colonies, as perceived by English officials, were not complimentary. And he was now convinced that the colonial Anglicans, along with the colonial governments, were being led to hell by the policymakers in England.

Johnson's attitude toward England and Englishmen had always been reverential. For over forty years he had corresponded with Anglican superiors who consistently failed to provide the colonial missionaries with the items he requested. But his admiration for the episcopal leaders remained intact. He was always prepared to believe that they were privy to information he did not have. They were contemporary heirs of the apostolic succession, men who embodied the archetypal values of a pure and pristine era. He seldom challenged their judgment or their motives. Similarly, his attitude toward English political leaders was courteous and deferential. He seemed to believe that an Englishman who was equipped with royal instructions possessed some magical ability to outperform elected colonial governors. He had unbounded faith in the crown's capacity to restore order in the American colonies. In fact, Johnson's vision of English institutions and officials was the vision of a provincial colonist who stood in awe of the mother country. In his philosophical and theological writings he had argued that all men were inherently depraved; his experiences with the Connecticut government, the New York Assembly, and the King's College trustees had confirmed his estimate of human nature. But he seemed to believe that English officials were immune to the corruptive influences of the world. England was the home of intellectual giants like Locke, Berkeley, and Newton. England was the cultural standard-bearer of the world, the model against which colonial architecture, philosophy, and laws must be measured. England was the great parent from whom colonial children must learn.

27. Johnson to Secretary, 25 June 1767, S.P.G. MSS, B, 23 : 195.

It was not a vision unique to Johnson. Many colonists, especially Anglicans, who looked toward England for political support and cultural leadership, tended to develop an exalted conception of things English. They were conscious that the American colonies were on the periphery of the cultural world. They borrowed their language, clothing styles, and many of their ideas from England. Even Benjamin Franklin, the proverbial first American, modeled his writing on the English literary masters, used Newtonian suggestions to investigate electricity, and lived comfortably in London for several years. But Franklin was able to fuse English and American cultural values. He could wear colonial homespun as well as English silk; he was at home in Philadelphia as well as London; he could, as Poor Richard, transform the English language into an American idiom.

Most colonists who were concerned about colonial culture, however, were unable to follow Franklin's lead. Like Johnson, they tended to exaggerate the differences between English and American society, to mimic the former and denigrate the latter. There was, to be sure, a certain inconsistency about Johnson's English bias. He loved the simple rural beauty of Stratford and he had seen his best friend, his son, and many of his ministerial candidates die of smallpox contracted in London. His belief in the power of education told him that the level of colonial culture could be improved. He admitted, for example, that "nature doubtless makes as good geniuses here as in any other parts of the world, and nothing is wanting but a regular education to polish and cultivate them." [28] And yet in spite of these reservations, Johnson was an Anglophile. Over the years he had developed the habit of looking toward England for cultural ideals and expecting English officials to save the colonists from themselves.[29]

The exchange of letters with Secker over the meaning of the colonial reaction to the Stamp Act signaled a dramatic change in Johnson's thinking. For the first time in his life he dared to criticize the policy-makers in England. He told Samuel Auchmuty that the ministers at Whitehall were "a pack of Courtiers, who

28. *Career*, 2 : 315.
29. See John Clive and Bernard Bailyn, "England's Cultural Provinces: Scotland and America," *William and Mary Quarterly*, 3rd ser. 11 (1954): 200–13, for a discussion of colonial attitudes toward English culture.

have no Religion at all." [30] When William Samuel, who was sent
to London in 1767 to present a land claim for Connecticut, reported that bribes, patronage, and underhanded deals were com-
monplace, Johnson replied: "What else can be expected from
such an unsettled state of the ministry, owing to such a perpetual
and violent jostling *in* and *out?*" [31] Auchmuty agreed with Johnson's description of the English political scene. "Every person
there," he wrote, "seems to be too busy in promoting his own
Interest, to pay the least regard to applications from this side the
water." [32] Both Johnson and Auchmuty were in general agreement with the assessment of Stephen Johnson, a Connecticut
Puritan who delivered a Fast Day sermon in which the English
officials responsible for the Stamp Act were described as "con-
trivers and authors . . . [governed by] a most venal, covetous
and arbitrary spirit of lawless ambition." [33]

Johnson was equally critical of the Anglican leadership in
England. No longer content to explain the persistent indifference
of the Anglican leaders to the problems of colonial missionaries
as the result of some grander vision, he expressed the suspicion
that English bishops had abandoned their religious calling and
had "dwindle[d] into mere worldly political creatures, instead of
truly spiritual persons." [34] It was a view that found support from
a colonial clergyman who had just returned from a two-year stay
in England, where he had met the Anglican bishops and concluded "they don't look like Gospel Bishops or ministers of
Christ. I can't find them in the Bible." [35] In 1765 Johnson confronted his Anglican superiors with the charge that "both the
Bible and the episcopate which the church at first received together from the Apostles, are both very fast sinking together in
this apostacizing age, both at home and abroad." [36] Why should

30. Auchmuty to Johnson, 26 July 1767, Johnson MSS, Hawks Papers.
31. S. Johnson to W. S. Johnson, 8 June 1767, *Career*, 1 : 404. William
Samuel's letters from England are gathered in Massachusetts Historical Society,
Collections, 5th ser. 9 : 214–490.
32. Auchmuty to Johnson, 21 March 1769, Johnson MSS, Hawks Papers.
33. Quoted in Heimert, *Religion and the American Mind*, p. 461.
34. Johnson to Archbishop of Canterbury, 10 November 1766, *Career*,
1 : 379.
35. Samson Occum in Sprague, *Annals*, 3 : 194.
36. Johnson to Secker, 5 September 1765, *Career*, 1 : 355.

colonial Anglicans look to England for help, he asked, when "the episcopate is more likely to be abolished at home than established abroad[?]" [37]

It was obviously not a question to which Johnson expected an answer. Nor was it, as some Anglican officials believed, just a spiteful comment by a cranky and overaged colonial missionary. Johnson's letters to England constituted a warning (and a warning that proved justified) that the officials at Whitehall and Canterbury were grossly out of touch with colonial affairs. For the first time Johnson openly admitted to himself and presented to his English superiors the distinct and growing possibility of a clash "between Old and New England," a possibility that English ignorance of America had allowed to develop. All of his previous prescriptions for religious and political reform of the colonies had been based on a naïve and provincial belief in the superiority of English leaders. Now he had concluded that English bishops and politicians were just as corruptible as the colonists. Human depravity was an international phenomenon. Yet, now that his former heroes and saviors were exposed as jealous and short-sighted men, Johnson could not conceive of any answers to the Anglo-American dilemma. Any effective colonial reform, he thought, was dependent on virtuous Englishmen. The simultaneous collapse of virtue in England and the colonies, he wrote his son, "seems to forbid all hopes for this century and probably till the millennium." [38]

Younger Anglican clerics who still had hope took note of Johnson's increasing age and pessimism and began to compete for his unofficial position as leader of the episcopal missionaries in the northern colonies. At a convention held in New Jersey in 1766, Thomas Bradbury Chandler turned back William Smith's bid for leadership and emerged as the new spokesman for colonial Anglicanism. Chandler was a Johnson protégé, a graduate of Yale (1745) who had read theology under Johnson at Stratford. A large and somewhat portly man, he even looked like Johnson.[39]

37. Johnson to Bishop of London, 15 July 1765, ibid., p. 354.
38. S. Johnson to W. S. Johnson, 22 April 1768, ibid., p. 439.
39. Samuel C. McCulloch, "Thomas Bradbury Chandler: Anglican Humanitarian in Colonial New Jersey," *British Humanitarianism* (Philadelphia, 1950), pp. 104–08; also Bridenbaugh, *Mitre and Sceptre*, pp. 204–06, 266–68.

Chandler agreed with Johnson that "our superiors . . . are governed altogether by political motives," but he was convinced that colonial Anglicans were obliged to persist in their pleas for bishops.[40] The Anglican convention of 1766 adopted Chandler's plan, which committed the colonial Anglicans to a public relations drive designed to persuade Puritans that the presence of episcopal bishops would not endanger the civil liberties of the colonists. Johnson appeared at an Anglican gathering in New York in May of 1766 to support the programs of his former disciple. He also wrote letters to Anglican clergy in Virginia, encouraging them to follow Chandler's lead.[41] With the approach of his seventieth birthday he could take solace in the realization that the colonial Anglicans were listening to his advice even if the English bishops were not. When colonial Anglicans fell into line behind Chandler, Johnson knew that the mantle had been passed.

Chandler's strategy was nothing more than an amalgam of the various proposals that Johnson had made during the previous forty years. He stressed the wholly spiritual duties of an Anglican bishop, the need to inform Anglicans in England about the peculiarities of the colonial situation, the political benefits that would accrue to the crown if the colonial episcopacy were more firmly established. But from 1766 onward, it was Chandler and not Johnson who managed the Anglican forces. After that date Johnson was merely a name that reminded younger Anglicans of earlier ecclesiastical wars, an old man who must be kept informed of current developments, a veteran who had retired from the fight and was watching with interest from the sidelines.[42]

One of the habits of mind that linked Johnson with his contemporaries, but separates him from modern social analysts, was his tendency to see political events as mere symptoms of some cosmic condition. It was, indeed, more than just a habit of mind; it was a conviction rooted in his psyche, central to his theology,

40. Chandler to Johnson, 20 August 1767, 7 July 1768, *Career*, 1 : 417, 444.
41. Johnson to J. Carwright, 10 April 1767, ibid., pp. 398–99.
42. Chandler's *Appeal to the Public in Behalf of the Church of England in America* (New York, 1767) was a concise statement of strategy as well as the literary signal that Chandler was now the unofficial Anglican leader.

and spelled out in his system of metaphysics. He had several different ways of expressing this conviction: God was the final and immediate cause of every natural event; the types were mere imitations of the archetypes; history was the unfolding of the divine mind. Each of these expressions required and received extensive explication in Johnson's formal treatises, but the conviction itself was a rather simple act of faith. Johnson believed that all the apparently unconnected and inconsistent events that constituted social and political life in this world played some prescribed role in an overarching cosmic scheme that men could not fully understand. As a result of this belief, when Johnson tried to make sense out of the political events surrounding the Stamp Act crisis, he perceived the corruption of English political and ecclesiastical officials and the disruptions produced by groups like the Sons of Liberty as moral warnings that indicated divine displeasure. All the considerations which would be central to a modern analysis of the imperial crises of the 1760s—the ambiguity of the relationship between Parliament and the colonial Assemblies, the expanding colonial population and economy, the bureaucratic inefficiency of the English administrative machinery, the financial problems produced by the French and Indian War —all these considerations were incidental to Johnson's analysis. He saw the problem in essentially moral terms: What was God saying to English America?

Sometime between 1763 and 1770 Johnson decided to write out his answer to that question in an elaborate treatise entitled "Raphael or The Genius of English America." [43] Under the guise of Raphael, "the guardian or genius of New England," who was described as "one of an order of intelligence superior to you, not clothed with flesh and blood," Johnson set down his personal analysis of the current imperial crisis. He cast the treatise in the form of a Platonic dialogue, in which Raphael, the main character, cuts through "the many empty debates in philosophy, religion and politics that obtain among the inhabitants" and

43. *Career*, 2 : 521–600. The precise date of authorship is unknown. Handwriting comparisons with letters written during the period lead me to conclude that Johnson wrote it during the Stamp Act crisis of 1765–1766.

entire enterprise.[58] And venality tended to feed on itself until honest men found it impossible to get elected or, once elected, to remain honest.

There was only one immediate solution, and it was merely a temporary measure. Until "the number of those that are truly qualified for so great and important a trust was greater," the number of representatives in Parliament and the colonial Assemblies must be reduced. A mechanism would have to be created so that only virtuous men could be elected to public office and they should then "take a great deal of pains to indoctrinate the bulk of the people . . . in the right understanding of the true public interest." [59] With fewer but more qualified representatives, moral reform could begin. Only if the virtuous few were able to resist the temptations that would surely come their way and institute programs designed to eliminate political corruption could the empire survive.

But the reduction of the number of representatives was, at best, a temporary expedient intended to hold the line until more lasting reforms were inaugurated. And Johnson pinned his hopes for lasting social reform on education. Only by rearranging the educational system so that it taught "self-denial and industry . . . , the foundation of all that is virtuous" could colonial society produce an intelligent electorate capable of selecting qualified representatives for public office. In fact Johnson, speaking as Raphael, suggested that the degeneration of moral standards was the direct result of inadequate schooling. He advised that the colonies establish a widespread network of secondary schools in which the bulk of the colonial population could be educated. Moreover, he recommended "a much longer course of instruction at the schools than there has been in this country before they are entered in the colleges." [60] The secondary schools should concentrate on Latin, Greek, and basic mathematics, because these subjects developed mental discipline and allowed students to "make their inclinations and appetites tame and pliable." The best secondary school graduates would then be

58. Ibid., pp. 546–75.
59. Ibid., pp. 574–75.
60. Ibid., p. 566.

admitted to the colleges, where they would learn how to use their rational faculties to analyze social and natural phenomena. The most accomplished of the college graduates would move on to professional school and undergo a four- to seven-year seasoning process that equipped them for the ministry, the bar, or political office. Only after an entire generation of colonists had passed through the expanded system of secondary schools would the country possess an intelligent and uncorrupt electorate. Only after a generation of students had had their minds and wills developed in college and in postgraduate training would the country possess a sufficient number of qualified social leaders.[61]

The comprehensive educational system that Johnson described in "Raphael" foreshadowed the plan that Thomas Jefferson proposed for Virginia years later, when the colonial problem was to retain the public virtue achieved during the war with Great Britain. But Johnson probably received his greatest inspiration from Plato's *Republic,* in which the education of the Guardians was made the foundation of republican government. (For that matter all of "Raphael" is modeled on the Platonic dialogues, with Raphael cast in the role of Socrates.) Yet Johnson's belief in the power of education also followed naturally from his own philosophy and from his experience as president of King's College. Despite his despondency over the deterioration of Anglo-American relations and his increasingly pessimistic view of the powers of human reason (he was still recommending *Moses' Principia* to his friends), Johnson refused to become a fatalist. To the end, he believed that even the most corrupt of men possessed a kernel of potential virtue which could be nourished and developed by skilled educators.

Perhaps the most astounding feature of Johnson's "Raphael," however, was the discussion of the relationship between church and state; Johnson advocated their complete separation. In times of widespread corruption, said Raphael, the church that was connected to the government invariably fell victim to the venality that infected the political leaders. As a result the church should be made "a distinct thing from civil government in order

61. Ibid., p. 557–58, 568.

to assure that there was as little temptation as possible to the officers of religion to betray its interests and rights to those of the world." [62] Johnson made it clear that his chief worry was not clerical infringement on civil liberties, but the corruption of religious leaders by politicians. No matter what motives underlay his recommendation that church and state be separated, it was a startling position for an Anglican missionary to take, since it contradicted the traditional episcopal assertion that both church and state had mutual obligations to support the other's interest. But then Johnson's personal experience as an Anglican missionary in New England had alerted him to the ways that established churches could use their political influence to oppress religious minorities. And more recently he had observed how the officials at Whitehall were able to use their control of bishoprics and benefices to obtain the support of the Anglican hierarchy for policies that ignored the requests of colonial missionaries. One of the central ironies of Johnson's life was that his experience as a colonial Anglican tended to confirm the old Puritan conviction that any church-state connection defiled the spiritual purity of the church. Perhaps he refrained from publishing "Raphael" because he was aware that his Anglican superiors would regard this argument as both insulting and absurd.

If the American colonists had been able to read "Raphael," they also would have been surprised by Johnson's advocacy of the separation of church and state. What the colonists would have taken for granted was the way Johnson saw the political discord of his time in essentially moral terms. Neither Johnson nor his contemporaries were turning their attention from religion to politics; rather, political issues were becoming the focal point for religious views. Politics was now the arena in which individual leaders exhibited their depravity or virtue, in which a nation showed itself degenerate or pure, in which God dispensed damnation or grace.

A good many colonists shared Johnson's moralistic perspective on the political crises of the 1760s, but read the spiritual signals

62. Ibid., p. 585.

differently. Disciples of Jonathan Edwards such as Samuel Hopkins and Joseph Bellamy, who called their religious movement the New Divinity, agreed with Johnson that the imperial conflict over sugar, stamps, and tea was a divine warning. The New Divinity clergy also preached that the colonists were exhibiting their sinful dispositions, and that political corruption was raging out of control. But Hopkins, Bellamy, and their many supporters accepted the Edwardean view that periods of gross public immorality were preliminary signs of an approaching apocalypse. The more severe the political crisis became, the more certain they were that the millennium was at hand. They regarded the pre-revolutionary contention as an indication that a second Great Awakening was on the way. While Johnson grew more despondent over the loss of public virtue, the New Divinity clergy encouraged the colonists to believe that the Kingdom of God was about to be established on earth.[63]

William Livingston was another colonist who agreed with Johnson that men were inherently depraved, and who regarded sectarianism and factionalism as social consequences of original sin. But Livingston thought that private vices could be channeled into institutions that forced the various factions to police one another. He believed, in other words, that intelligent men could devise social mechanisms that used human weakness against itself. Livingston, like Johnson, saw the social malaise of the time as a victory of private gain over public good, but he did not believe, as did Johnson, that reform depended upon the election of a few properly educated leaders. Livingston had little faith in any political system that gave men arbitrary power, no matter how virtuous those men appeared. In his view human nature could not be changed; but institutions could and should be restructured so as to force elected representatives to act in the public interest. In Johnson's view, institutions were no better than the men who ran them. The only way to reform society was

---

63. See, for example, Bellamy's *The Works of Joseph Bellamy, D.D.*, vol. 2, *The Wisdom of God in the Permission of Sin* (Boston, 1850), pp. 5–8, and vol. 1, *The Millennium* (Boston, 1850), pp. 452–59. See also Heimert, *Religion and the American Mind*, pp. 340–44.

to reform men. Livingston, in effect, began with certain Puritan assumptions about man and with them constructed a modern political theory of checks and balances. Johnson began with the same assumptions and constructed an educational program designed to produce an enlightened elite.[64]

Finally, there was a moralistic vision with which Johnson disagreed completely. It was a vision that drew upon the ecclesiastical arguments of Dickinson, Hobart, Welles, and Mayhew. It was a vision that resurrected the hopes and fears of the original Puritan migrants to New England. It was the vision Johnson had been fighting against for fifty years. According to this view the sectarian and factional divisions within the colonies were the direct result of subversion and intrigue by Anglican agents. As the political conflicts over the right of Parliament to tax the colonists became more severe, Puritan ministers of several denominations warned that the political attack on colonial rights was intended to prepare the colonies for eventual anglicization. An Ezra Stiles sermon of 1760 had proven to be prophetic. At that early date Stiles had called for a "Christian Union" of all Puritan sects to protect themselves against the encroachments of episcopacy. In 1766 eighty Puritan clergymen gathered in New York City to discuss plans for a united front against the political and religious attacks from England and agreed to meet annually thereafter to update their strategy. As relations between England and America became more strained, this anti-Anglican group was instrumental in causing the bulk of the colonists to associate political corruption with the Church of England, English politicians, and even English culture. While Johnson tried to persuade his colonial friends that the political problems of the day transcended national and denominational boundaries, and demanded a Christian union of all moral men, Presbyterian and Congregationalist clergy delivered election sermons in which they recalled the old image of America as a city on a hill, once separated from the corruption of the Anglican church, but now endangered by the religio-political agents of Canterbury and

64. See above, chap. 9, for a discussion of Livingston's political theory.

Whitehall. The very religion that Johnson represented had become a touchstone which colonists used to measure their purity and, eventually, their patriotism.[65]

The destiny of the colonies concerned Johnson deeply, but he kept his thoughts to himself and kept himself occupied with more mundane projects. According to Johnson's own account, he "chiefly labored . . . in . . . the Holy Scriptures in their sacred originals and especially the Hebrew language in which the holy oracles were from the beginning delivered. This was always his delight and therefore now his chief business." [66] The business of Hebrew involved the education of his two grandchildren, Charles and Billy, the sons of William Samuel. Billy was his favorite and most avid student, even though Johnson admitted that "his play and mates somewhat alienate him from his Hebrew." In fact, Billy took to Hebrew and the Bible with the same enthusiasm as had his grandfather many years earlier. In March of 1767, Johnson wrote William Samuel that Billy, who was six years old,

> has perfectly learned both his Greek and Hebrew letters. I wrote out the Lord's Prayer for him in Greek and he reads it, and has got it by heart, and says it prettily, and besides has begun to read out the Bible in English (and has read near 30 Chapters in Genesis) and is greatly delighted in the stories.[67]

Two years earlier he had published in a single volume an English grammar and catechism for children, texts he had composed to facilitate the education of Billy and Charles and that he wanted to share with the public. He was also busy trying to publicize the significance of Hebrew, although he admitted that it was a subject that "few . . . know or desire to know anything about." [68] He eventually convinced a London publisher to ac-

65. Ezra Stiles, *A Discourse on the Christian Union* (Boston, 1761); Bridenbaugh, *Mitre and Sceptre,* pp. 270–78.
66. *Career,* 1 : 46.
67. S. Johnson to W. S. Johnson, 12 March 1767, ibid., p. 439.
68. Johnson to Bishop Lowth, 25 June 1767, ibid., p. 409.

cept his Hebrew grammar in 1767 and to come out with a revised edition in 1771.[69]

He thought, he wrote, he taught, he published, and, most of all, he worried about William Samuel. He was haunted by the possibility that the smallpox would strike down his only remaining son while he was in England, just as it had taken his two wives, his other son, and so many of his friends and fellow missionaries. Or perhaps God would see fit to end his own life before William Samuel returned. The infirmities of old age had already required him to accept George Kneeland as an assistant to handle parish duties. The recurrent leg trouble and the periodic paralysis of his right arm were surely physical signs of an approaching divine judgment. But he was determined to hang on until William Samuel returned home.[70]

In 1771 he kept himself alive intellectually by writing a short autobiography. It was a modest piece, sixty paragraphs long, that related the high and low spots of Johnson's life as the old man remembered them. And therein lay the problem. He tended to read the Hebraic theories of John Hutchinson back into his early life, before his interest in Hebrew was anything more than a curiosity. He slighted his youthful confidence in reason and natural philosophy. He described his desertion of the Puritan churches and acceptance of episcopacy as if it was a rather facile and rational recognition of truth instead of an agonizing transferral of allegiance.

Not only the Puritan churches, but Ames, Ramus, and the entire content of Puritan theology and metaphysics—what Johnson called the old learning—were written off in the autobiography as "a curious cobweb." Johnson either failed to understand or simply did not record the countless ways that he remained tied to New England Puritanism: his lifelong retention of an exceedingly pessimistic estimate of man; his acceptance of the essential Platonism of Ames and Ramus; his insistence on a

69. For correspondence on the Hebrew grammar, see Chandler to Johnson, 22 January 1768; Stephen Sewall to Johnson, 12 July 1769; S. Johnson to W. S. Johnson, 16 September 1769; Johnson to Parkhurst, 1 November 1771, ibid., pp. 432, 457, 461, 480–81.

70. Ibid., p. 48, for admission of Kneeland as a permanent assistant. See S. Johnson to W. S. Johnson, 24 November 1769, for an account of his health.

wholly sovereign deity; his willingness to allow a large measure
of local control in church affairs; his lifelong belief in the
value of strong educational institutions; his conviction that
moral considerations underlay all human activity; even his final
retreat to the pure and uncorrupted language of Scripture. Not
all of these religious and intellectual tendencies were the ex-
clusive preserve of New England or Puritanism. But Johnson had
first been exposed to this assemblage of ideas and attitudes in
New England, especially at Yale, the cradle of the so-called old
learning. Moreover he had been attracted to those English
philosophers and philosophies that allowed him to sustain the
religious and moral perspective that was central to the Puritan
corpus. He had formed mental habits and acquired an intellectual disposition during his early years that stayed with him
to the grave. But no part of his intellectual debt was recognized
in his autobiography.[71]

In October of 1771, just before Johnson finished his autobiography, God answered his prayers and returned William Samuel
to Stratford. It was a time of "inexpressible joy and thankful-
ness" for the entire Johnson family.[72] Johnson was convinced
that God had sustained him until his son was safely home. There
was no longer any reason to persevere. On 6 January 1772, he
told his family that "he found his strength failing him; that he
must soon leave them, but he was going home." He supposedly
expressed the wish that he "might resemble in the manner of his
death his good friend Bishop Berkeley." [73] A few hours later,
he expired in a chair; like Berkeley, without a sound.[74]

71. The autobiography is in ibid., pp. 1–39.
72. Ibid., p. 49.
73. Chandler, *Life of Johnson*, p. 123.
74. W. S. Johnson to Bishop Lowth, 13 January 1172, *Career*, 1 : 486.

Bibliographical Essay

What follows is a discussion of some of the primary and secondary sources that affected my thinking on Johnson and eighteenth-century America. Although it is a selective and critical account and not a comprehensive listing, it does include all of the historical material that bears directly on Johnson. And the essay format allows me to comment on some of the more controversial books and articles, to make clear my own position in these professional arguments, and to expose the way in which I have come to terms with the existent literature; that is, the way in which my own ideas evolved as I grappled with the complexities of one man's life and the intellectual forces that shaped it.

General Sources

Johnson's letters, sermons, notebooks, and autobiography are to be found in the Johnson Papers in the Special Collections Room of the Columbia University Library. Approximately half of the Johnson material has been published, most of it in Herbert and Carol Schneider, eds., *Samuel Johnson: His Career and Writings*, 4 vols. (New York, 1929). Volume 1 of the Schneider collection contains the autobiography and personal or family correspondence. Volume 2 includes Johnson's philosophical treatises. Volume 3 is devoted to Johnson's religious essays, sermons, and ecclesiastical correspondence. Volume 4 covers his presidency of King's College. Not included in either the Johnson Papers or the Schneider volumes are many of Johnson's letters to English Anglicans. These are located in the Transcripts of the Correspondence between the Society for the Propagation of the Gospel in Foreign Parts and Its Missionaries, which are available on microfilm. Series "A" (26 reels) and series "B" (26 reels) contain many

letters to and from Johnson that are not to be found elsewhere. The
Columbiana Room of the Columbia University Library also possesses
a great deal of manuscript material relating to King's College during Johnson's tenure, including some Johnson letters. There is a
sizable collection of Johnson's correspondence with Charles Inglis,
Samuel Auchmuty, and Thomas Bradbury Chandler in the Archives of
the Episcopal Church in America, formerly in possession of the New
York Historical Society but now located in Austin, Texas. Finally,
I found miscellaneous Johnson documents at the Connecticut Historical Society Library in Hartford and at the Yale University Library
(Sterling). A calendar of the Johnson manuscripts is in the Columbia
University Library and a chronological bibliography is to be found
in *Career*, 4 : 285–361.

There are two published biographies of Johnson: Thomas Bradbury Chandler's *The Life of Samuel Johnson, D.D.* (New York, 1805)
and E. E. Beardsley's *Life and Correspondence of Samuel Johnson*
(Hartford, 1873). Although these books provide a narrative history
of Johnson's life and contain primary source material unavailable
elsewhere, they are both written by Anglicans anxious to applaud
Johnson's missionary activities. Neither author provides an analysis
of Johnson's intellectual accomplishments. And both books rely heavily
on Johnson's autobiography, which contains factual errors and the
kind of interpretive bias one normally associates with memoirs from
the edge of the grave. Herbert Schneider's essay, "The Mind of Samuel
Johnson" (*Career*, 2 : 3–22), discusses Johnson's intellectual development, but it is an abbreviated account that ignores Johnson's theology,
his ecclesiology, and his educational views, and drastically oversim-
plifies the intellectual context within which he operated.

Charles Evans' *American Bibliography: A Chronological Dictionary
of all Books, Pamphlets and Periodical Publications Printed in the
United States of America* (Chicago, 1903–04) allowed me to locate all
material published in the colonies and to read on microcards the
pieces relevant to Johnson. What these documents mean is a matter
of perception and interpretation. Like most colonial historians, I
am indebted to Perry Miller, most especially to his *The New England Mind: The Seventeenth Century* (New York, 1939) and *The
New England Mind: From Colony to Province* (Cambridge, Mass.,
1953). Miller's work has become a classic, but his elaborate prose style,
his tendency toward melodrama, and his ability to impose his own
coherence and order on ambiguous historical developments recently
have come under criticism. Summations of the revisionist scholarship

critical of Miller can be found in David D. Hall, "Understanding the Puritans," in Herbert Bass, ed., *The State of American History* (Chicago, 1970), and in Michael McGiffert, "American Puritan Studies of the 1960's," *William and Mary Quarterly*, 3rd ser. 27 (1970): 36–67. The work of Edmund S. Morgan, especially his *Visible Saints: The History of a Puritan Idea* (Ithaca, 1963), represents a refinement of the Miller corpus. And Morgan's *The Gentle Puritan: A Life of Ezra Stiles, 1727–1795* (New Haven, 1961) is a subtle discussion of what happened to several Puritan ideas in the first half of the eighteenth century and a book that more historians should read. Finally, a new book by Robert Middlekauf, *The Mathers: Three Generations of Puritan Intellectuals, 1596–1728* (New York, 1971), is a reassessment of the meaning of New England Puritanism that continues the modification of Miller's majestic interpretation.

While I was writing this book, a flock of demographic studies concentrating on New England community life appeared. The work of Richard Bushman, John Demos, Philip Greven, Kenneth Lockridge, and Michael Zuckerman has forced colonial historians to revitalize and revise many of their assumptions about the way New England society developed. I was particularly impressed by Lockridge's *A New England Town: The First Hundred Years: Dedham, Massachusetts, 1636–1736* (New York, 1970) because of the way it extracted intellectual meaning from local records. Equally insightful and more relevant for Connecticut is Bushman's *From Puritan to Yankee: Character and Social Order in Connecticut, 1690–1765* (Cambridge, Mass., 1967), which documents the disintegration of the old Puritan ideology under the impact of shifting social conditions. Bushman's book gave me the courage to generalize about Johnson's intellectual development by describing the evolving social context within which he operated and against which he reacted. Although much of my own work concentrates on the relationship among conflicting ideas rather than the relationship between ideas and the social arena in which they operated, the continual advance of demographic research promises to make possible a more sophisticated version of colonial intellectual history that does justice to ideas as well as their social origins and consequences.

Chapter One

For the background of colonial Connecticut, I have relied heavily on J. H. Trumbull and Charles J. Hoadley, eds., *Public Records of the Colony of Connecticut,* 15 vols. (Hartford, 1850–90). The volumes are well indexed and provide the best collection of primary source documents. Johnson's great-grandfather, Robert Johnson, and grandfather, William Johnson, are mentioned frequently in Charles J. Hoadley, ed., *Records of the Colony and Plantation of New Haven, 1638–49* (Hartford, 1857). The best secondary account of the founding of Connecticut is still Charles Andrews, *The Colonial Period of American History,* 4 vols. (New Haven, 1936), 2 : 67–194. The best personal accounts of daily life in colonial Connecticut are Sarah Knight, *The Journal of Madame Knight* (New York, 1935), the *Diary* of Joshua Hempstead, printed in the New London Historical Society, *Collections,* vol. 1, and Franklin B. Dexter, ed., *The Literary Diary of Ezra Stiles,* 3 vols. (New Haven, 1901). John J. Carman, ed., *American Husbandry* (New York, 1939) has some spicy comments on farming in colonial New England. On the local level, the Guilford Records, located in the Guilford Town Hall, are fragmentary and often illegible, although there are manuscript copies of certain sections of them that are useful. Bernard C. Steiner, *A History of the Plantation of Menunkatuck* (Baltimore, 1897), and Ralph D. Smith, *The History of Guilford* (Albany, 1877), are excellent local histories of the area.

The best index of the colony's school systems is in *Connecticut Records.* Legible sections of the Guilford Records pertain to the tax drain and its effect on schooling. The best secondary account of the New England grammar schools is Robert Middlekauf's *Ancients and Axioms* (New Haven, 1963). Clifford K. Shipton, "Secondary Education in the Puritan Colonies," *New England Quarterly* 8 (1934): 646–61, and Kenneth B. Murdock, "The Teaching of Latin and Greek at the Boston Latin School in 1712," Colonial Society of Massachusetts, *Transactions* 27 (Boston, 1932): 21–29, are helpful. There is useful material in S. E. Morison, *The Intellectual Life of Colonial New England* (New York, 1956), and Thomas G. Wright, *Literary Cultures of Early New England* (New Haven, 1920).

The ecclesiastical background of New England Puritanism has been treated extensively by earlier historians. Williston Walker's *The Creeds and Platforms of Congregationalism* (Boston, 1960) is indispensable. The sermons of Solomon Stoddard and Cotton Mather, along with the Connecticut election and ordination sermons from 1713 to 1740, can be located in Evans, *American Bibliography,* and read on microcards from Clifford K. Shipton's *Early American Imprints, 1639–1800.* They are filled with debates about church discipline.

Perry Miller's "Solomon Stoddard, 1643–1729," *Harvard Theological Review* 34 (1941): 277–320, and "The Half-Way Covenant," *New England Quarterly* 6 (1933): 676–715, are concise statements of the ecclesiastical problem attendant on the demand for a pure church. Two recent and incisive books, which I read in dissertation form, were Robert Pope's *The Half-Way Covenant: Church Membership in Puritan New England* (Princeton, 1969) and David Hall's *The Faithful Shepherd: A History of New England Ministry in the Seventeenth Century* (Chapel Hill, 1973), both of which deal extensively with ecclesiastical developments.

Chapter Two

The essential primary source for the history of the Collegiate School is Franklin B. Dexter's *Documentary History of Yale University Under the Original Charter of the Collegiate School of Connecticut, 1701–1745* (New Haven, 1916). Equally valuable is Dexter's *Biographical Sketches of the Graduates of Yale College with Annals of the College History*, 6 vols. (New York, 1885–1912). The best secondary account of the intellectual and religious climate at early Yale is the doctoral dissertation by Richard Warch, "Yale College, 1701–1740" (Yale University, 1968). Earlier secondary works which eulogize or mythologize the Collegiate School are Edwin Oviatt, *The Beginnings of Yale, 1701–1726* (New Haven, 1916), Ebenezer Baldwin, *Annals of Yale College* (New Haven, 1938), and W. L. Kingsley, ed., *Yale College: A Sketch of Its History* (New York, 1879). S. E. Morison's majestic *Harvard College in the Seventeenth Century*, 2 vols. (Cambridge, Mass., 1936), is filled with material directly connected with the Yale curriculum. The most recent and best overview of the entire colonial educational landscape is by Lawrence A. Cremin: *American Education: The Colonial Experience, 1607–1783* (New York, 1970), which has some insightful comments on the social functions of colonial schools and a staggering bibliography, but says very little about early Yale.

The best primary accounts of the Yale curriculum are Johnson's *Technologia* and *Synopsis Philosophiae Naturalis*. The Yale library of 1742 is preserved and contains many of the books used during Johnson's years, including Abraham Pierson's manuscript notebook and textbooks by Burgersdicius, Heerebord, Magirus, and Wollebius (all cited in footnotes). For an understanding of William Ames, see John D. Eusden, ed., *The Marrow of Theology: William Ames, 1576–1633* (Boston, 1968).

Ramist logic is handled in brilliant fashion by Walter J. Ong, *Ramus, Method and the Decay of Dialogue* (Cambridge, Mass., 1958), which relates Ramist methodology to the rise of printing and McLuhan-like trends. Ong's book replaces Miller's treatment of Ramus in *The New England Mind: The Seventeenth Century,* which first identified the significance of Ramist logic for New England thought. In addition to the books and articles cited in the footnotes, I was impressed by Keith Sprunger's "Ames, Ramus, and the Method of Puritan Theology," *Harvard Theological Review* 59 (1966): 133–51. The best discussion of scholastic logic is in William S. Howell, *Logic and Rhetoric in England, 1500–1700* (Princeton, 1956).

There are some excellent books that suggest the relationship between college curricula and intellectual trends. Robert S. Guttchen and Bertram Bandman, eds., *Philosophical Essays on Curriculum* (Philadelphia, 1969), and G. W. Ford and Lawrence Pugno, eds., *The Structure of Knowledge and the Curriculum* (Chicago, 1964), are difficult but worthwhile reading. Cremin's book (cited above) replaces Colyer Meriwether, *Our Colonial Curriculum, 1607–1776* (Washington, 1907), Theodore Hornberger, *Scientific Thought in the American Colleges* (Austin, 1945), and James J. Walsh, "Scholasticism in the Colonial Colleges," *New England Quarterly* 5 (1932): 483–90. Another article by Keith Sprunger, "Technometria: A Prologue to Puritan Theology," *Journal of the History of Ideas* 29 (1968): 115–22, suggests the way in which curricular structure reinforced doctrines essential to Puritan epistemology.

Chapter Three

Johnson's activities while a tutor at Yale are recorded in the Yale histories cited above. His own account, "Some Historical Remarks Concerning the Collegiate School of Connecticut in New Haven," in Dexter, *Doc. Hist.,* pp. 149–63, says precious little about what he was teaching. The 1718 theses, the first theses published at Yale, provide evidence of changes in the logic, mathematics, and metaphysics courses. Johnson's "Revised Encyclopedia" and "Logic" indicate alterations in his approach toward learning. Both are in *Career,* 2 : 201–44. His Mathematical Notes, 1717–18, are preserved at Columbia and document his efforts to master trigonometry. Lao G. Simons, "Introduction of Algebra into American Schools in the Eighteenth Century," U.S. Bureau of Education, *Bulletin* 18 (1924): 30–40, credits Johnson with first teaching algebra at Yale.

The books that Johnson found so enlightening are listed and discussed in Ann S. Pratt, *Papers in Honor of Andrew Keogh* (New Haven, 1938). For Locke I used A. C. Fraser, ed., *An Essay Concerning Human Understanding*, 2 vols. (London, 1894); for Bacon, I found G. W. Kitchin, ed., *Advancement of Learning* (London, 1915), complete and convenient. The watered-down versions of Locke and Newton are available in the Yale library of 1742, especially William Derham, *Astro-Theology* (London, 1715); William Whiston, *Astronomical Principles of Religion* (London, 1717); and John Ward, *The Young Mathematician's Guide* (London, 1727). For a discussion of Newtonian science and religion see E. A. Burtt, *The Metaphysical Foundations of Modern Physical Science* (London, 1925); G. N. Clark, *Science and Social Welfare in the Age of Newton* (Oxford, 1937); C. Van De Wetering, "God, Science and the Puritan Dilemma," *New England Quarterly* 38 (1965): 494–507. The old account of Johnson's early conversion to the New Learning is by Theodore Hornberger, "Samuel Johnson of Yale," ibid. 8 (1935): 372–85.

Historical accounts of the American Enlightenment disagree over such fundamental issues as when and how the Enlightenment happened to America, if it happened at all. Carl Becker's classic, *The Heavenly City of the Eighteenth-Century Philosophers* (New Haven, 1932), emphasizes the extent to which the philosophes remained wedded to mythical, unscientific, and religious ideas, in spite of their secular and scientific proclamations. Peter Gay's more recent work, *The Enlightenment: An Interpretation*, 2 vols. (New York, 1966–69), argues that the distinguishing feature of the philosophes was their "critical paganism," their denial of traditional Christian mythology. While Gay's work seems to me to make sense of European thinkers like Hume and Voltaire, I do not think it satisfactorily explains what happened in America. In the American colonies, especially in New England, religion did not perform the same function that Gay says it performed in Europe. In Europe the Catholic and Anglican churches provided men with an intellectually comforting set of doctrines that acted as a mental sedative and discouraged scientific investigation. In America, especially in New England, Puritanism was a disquieting and discomforting force that encouraged introspection and self-doubt. Colonists like Benjamin Franklin, who rejected religion in favor of secular wisdom, were distinctly less anxious, less skeptical, and less modern than their Puritan predecessors. Gay's *A Loss of Mastery: Puritan Historians in Colonial America* (Berkeley, 1966), by emphasizing "the Europeanness of the early American experience," dismisses

American thinkers like Jonathan Edwards as tragically parochial in their attempt to fuse Newtonian and Lockean insights with Puritan religious doctrines. Here, I would suggest, Gay misunderstands the extent to which the relationship between religion and science operated in the American intellectual environment differently from Europe. To adopt Gay's criteria for modernity and enlightenment is to impose European standards on a culture in which religion played a different role and to skim over intellectual distinctions that obsessed colonists like Edwards and Johnson. The distinguishing feature of the American philosophe was the tendency to combine the modern psychological insights of Puritan religion with the modern philosophical and scientific insights of secular learning, not the tendency to reject revealed religion in favor of enlightened ideas. What makes Johnson historically significant is that he was one of the first colonists to understand this intellectual dilemma.

Chapter Four

Historians have only recently begun to point out the emergence of an anglicized segment of New England society in the first half of the eighteenth century. The forthcoming book by John Murrin, *Anglicizing an American Colony: The Transformation of Provincial Massachusetts,* promises to deal with this attraction to English culture more thoroughly than any previous account. T. H. Breen's *The Character of the Good Ruler: Puritan Political Ideas in New England, 1630– 1730* (New Haven, 1970) contends that an English-oriented court party became influential in Massachusetts political life after the overthrow of Andros. Kenneth Lockridge's *A New England Town* suggests that the increase in population, the lack of available land, and the greater complexity of life in local communities was rapidly turning colonial New England toward social patterns reminiscent of England and Europe. Lockridge, in other words, locates the source of anglicization in demographic trends and not simply in the political alliances that formed around royal officials in the colonies. I would argue that Johnson's attraction to England, which took the extreme form of conversion to Anglicanism, was motivated by a genuine concern about ordination procedures, which developed in response to ecclesiastical problems produced by increased church membership, as well as by fascination with the cultural and intellectual trappings associated with episcopacy.

There is a need for more secondary work on latitudinarianism.

G. R. Cragg's *From Puritanism to the Age of Reason* (Cambridge, 1950) is an excellent survey, but too short and general. John Hunt's *Religious Thought in England,* 3 vols. (London, 1870–72), is a dated survey of the chief thinkers, as is John Tullock's *Rational Theology and Christian Philosophy in England in the Seventeenth Century,* 2 vols. (London, 1872). Martin Griffin's "Latitudinarianism in the Seventeenth-Century Church of England," (Ph.D. diss., Yale University, 1962), has information that cannot be found in any other secondary work. Among the host of primary works by Cudworth, More, Chillingworth, Tillotson, and Whitby (cited in footnotes 24 to 29), I found Stillingfleet's *Irenicum* most helpful.

More specific ecclesiastical works on the church and the ministry by Peter King, William Sclater, John Potter, Edmund Calamy, and Benjamin Hoadley are cited in footnotes 41–43, 51. James L. Ainslie's *The Doctrines of Ministerial Order in the Reformed Churches of the Sixteenth and Seventeenth Century* (Edinburgh, 1940) provides an overview of ministerial problems in England and Europe. Rosalie Colie's *Light and Enlightenment: A Study of the Cambridge Platonists and the Dutch Arminians* (Cambridge, Mass., 1957) gives the intellectual background of these religious disputes.

The best source for New England's ecclesiastical debates is the contemporary literature listed in Evans. I found the sermons of Ebenezer Pemberton and Solomon Stoddard to be the most revealing. Cotton Mather's *Magnalia Christi Americana* (London, 1702) reflects the ministerial anxiety over church procedures. Johnson's autobiography is a gross distortion of the Puritan position on ecclesiology. The S.P.G. Transcripts, A, IX–X contain previously unexamined material on early Connecticut Anglicans. For the popular response to Johnson's conversion, I used three New England papers: *The Boston Gazette, The Boston News-Letter,* and *The New England Courant.*

Chapter Five

The best account of colonial Anglicanism is still Carl Bridenbaugh's *Mitre and Sceptre: Transatlantic Faiths, Personalities, and Politics, 1689–1775* (New York, 1962), which does not cover the topic so completely as its title suggests and is largely concerned with the coming of the American Revolution. Bruce Steiner's "New England Anglicanism: A Genteel Faith?" *William and Mary Quarterly,* 3rd ser. 27 (1970): 122–35, is a sound social analysis based on both literary and statistical evidence. The Boston brand of Anglicanism is well covered by Henry W. Foote, *Annals of King's Chapel,* 2 vols. (Boston, 1882–96), which includes a good deal of primary material. William S. Perry, ed., *Historical Collections Relating to the American Colonial Church,* 5 vols. (Hartford, 1870–78), vol. 3, provides the documents for Massachusetts. Several letters of Timothy Cutler are printed in John Nichols, *Illustrations of the Literary History of the Eighteenth Century,* 8 vols. (London, 1817–58), vol. 4. Biographies of Anglican and Puritan disputants are in Dexter, *Yale Biographies*; Shipton and Sibley, eds., *Biographical Sketches of Those Who Attended Harvard College,* 14 vols. (Cambridge, Mass., 1873–1970); and William Sprague, ed., *Annals of the American Pulpit,* 6 vols. (New York, 1857–60).

Johnson's journal, in the Johnson Papers, tells the story of his year in England. Beardsley, *Life and Correspondence,* pp. 23–50, prints portions of the journal. The best descriptions of Stratford are in Samuel Orcutt's *A History of the Old Town of Stratford and the City of Bridgeport, Connecticut* (New Haven, 1866) and William Wilcoxson's *History of Stratford* (Stratford, 1939).

Connecticut Anglicanism is the subject of Hawks and Perry, eds., *Documentary History of the Protestant Episcopal Church in the United States of America Containing Numerous Hitherto Unpublished Documents Concerning the Church in Connecticut,* 2 vols. (New York, 1863–64). This collection includes material from the S.P.G. Transcripts and from letters deposited at Lambeth Palace. E. E. Beardsley's *A History of the Episcopal Church in Connecticut,* 2 vols. (New York, 1869) is an uneven secondary account partial to Johnson. Hector G. L. M. Kinloch, "Anglican Clergy in Connecticut, 1701–1785" (Ph.D. diss., Yale University, 1959), provides little in the way of analysis but a good deal of raw data on the Anglican missionaries, and its appendix helps to locate documents in the S.P.G. Transcripts.

Chapter Six

The previously cited works by Bridenbaugh and Steiner are central to an understanding of Johnson's missionary activities. Johnson's pragmatic attitude toward Anglican ecclesiastical policy tends to illustrate the point suggested by Daniel Boorstin in *The Americans: The Colonial Experience* (New York, 1958). The best secondary account of the S.P.G. machinery is still Arthur Lyon Cross, *The Anglican Episcopate and the American Colonies* (Hamden, 1964). Another dissertation, this one by Borden W. Painter, Jr., "The Anglican Vestry in Colonial America" (Yale University, 1965), aided my analysis of missionary work on the local level. M. Louise Greene, *The Development of Religious Liberty in Connecticut* (Boston, 1905), is the old but reliable account of the conflict among Anglicans, Baptists, Quakers, and Presbyterians. Norman Sykes has written a number of illuminating books on English Anglicans that clarify what was going on in London and Canterbury while Johnson was grubbing in the provinces. I found his *Church and State in England in the XVIIIth Century* (Hamden, 1962), *Edmund Gibson* (London, 1926), and *From Sheldon to Secker* (Cambridge, 1959) most helpful. There are innumerable new collections of documents on the Great Awakening, although the best history of the movement in New England remains Edwin L. Gaustad's *The Great Awakening in New England* (New York, 1957).

Chapter Seven

Johnson's sermons were the main depositories for his theological principles. Schneider has published some of the sermons, but a majority of the informative and interesting items remain in the Johnson manuscripts, unpublished. The longer sermons, including the *Aristocles to Authades* series, are in *Career*, vol. 3.

The theological tracts of the Puritan divines are listed in Evans. Certainly Jonathan Edwards, Jr., ed., *The Works of President Edwards*, 4 vols. (New York, 1843), is central to an understanding of the period. I found that John White, *New England's Lamentations* (Boston, 1734); Charles Chauncy, *Seasonable Thoughts on the State of Religion in New England* (Boston, 1743); and Thomas Prince, Jr., ed., *The Christian History*, 2 vols. (Boston, 1744–45) stated the theological issues in their clearest form.

Among the chief secondary works on theology, Perry Miller's *The New England Mind: The Seventeenth Century* is basic. Norman Pettit's *The Heart Prepared* (New Haven, 1966) clarifies the Puritan conception of the conversion process. Conrad Wright's *The Beginnings of Unitarianism in America* (Boston, 1966) is a superb summary of the conflict between orthodox and liberal New England theologians in the eighteenth century. An old article by F. A. Christie, "The Beginnings of Arminianism in New England," American Society of Church History, *Papers* 3 (1912): 153–71, is still useful. In a more recent article by Gerald J. Goodwin, "The Myth of 'Arminian-Calvinism,'" *New England Quarterly* 41 (1968): 213–37, the Arminian heresy is discussed as a clearly definable theological position. Although I would agree that New Englanders discussed Arminianism with precision in the seventeenth century, I believe the term was misused and misunderstood by many Puritan ministers in the eighteenth century.

Chapter Eight

The secondary material on American philosophy in general, and Johnson in particular, is disappointing. Miller's two volumes on *The New England Mind* and his biography of *Jonathan Edwards* (New York, 1959) identify the essential philosophical problems that New Englanders faced in the seventeenth and eighteenth centuries, but he lacked the technical training in philosophy necessary to analyze epistemological and metaphysical problems with precision. Both I. W. Riley's *American Philosophy: The Early Schools* (New York, 1907) and Herbert Schneider's *A History of American Philosophy* (New York, 1963) lack technical rigor as well as the historical sense that informs Miller's work. Vincent Burranelli, in "Colonial Philosophy," *William and Mary Quarterly*, 3rd ser. 16 (1959): 343–62, correctly identifies the need for a rigorous analysis of early American philosophers that might serve as a foundation for a new intellectual history of the period. Professor Murray Murphey is currently engaged in a reinterpretation of colonial philosophy that will supplant Woodbridge and Schneider and infuse some philosophical structure into American intellectual history.

Essential to an understanding of eighteenth-century American philosophy is a comprehension of the way religious and philosophical trends blended together and conflicted. Herbert Morais' *Deism in the Eighteenth Century* (New York, 1960) is a rudimentary start in this direction. What is needed is an American version of Sir Leslie Stephen's *History of English Thought in the Eighteenth Century*, 2 vols. (New York, 1902). For the influence of Plato on both colonial and English philosophy, see John Muirhead, *The Platonic Tradition in Anglo-Saxon Philosophy*, 2 vols. (New York, 1902).

A superficial treatment of Johnson's metaphysics can be found in most surveys of American philosophy, including Woodbridge and Schneider. A recent exception to this cursory approach is Norman Fiering's "President Samuel Johnson and the Circle of Knowledge," *William and Mary Quarterly*, 3rd ser. 28 (1971): 199–236, which relates Johnson's philosophy to his *Technologia* and points out the connection between Johnson's philosophical efforts and the rise of moral philosophy.

I used the A. C. Fraser edition of *The Works of George Berkeley*,

4 vols. (Oxford, 1901). The best secondary account is by John Wild, *George Berkeley: A Study of His Life and Philosophy* (Cambridge, Mass., 1936), although Wild's discussion of Johnson has several factual errors (and I also disagree with his interpretation of Johnson). Other works on Berkeley that I found helpful are G. Dawes Hicks, *Berkeley* (London, 1932) and R. A. Hoernlé, *Idealism as a Philosophical Doctrine* (London, 1924).

Chapter Nine

The best way to get at Johnson's role in the founding of King's College is through *Career,* vol. 4. The place to begin an overview is Beverley McAnear's review article, "American Imprints Concerning King's College," *Papers of the Bibliographical Society* 44 (1950): 301–39. Most of the primary literature is located and described in McAnear's article and can be found in either Evans or in the Columbiana Room of Columbia Library.

There is no adequate, much less definitive, history of early Columbia. John Howard Van Amringe, et al., *A History of Columbia University* (New York, 1904), cries out for a successor. Bits and pieces can be garnered from Cremin, *American Education*; Hofstadter and Metzger, *The Development of Academic Freedom*; Rudolph, *The American College and University*; and Hornberger, *Scientific Thought.*

There is no shortage of material on colonial New York. Stanley Katz's *Newcastle's New York: Anglo-American Politics, 1732–1753* (Cambridge, Mass., 1968) is a provocative secondary account. William Smith, Jr., *A History of the Late Province of New York, from its Discovery to 1762* (New York, 1829–30), is at once a historical narrative and a primary source written by a member of the Livingston faction. E. B. O'Callaghan, ed., *Documents Relative to the Colonial History of the State of New York*, 15 vols. (Albany, 1853–87), is the best collection of letters and documents. The Anglican role in New York politics is handled briefly in John B. Langstaff, "Anglican Origins of Columbia University," *Historical Magazine of the Protestant Episcopal Church* 9 (1940): 257–66, and Milton Klein, "Church, State and Education: Testing the Issue in Colonial New York," *New York History* 45 (1964): 291–303.

A satisfactory account of the relationship between William Livingston's life and ideas has yet to be published. Milton Klein's "The American Whig: William Livingston of New York" (Ph.D. diss., Columbia University, 1954) is a superb study that goes far beyond

Theodore Sedgwick's *A Memoir of the Life of William Livingston* (New York, 1833); but Klein's dissertation has yet to be published. Klein has published a succinct and suggestive fifty-page sketch in his edition of *The Independent Reflector . . . by William Livingston and Others* (Cambridge, Mass., 1963). Katz's previously cited book on New York uses several of the ideas Bernard Bailyn first suggested in *The Ideological Origins of the American Revolution* (Cambridge, Mass., 1967) and *The Origins of American Politics* (New York, 1968) in order to make sense of New York politics. The more I read the Livingston articles in *The Independent Reflector,* the *New York Mercury,* and *The Occasional Reverberatory,* as well as his letters to Noah Welles (in the Johnson Papers, Yale University Library), the more certain I became that Livingston most clearly articulated a mature version of the political ideology that Bailyn describes.

Chapter Ten

Although a good many historians have recently begun to research early American higher education, there is, as yet, very little in the way of secondary literature to assist someone interested in understanding the first decade of King's College. After I had gone through the College Papers in the Columbiana Room of Columbia University Library, I was directed to David C. Humphrey's "King's College in the City of New York, 1754–1776" (Ph.D. diss., Northwestern University, 1968), which is a long and solid study that supports my view of Johnson's presidency. Of all the archival material, I found *Early Minutes of the Trustees* most informative.

The most significant of the published primary sources are *Journal of the Votes and Proceedings of the General Assembly . . . 1743 . . . 1765* (New York, 1766) and articles in the *New York Mercury* and *New York Gazette or Weekly Post-Boy.* Taken together, these publications allow one to know how the various factions were jockeying for position in the college dispute.

If the College Papers at Columbia are indicative of the collections available at other schools founded in eighteenth-century America, then there is an abundance of material for historical research on the following questions: who went to college in colonial America? how did they choose a college? did the role of colleges and the view of education change after the Great Awakening? how did the sectarianism in the colleges eventually produce a desire for secularization? Two old but valuable studies that deal with these questions are Bailey Burritt's

Professional Distribution of College and University Graduates (Washington, 1912) and Beverley McAnear, "The Selection of an Alma Mater by Pre-Revolutionary Students," *Pennsylvania Magazine of History and Biography* 73 (1949): 432–35.

Chapter Eleven

The current belief that we are experiencing a crisis in American education has stimulated a searching re-examination of what education is or should be and how it differs from socialization. Cremin's *American Education* suggests that it was in the eighteenth century that America began to invest so much hope and power in schools. And although the provocative recent books by Jonathan Kozol, Edgar Friedenberg, and Charles Silberman address several problems unique to the twentieth century, a look at John Locke's essays, conveniently and elegantly edited by James L. Axtell in *The Educational Writings of John Locke* (Cambridge, 1968), suggests that many of our educational problems are, in Johnson's terms, archetypal. Which is to say that men have long been interested in how they learn and what difference it makes. As I try to suggest, the New England Puritans thought about these questions in the seventeenth century, but used theological rather than psychological or educational language to express their opinions. See Perry Miller's "Preparation for Salvation in Seventeenth Century New England," *Journal of the History of Ideas* 4 (1943): 253–86, for the most succinct statement of Puritan religious psychology.

In this chapter, as in chapter 2, I am using college curricula as a way of measuring the significance that Johnson and other colonial thinkers attributed to certain "enlightened" or "unenlightened" ideas. An earlier and similar approach is Francis L. Broderick's "Pulpit, Physics and Politics: The Curriculum of the College of New Jersey, 1746–1794," *William and Mary Quarterly*, 3rd ser. 6 (1949): 42–68. The study of science in the colonies has been analyzed by Hornberger, *Scientific Thought*; Brook Hindle, *The Pursuit of Science in Revolutionary America* (Chapel Hill, 1956); and John E. Van De Wetering, "God, Science and the Puritan Dilemma," *New England Quarterly* 38 (1965): 494–507. For Thomas Clap's career as a minister, college president, and scientist, see Louis Tucker, *Puritan Protagonist: President Thomas Clap of Yale College* (Chapel Hill, 1962).

The role of moral philosophy in American colleges has been explored by historians of the nineteenth century, but has not received much attention from colonialists. Norman Fiering's "Moral Philosophy in America, 1650–1750, and Its British Context" (Ph.D., diss., Columbia University, 1969) summarizes and surpasses all previous work.

Chapter Twelve

The central secondary work on the relationship between religion and politics in the prerevolutionary period is Alan Heimert's *Religion and the American Mind: From the Great Awakening to the Revolution* (Cambridge, Mass., 1966), which is a seriously flawed masterpiece. I would agree with many of the historians who have questioned Heimert's overdrawn connection between the New Lights and the adherents of American independence, but I also think that Heimert has focused historical attention on the religious psychology that underlay political opposition to the crown. Once again, Perry Miller was the first to identify the way religious and political ideas fused in his "From the Covenant to the Revival," in James Ward Smith and A. L. Jameson, eds., *The Shaping of American Religion*, in *Religion in American Life* (Princeton, 1961). Edmund S. Morgan has also explored the way colonists buttressed their political views with ideas lifted from Puritanism in "The Puritan Ethic and the American Revolution," *William and Mary Quarterly*, 3rd ser. 24 (1967): 3–43.

In fact the whole debate over the ideology of the American Revolution has recently taken a turn towards a greater awareness of the dynamic role religion played in arousing the colonists to recognize their common grievances against Great Britain. It was not simply, as Carl Bridenbaugh's *Mitre and Sceptre* suggested, that religious opposition to Anglicanism united the colonies. Gordon Wood's "Rhetoric and Reality in the American Revolution," *William and Mary Quarterly*, 3rd ser. 23 (1966): 3–32, and Bailyn's *Origins of American Politics* both point toward a deeper and more subtle interpretation in which suspicion of wealth, distrust of human nature, and belief in an approaching millennium—all tendencies of Puritan religion—gave vitality and meaning to the movement for political independence. Max Weber's *The Protestant Ethic and the Spirit of Capitalism* (New York, 1957) is, of course, the classic statement of the way religious attitudes affect things secular.

Index